Breakaway

Family conflict and the
teenage girl

For Judy, my twin

Angela Willans

Breakaway

*Family conflict and
the teenage girl*

Temple Smith·London

First published in Great Britain 1977
by Maurice Temple Smith Ltd
37 Great Russell Street, London WC1
© 1977 Angela Willans
ISBN 0 85117 1346 paperback
ISBN 0 85117 129X cased

Photoset by Amos Typesetters, Hockley, Essex
· Printed in Great Britain by
Billing & Sons Ltd
Guildford, London & Worcester

Contents

Acknowledgements

I would like to thank a number of people who helped me in various ways with this book.

Firstly, my thanks go to all the girls who talked to me about their breakaway experiences and what led up to them, and to the mothers who also gave me their views. Every one of them hoped that in telling me her story she would help other girls and other parents towards a better understanding. It was my hope too. If that is not the result, it is not the fault of those who talked to me. I am deeply indebted to them all.

I wish to acknowledge the generous help of the many counsellors, social workers and the staff of statutory and voluntary agencies who gave me the benefit of their knowledge and work in the area of young people's problems. I am particularly grateful to the following: Isobel Allen of Political and Economic Planning; Rosamund Blackler and Susan Ramsden of Girls Alone in London Service (GALS); Anne Bogood, Chairman of the National Association of Young People's Counselling and Advisory Services (NAYPCAS); Margarat Bramall, Director of the National Council for One-Parent Families; Michael Butler, Albany Trust; Michael da Costa of the University Counselling Service, Norwich; Donald Godden, Publications Officer of the National Marriage Guidance Council; Dr James Hemming; Carol Kayira, founder of 'Harmony'; Thelma Kellgren, Organising Secretary of 'Stop Over', Manchester; June Lightfoot of Campaign for the Homeless and Rootless (CHAR); Diane Munday, British Pregnancy Advisory Service; Nancy Pearce, Counsellor with an anorexic group; Joe Pimlott of Middleton, Manchester;

Acknowledgements

Dr Faith Spicer; John Tayler, Chairman of 'Off the Record', Bristol.

In addition, I am indebted to Pat Bramley, Caroline Francis and Anne Thomas for help with my researches; to Deana Seal for secretarial help and to my daughters, Sarah and Lucy, for any number of reasons.

Finally, I want to thank, for all that they have taught me, the thousands of readers of *Woman's Own* magazine who have confided their troubles to me during the fourteen years that I've been Mary Grant.

Introduction

There is a new wave of teenage girls breaking away from the family. The old waves are still coming, and getting bigger. There are still girls who just can't take home-life any longer, or who get kicked out, and who take off for the big city centres. Last Christmas, in London alone, there were an estimated two thousand of these homeless, runaway girls. In 1975 there was a twenty-five per cent increase in girls and women held in custody. All the helping agencies and emergency aid centres for girls adrift or in trouble report a rapidly increasing need of their services.

But alongside this increase is the largely undocumented but growing number of adolescent girls who are breaking with their families in a different way. They are not delinquent or disturbed; most of them don't come up against the law or end up in emergency accommodation, they don't necessarily even leave home. They are either choosing, or being driven into, attitudes to life and relationships which are totally different from their parents' expectations for them. They are going *to* something they want as well as *from* something they don't want. They are party to conflicts that mostly take place behind their own front doors. There is no social intervention in these conflicts. The girls never become a statistic or get to have their stories researched and recorded.

Yet we can all see that there are more girls hitching lifts on the motorways; more girls following off-beat religions and cults; more girls joining communes and squats; more girls living with their boyfriends; and if not more, at least no fewer girls — in spite of the pill — getting pregnant and facing the choices of abortion, adoption or keeping the baby; and more girls defying their parents in symbolic ways, like kicking over the class divisions and dropping out of the school-training-job-marriage pattern.

There are also more girls with identity problems. The in-put of models and opportunities for comparison, from magazines, books, television, the pop culture, higher earning-power at a younger age and even the defensiveness of many parents against being taken for 'squares' — all these pressures are enormous and may be less helpful than confusing when it comes to answering 'Who am I? Where am I going?' Another difficulty for some girls is that while the nuclear family has contracted in size, or perhaps because it has contracted, the emotional life within it has hotted up and become more complex, more subject to crossed wires and ambiguities.

So, added together, these new and different breakaways are a striking social phenonemon. From the letters that come to me as Mary Grant I know that it worries parents, splits families apart and sometimes leads to desperate situations for the daughters. For a long time I've wanted to know what lies behind it.

Is it all, or anything, to do with women's lib? Are the pressures on the breakaway girl mainly from without — in the open, plural society? Or from within — in the changing nature of family relationships? What are the breakaway girls travelling to? And what are they leaving behind? What have parents and daughters said and done to each other to reach this sea-change in the family's life?

Some of the answers to these questions are in these stories of family conflict. I simply set out to listen to a number of girls, and a few mothers, who have been involved in a 'breakaway', and to examine some of the conclusions that their experiences seem to offer.

PART ONE

The clash of values

1 Class, culture and choices

One of the most noticeable ways in which girls make the first break from their parents' expectations is to choose their friends — or get chosen by them — from a different social class. If they go up the scale, nobody minds. But the other way, when girls from actual or aspiring middle-class homes go out with working-class boys, is one of the commonest problems in my 'Mary Grant' mail.

It's mainly parents who write. They write in tones of disappointment and shock that a daughter is going out with a boy 'who's not good enough for her', 'can hardly read or write when she's got eight O-levels', 'has been in prison or up in court', 'is only a labourer' or 'doesn't have a job'. But there are also many letters from the girls themselves, lamenting their parents' opposition to a boyfriend 'because he's not as well-educated as me', 'because he works on a building site', 'because he doesn't talk very well' or 'because they think his family are a rough lot'.

If, in addition to having less formal education and coming from a working-class home, the boy is sexually aggressive — enough, in some cases, to ignore the age of consent — takes drugs, has a property-owning attitude to women, and despises the middle-class ethics of stability, orderliness and hard work, then parents feel very threatened indeed by his potential influence on their daughter.

In Sally's story, the vehement reactions of her parents to her boyfriend, Steve, are evident even before they had met him. The one conscious reason for the chilly feelings that remain between Alison and her parents, after all the turmoil of her anorexic illness and her leaving home, is her choice of boyfriend — 'He's not what my parents call my type. I think they mean class. Education and money-wise'. The mothers of Kate and Fran describe their bafflement and despair when their daughters took up with 'frightful' boys. Kate's mother says, 'This is what I can't understand, that they do like these awful herberts'. Well, why do they? The girls themselves give us several clues to their personal reasons, as far as they are aware of them. But there are a number of general reasons for this form of family conflict.

One interesting point is that most of the girls concerned are younger teenagers — fifteen to seventeen. It's almost as if the socially unacceptable liaison is for both a kind of baptism. For the girl, this is likely to be the first time she has actually paired up with a boy on one-to-one dates. The middle-class boys she mixes with are perhaps not so accustomed to early dating as working-class teenagers are, and are probably a good deal more inhibited about picking up a girl in a club or disco. So, in the early teens, it's the working-class boy who gets the bird. There's also the pub culture to ease the relationship once it's made. In places where there are few meeting-places for youngsters or cheap sources of entertainment on an evening together, the pub is often the only answer. But middle-class boys are not so apt to centre their social lives on the local. It just isn't their scene. So again the working-class boy is frequently the route to the 'getting out' and 'having a boyfriend' that the fifteen to sixteen-year-old longs for. And we shouldn't underestimate how much she longs for that. To be sixteen and to have to say that you're not going out with anyone or that you don't have a boyfriend is tantamount to saying that you're a non-starter as a woman, the bottom of the heap, a kind of outcast. So it's not surprising that girls will not only fantasise about having a 'boyfriend' when they mean a boy smiled at them once on the bus but will also grasp at any potential relationship which promises the coveted status of 'going out with a boy'. And to start with, they'll fight tooth and nail against parents' disapproval, and deceive and connive every which-way in order to maintain this status — at least until they're in a position to be the one to end it.

This sounds calculating but, of course, it isn't. I believe that there's a strong pull for girls, in the instinctive search for a suitable mate, to find what they don't want en route to finding what they do want. We sometimes forget, too, that immaturity is not a flaw in the young but part of the very stage of being young. No one matures until they've first been immature.

On the boy's side, some obviously get a bit of kudos among their mates from pulling a middle-class girl. Some are frankly in it for the pickings — Kate, for instance, describes how she kept her boyfriend in cigarettes and paid for his drinks as well as her own, and that's not unusual. Some genuinely don't recognise social divisions — or, if they do, believe they don't matter — and hope to become acceptable, in due course, to their girlfriend's parents. The stories of Sally, Kate and Fran (as told by her mother) show what enormous barriers still linger between the social classes when it comes to sexual pairing.

James Hemming believes that physical attraction, at least on the girl's side, is a strong point in these class mixings. He says, 'I think that middle-class boys are often a bit too smooth for the middle-class girl and the unadulterated masculinity of the working-class male can be very attractive. You quite often find that a fine-structured girl — fine in every way, physically, emotionally and mentally — will find tremendous pull in the antithesis of a masculine young male.

'I think the trouble with the middle-class is that they are de-sexing mankind. The men are not allowed to be men any more. They are getting out of touch with the animal in us.

'I know a case right now in which the girl knew what was going on. She was swept off her feet — I think that's the phrase — by this strong Nordic type, a nice young man doing a labouring sort of job. I mean, this wasn't a matter of anybody taking advantage of anyone else. She was enormously attracted to him and she started sleeping with him and that was fine. But she knew it would be fatal to marry him. He couldn't keep up with her conversation and when she was with her friends he was just dumb, not saying a thing. But time passed and he was very anxious to

match up to her, taking classes in this and that and now
they've got married. It's a lovely story. But I don't know
how it will work out.

'This was notorious too in the early days of the war when
the smoothy ladies went into munitions and met these
males radiating a degree of masculinity they'd never
encountered in their ex-public-school types. That was the
appeal — and they just said "yes".'

It's easier for girls nowadays to do the same. They don't
have to work in a factory to meet working-class males. In
this sense, our society is less divisive than it was. People
with different accents, different incomes, different educa-
tions, rub shoulders with each other socially. Snobbery is
becoming a characteristic that people keep hidden or
rationalise into a matter of 'good taste' or 'bad taste' — 'It's
not that I disapprove of his accent — it's just that I dislike
lazy speech . . .' In fact, one could almost say that the
question of 'Would I let my daughter marry/sleep with a
labourer?' has become the last stronghold of the slowly-
eroding class divisiveness. If you're an eighteen-year-old
girl you can no longer shock your parents by swearing,
wearing ragged jeans, sporting lank, straggly locks or even
by getting a job washing up in a hotel — you can only shock
them by falling for a boy who does these things.

Another factor in these ill-matched relationships is
hostility. It may be unconscious, but I've no doubt that in
most cases the girl is making some kind of protest against
parental control and values when she brings home a boy
who talks differently, rolls his own fags, drinks beer rather
than wine, treats her like an old boot and later brutally puts
his finger on the more artificial and hypocritical elements of
middle-class family life. This is music to the ears of a girl
who's at the stage of questioning everything her parents do
and say. And the boyfriend who she *knows* will be
unacceptable to her parents is a highly satisfying form of
symbolic defiance.

There is the boy's hostility too. There is still a good deal of
class-hatred and resentment, upwards as well as downwards. I suspect it's often a spin-off from the boy's parents'
recollected resentments rather than freshly minted by the
boy himself. But it comes out in a mocking kind of

put-down of the customs and speech and materialism of the middle-class home. And for a short time, this serves both the girl and the boy in their struggles to distance themselves from their backgrounds. Sometimes, incidentally, this is a step towards accepting their own backgrounds. Sometimes it's a step towards rejecting them. But the distancing itself, in one form or another, is common to all adolescents at the breakaway stage.

A clash of cultural values, rather than of class, can be just as disrupting. This is clearly shown in the story of Elizabeth's involvement with transcendental meditation, as told by Elizabeth herself and by her mother, Carol. Here, there was no question of crossing the classes. Transcendental meditation, in common with most fringe semi-religious cults, has no particular class image. It has even acquired a certain charisma through being associated with the Beatles and by being accepted as an aid to relaxation in some areas of the medical and educational establishment, particularly in the States.

But the gap between its aims and values on the one hand and those of Elizabeth's parents on the other turns out to be unbridgeable. The predominant note in both mother's and daughter's accounts of how this gap developed is not so much disapproval of each other's values — although there is that — as total non-comprehension of the essential difference in their stances for living.

I found this to be a feature of many family conflicts. Parents not only expressed their bewilderment at the route a daughter took to 'find herself' and discover some meaning and purpose to her life; they frequently asked why she needed to 'find herself' at all. What was wrong, they wondered, with simply becoming an extension of their lives, mixing with the same kind of people, inheriting the same goals and leaving the meaning and significance of life to take care of itself — or to be taken care of by traditional religions and ethics? Why all this fuss about the 'inner life' and personal standards? Why go back to square one when there's a ready-made structure for you right here?

But the rapid changes that have taken place in the lifetime of today's young adults — the threatened popula-

tion explosion, the collapse of absolute rules and the
emergence of situational ethics, the growing awareness of
limits to the earth's resources, the greater mobility of the
working population, the growth of the media — all these
things have threatened people's individuality and
autonomy. They perceive the risk of becoming mere
cyphers, manipulated by other faceless, impersonal forces.
They question how much of their lives they can actually
control for themselves. They are ticketed, docketed,
categorised from the moment they're born. They resist this
by making exploratory journeys into the 'self' via mystical
cults, way-out religions, encounter groups. And since they
retain the tribal element in human nature they pursue these
things in the company of other people. They opt for
alternative life-styles — small communities, back to the
land or to manual crafts, often dismissing the values of their
parents in favour of the values of the generations before
them.

It takes very confident parents to accept these dramatic
departures from their values without feeling personally
rejected and threatened. The commonest cry from parents
with breakaway daughters is 'Where did we go wrong?'
And there is evidence of the sheer terror engendered in the
parent-generation by these alternative value-systems and
life-styles in the escalation of such authoritarian and
would-be censoring bodies as the Festival of Light, the
Responsible Society, and the Viewers' and Listeners'
Association. They are holding change at bay — or attempting to — and it's what many threatened and bewildered
parents are also trying unwittingly to do when they clash
with their children over class and culture differences.

Children too, of course, can be equally rigid in their total
rejection of the former generation's way of managing their
lives, and in their belief that what they find to put in its
place is always better. The ability to tolerate difference,
without the necessity to pronounce it better or worse, is
perhaps what most oils the wheels of family and society —
and the lack of it leads more quickly than anything else to a
grinding halt in communications. Many parents have been
chewing their nails for some years about whether self-
expression, and a more or less free choice of goals and

standards, are really as helpful as a tighter structure for the business of learning and growing and fitting in with the world.

There's obviously a case for adapting one's methods of upbringing to the individual child. It's been established that extreme convergers thrive on a tight, clearly bounded, orderly setting out of what they can do and can't do. They are safest with absolute rules about right and wrong. And the extreme divergers need space and choice in order to spread their minds laterally and develop their creative potential. But what of the majority, the youngsters between these two extremes? Are they happy with the freedom to be themselves? If so, at what age? Do they take happily to the responsibility for creating their own standards?

Many parents don't think so, nor do many adolescents. Repeatedly, in talking with girls who regard themselves as failures, I've heard the phrases 'I wish now they'd made me do my homework', 'If only Dad had stopped me going out that night', 'They said I could leave school at sixteen if I wanted to so I did. But if they'd made me stay I'd have been at University now instead of this rotten dead-end job . . .'

Many runaway girls significantly leave some indication of where they've gone to—far more than those who do the opposite and leave no trace of their whereabouts. Are they saying 'Come and fetch me'? Many girls, like Kate, leave their 'secret' diaries and letters in full view of their parents. Are they saying 'I can't tell you what's happening in my life, but I want you to know and to do something about it'? In many of the accounts of wild behaviour I've listened to I've also heard an undercurrent of 'Why doesn't someone bust right in and stop me?' Some girls scare themselves out of their wits by the situations they fall into — not from choice, but from sheer lack of barriers which declare how far they can actually go without regretting it later. A few mistakes are all right; they're necessary, in fact. Several mistakes are all right too. But it's the piling-up of one mistake after another, with no pause to learn from them and no one to say 'That's enough' that puts anyone, adult or youngster, into the kind of frightening limbo which spells insecurity and which Kate, Fran, Emma, Tracy and

Cheryl experienced and describe in this book.

Although my listenings were mainly limited to girls who had not come up against the law, there is an analogy between their needs and the needs of girls who have ended up in some sort of custodial care. At Cumberlow Lodge in London about four hundred girls aged between fourteen and sixteen are held in custody per year. The operative word is 'held'. Tom Hart, who runs Cumberlow Lodge, says 'The interesting thing is that the majority of them appear to experience an overwhelming sense of relief, of security if you like, that they are somewhere, for the time being at any rate, they can't be sent away or moved on . . . It's a place where many of the pressures they have felt outside can be temporarily removed. Many of these children are terrified of what is happening to them in the great outside world.'

There may similarly be a case for parents of non-disturbed, non-delinquent adolescents to hold them tightly at home when the pressures outside become too much. This is perhaps what many parents do without realising it when they lay down rules about home-coming, going out, choice of friends, being chaperoned, etc. Unless they're unreasonable rules, made without any consultation with the daughter, they can be regarded as safe boundaries, which 'hold' the girl against the pressure of life.

Many agencies for helping young people observe this covert wish for structure. They speak of the bewilderment at the breadth of choice before the adolescent, the enormous amount of decision-making involved in everyday life. 'Shall I sleep with my boyfriend? Is it right or wrong to kiss on your first date? Do other girls do this? Is it all right to do that?' And on top of this confusion is the increasing competitiveness between girls, based on looks. In some cultures adolescent dances, for example, are highly structured; everyone must be brought in and it's bad manners to leave any wallflowers. But in our discos plain girls can sit about all evening and end up dancing with each other, while the pretty girls are turning down partners between every dance. When there are no rules it's not the weakest who go to the wall but the boy or girl with the least confidence in his or her appearance. And appearance, in its turn, is equated with lovability.

How, in the absence of structure, does a girl acquire the personal strength to build up her own standards? It's often believed that she only does this by relating to her contemporaries, by trying and testing and comparing as she makes and breaks friendships through the turbulent years of adolescence. Her own age group is thought to be where a girl's self-image is finally minted.

But the girls' accounts of their lives in this book show how strongly all of them draw their feelings about themselves from their parents. In a recent survey of Sixth Formers, James Hemming found that, in a rating of what the boys and girls considered to be the most formative influences on their growing-up years, parents came out comfortably on top and mothers had considerably more first places than fathers. However, everyone who listens to women's problems knows how tenacious are the negative comments that a father makes about a daughter in her adolescence. Married women who seek counselling help for marital problems recall a father's remark from twenty years ago which has devastatingly remained as an authoritative statement about them rather than simply an opinion. A girl expects a certain amount of friction with her mother — there is a modicum of rivalry here as between all women. If her mother calls her 'fatso' she'll put it down to jealousy or even consider it's time to go on a diet. If father says it, she may well go on thinking of herself as unattractively fat at every low or troubled point in her life, even if there's irrefutable evidence that she's not. Fathers have tremendous power to build up or knock down a daughter's confidence. Unfortunately, in an indirect way, his absence from the home — as after divorce — can be interpreted by some daughters as a put-down or rejection. The case-histories in this book which concern a home broken by divorce (Emma's story and Jane's story) seem to me to show something of these after-effects, though they are not necessarily damaging for all time. It's just that a girl who lacks the feeling that her father thinks of her as totally acceptable seems to have a harder struggle to acquire that feeling for herself.

And what of mothers? Their task now is radically different from that of mothers even twenty years ago. We have completely abandoned the kind of society in which each member had a structured place and knew where he or she belonged. In that kind of society, a child's upbringing was primarily designed to fit him or her to the parents' life-system. Within that system everyone was supported by other members. There was inbuilt security, simply by the adolescent's extension of the parents' lives.

But now it's all systems go. And in the open, unsupporting society we have now the child's primary need is not to fit in but to survive as an independent, autonomous individual.

That now is a mother's task — to set her child free to be herself — which often means allowing her to have totally different ideas about life and relationships. It also means having firm boundaries and standards which a daughter can either follow or break away from — or a bit of both — as suits her best.

Several of the stories in this book show how difficult this is for parents — the combination of 'holding' and 'freeing' their daughters. It may be that Kate, at one time, had too little holding and too much freedom — although she agrees that there seems to be just the right balance now. Sally experienced her parents' expectations for her as totally rigid — a matter of keeping in line and following their 'good taste' in values, friends and life-aims. It was a vice-like holding from which she perhaps had to break away as drastically as she did, flouting *all* their dearly-held views in one fell swoop.

And Alison's breakaway, which she and her mother recount in Part Two, is perhaps another example of a protest against too much control exercised by the parents, or at any rate control without consultation. She could, in the end, only be free when she left home altogether.

'What I'd always look for in a man now is
that kind of strength Steve and my father
just haven't got. I suppose it's
self-confidence really — not having to be
dead right all the time . . . seeing the grey
bits instead of everything in black and
white.'

2   Sally and the motorbike boy

*Sally is eighteen and is taking a language course at a residential
college in Oxford. Her parents live in a Tudor-style house with
tennis court and swimming pool. Her father is a minor industrial
tycoon. He makes plastic articles.*
*Sally is a well-developed redhead. She has long hair and a
Burne-Jones look about her. When we talked she was wearing a
floor-length green caftan and a lot of eye make-up. She is very
striking-looking and gives the impression of always getting her
own way.*
*Eighteen months ago she fell in love with an unemployed motor
mechanic who was living in a squat in Paignton. This is her story
of their love affair and the effect it had on her family.*

I fell for Steve because he was uncomplicated, exciting and
different. At first, I thought he was strong as well. Up to
then, my life and everyone I came across had been so
proper and 'nice' and totally wet. At home and school —
the whole idea seemed to be that I should grow up as a sort
of non-person, doing what my parents did, talking and
thinking like them and generally making sure to 'keep in
line' (one of my father's favourite expressions).

My mother's big thing is 'good taste'. This makes her
scared to make any changes or decisions — she's frightened
the result might be in bad taste. She's worn the same colour
in clothes — navy blue and white touches are her favourite
— the same shade of lipstick and the same hair style for as
long as I can remember. She's only about forty-five but for

at least the last ten years she's been pulling the line about
'not getting any younger' and 'at my time of life one wants a
bit of peace and harmony' whenever any disagreements
cropped up.

Of course, she was busy 'keeping in line' for my father
too. This is basically what he expects from all women. He
doesn't like them to have opinions of their own, only back
his up. That's why there were never any real discussions in
our house, about politics or class or people, certainly never
about *feelings*. He'd get uptight if you began to examine
anything or question it. At school I went Socialist really; it
was all to do with my thing about people. I feel they should
always come before 'things' — property, money and all
that. But after once piping up about this at home and being
put down by my father I never mentioned it again. But it
went on underneath.

  I knew I hadn't a clue about working-people at all, I'd
never met any. So I had a pretty idealised picture of them. I
guess I felt that, given the chance, every backstreet boy
could have all the things my father had, only with a lot
more appreciation and human understanding. It never
occurred to me that not every backstreet boy would
necessarily want all this. But it was what partly made me go
for Steve — the business of crusading for his class, thinking
I could level things up a bit somehow by giving him the
benefit of my advantages. But what advantages? It makes
me laugh now. I was an arrogant bitch all right. There was
more of your actual spontaneous feelings about people and
life generally in Steve's little finger than in the whole of my
family. Trouble was, there just wasn't any thought as well.
He never knew what he felt and then worked out whether
or how to take any action about it. He just felt things, and
then acted on them straightaway, never mind what the
consequences might be. He never had any thought-out
reasons for doing anything, no logic. It was one of the
things we argued about most — his maddening lack of
logic. For instance, he'd spend ten pence on a bus-ride to
get to the market to buy a tin of peas that was two pence
cheaper than a tin at the corner shop. If I pointed this out to
him he'd just get cross and say 'Oh, you don't understand.'
In that way he was a bit like my father, anything that didn't

fit in with his ideas was just wrong or stupid. I think this is a sign of terrible weakness, not being able to allow anyone else's point of view to be just *different*.

What I'd always look for in a man now is that kind of strength Steve and my father just haven't got — I suppose it's self-confidence really — not having to be dead right all the time, being able to chew things over and see things all round, seeing the grey bits instead of everything in black and white. Honestly, I'm not being smug.

After I left school at sixteen I didn't know what I wanted to do. So I hung about at home for a whole year. I went to stay with girls I'd known at school and that way I got a bit of life but they all had things going for them, college or something, so I felt a bit left out. I had various adventures with boys that I met with my friends, or ones I still knew near my home but it was all a bit feeble. I went to some art classes at the tech two mornings a week and an evening typing class once a week. I didn't feel I was going anywhere in particular; but my parents, I realise now, were content and didn't view me as any kind of a problem because they took it for granted that what I was going to do eventually was make a 'good marriage' and that the things I was doing were, in their eyes, quite adequate preparation for that. They didn't think I was marking time, but to me it felt that that was all I was doing.

Then I was asked to go with a couple of other girls to this camp near Paignton. The idea was to hire a chalet together for a fortnight. My parents were delighted; they were going to Ibiza themselves anyway and I know they never liked the idea of me being alone at home. To them, this meant all-night parties and yobo gate-crashers and all the rest — drugs and orgies, the lot. So I went, with their blessing.

Steve and a crowd of his mates picked up the three of us — my girlfriends and me — on the beach. I noticed Steve long before they spoke to us. He wasn't the best-looking, or the obvious leader or anything. He just looked the most interesting. He clowned a lot better than the rest, looking more natural at it — I realise now this was because, in a way, he's stayed a lot more childish than his mates. He's very quick-moving and direct. He talks fast too, full of catchphrases and odd bits of slang and words I've never

heard of. What with his accent as well, it took me a while to
understand everything he said.

We agreed to meet that evening at a disco and that was
the beginning of it. I felt really happy when I walked back to
the chalet for lunch. Fiona and Debbie were rather
boot-faced and tutty, saying things like 'Did you notice that
dark boy's *filthy* nails?' and 'Did you hear the way one of
them kept saying "bollocks"?' and 'What did you find to
talk about all that time?' But when I said I was going to meet
Steve later they just looked stunned and then shut up. In a
way, I think they were relieved that I'd got something to do
without them — I'd been moaning at them a helluva lot to
stop tanning themselves on the beach and come here, there
and everywhere.

I hadn't the guts to go anywhere on my own, you see.
I've always seemed to need company when I'm doing
anything new. In a way, I'm quite timid socially. That's
why it was so easy for Steve to lead me into anything he
wanted to do and take charge of me the way he did. I just
wasn't truly a very independent kind of person then. But
I'm getting nearer it now. Perhaps it needed someone else
to show me how. Parents can't do that — not mine anyway.
They don't deep down really want you to be independent
in the sense of not giving a fig for their approval anymore.
They want you to stay dependent on their good opinion of
you, if you know what I mean. That way, if you end up
successful you can be a credit to them. And if you end up a
bad lot, they can always say you thought you could do
without them but you were wrong.

After the evening at the disco I spent all my time with
Steve, and when it came to the end of the fortnight, Steve
took it for granted I was going to stay on with him in
Paignton in the room he had in a squat. So we worked out a
scheme for telling my parents that I'd found a job in a
boutique and had a nice room in a boarding-house and
wanted to stay for a few more weeks. And then I rang home
and told them and said all the right things like I'd keep in
touch by phone and please let me stay as I'd made some
nice friends down there and one of them had been to
Oundle and was taking me out and acting very properly as
his widowed mother was down here too — and it all

worked like magic. I felt a bit ashamed afterwards at how easy it was. But I think they'd got a bit fed up with me during that year at home, not getting on and not meeting any eligible men and being in the way of their bridge parties.

Every day was free to do as you liked. It was new to me, having no one to plan the day for you, suggesting you got this done and that done, like my mother does. She had lists and calendars all over the house — about shopping and engagements and taking library books back and ringing the plumber and appointments with the dentist. There were times to water the indoor plants and times to feed the dog and times to take her car to be serviced and times to do her household accounts. I'd lived with this all my life — and it was fantastic the feeling of freedom I had those few weeks in the squat — no clocks or calendars or timetables. I didn't realise it was possible to live like that.

In private, he was all for closeness and touching and hugging; it was as if he could never get enough of it. Sitting in the squat together in the evenings, with the radio on, he'd always have his arm round me or we'd hold each other if no one else was around. Sleeping together wasn't so easy in the squat as it was later on, when we moved up North, but he wasn't all that sexy in the sense of forever wanting actually to make love. He'd want to cuddle and kiss at night but often he'd just want to fall asleep like that rather than go on to have sex. He could be very tender and playful but when he did want sex, he was pretty direct and brusque about it — no question of asking permission — I liked that but there was no question of being 'too tired' or anything like that if I didn't feel like it. He was very touchy about being rejected sexually — which figures — but then I nearly always did feel like it when he did. I found him exciting and attractive and very loving in those early days. I was crazy about him actually.

We were together in Paignton for nearly three weeks. It ended rather abruptly when his motorbike got smashed, and he was banned from driving for a year. He was lost without a bike. He began to change after that. I can see now that it was the beginning of the end for us. But we didn't know it then; it just seemed like a change in the way we

were living, not a change in us. The truth is that owning a
bike and riding one and racing with his friends and having
a bird behind — that was what life was all about for him. So,
of course, he felt a different person, *was* a different person,
without any of that.

I felt very sorry for him; he'd become so different without
his beloved bike, like a child who'd had his favourite toy
smashed, that I'd have done anything to comfort him and
make him happy. Besides, I was as steamed up as he was
about the injustice of it all — his kind of persecution
complex was terribly catching. So I decided to go home
straightaway and get help from my parents. I was so caught
up in Steve's world I really expected that all I had to do was
tell them our troubles and they'd rush to help me — with
money, by pulling strings for Steve, and even perhaps by
saying, 'Both of you come and stay here at home till you get
on your feet.' So I went back on the train happy and
excited.

But it was ghastly when I got there. We had drinks before
the meal, just as we used to in the old days when it was a
matter of mother and me sitting there looking decorative
and listening to Daddy's monologues about work and golf
and the dreadful unions. Only this time I was tired and a bit
scruffy and doing all the talking at first. Both of them went
on a lot about my appearance, but until they realised what
kind of crowd I was going with they were all sympathetic
and sweet, thinking that it was only being exploited by the
(imaginary) shop I worked for that had reduced me to such
poverty and fatigue.

Then my father started on about 'this chap' I'd told my
mother about meeting down there — 'Who is he? Do I
know his people? Are you going to bring him here? Why
didn't he come with you now?' and so on.

So then I told them about Steve; if it hadn't been so
upsetting it would have been funny to see how slowly it
dawned on them that my boyfriend was what they'd
always referred to as 'the dregs' — long-haired, unemployed, in trouble with the law. As each detail came out you
could see my father changing his whole idea about *me*. In
one moment of fury, he called me a 'common slut' — and
they didn't even know then that I was sleeping with Steve

though I guess it was in their minds, wondering how far we'd gone. He utterly refused to help him in any way, and I simply couldn't understand this except on the grounds of sheer snobbery.

My mother couldn't do much more, while all this was going on, than make little tut-tutting noises, and now and again saying 'Oh Sally — how could you?' and asking frivolous questions, which seemed pointless to me but I suppose they meant a lot to her, like how did I manage to wash regularly 'in that hostel-place' (she had no idea what a squat was) and what had happened to the nice blue suit I travelled to Paignton in at the start of my holiday? She was completely bewildered, knocked for six and desperately wanted to understand. But my father was out-and-out angry and jealous. He realised this was the first boy I'd fallen in love with. He didn't want to understand anything; he just wanted to put a stop to it. He finally said the only decent thing to do was to break it off with him. And when I said I couldn't ring him and had promised to go back to Paignton the next day anyway, he grudgingly said that was the way I'd have to end it then, by going to Steve and telling him so — 'But you make sure you're back, alone, in this house by next weekend or I'll get in touch with the police all right and it won't be to save your friend's neck. It'll be to break it . . .'

When I got back to Paignton, I found Steve in the squat alone with some cans of beer. He was pleased to see me but not a bit surprised that I'd had no luck with my parents. He said he hadn't expected 'any favours from their sort'; he was also pleased underneath that I'd had such a big row with my father. I realise now that he'd have been much less content if they'd given us their blessing and help. He really prided himself on being unacceptable to anyone in authority, or well-off, or in a higher class. It was part of his persecution thing.

It was past the season for getting jobs in Paignton. The camps were closing, so were the cafés and restaurants. Steve said the only thing to do was to go to his home town. So we set off in no particular hurry to hitch North. We stayed a couple of times in bed-and-breakfast places, little back rooms in tiny private houses. It only cost about £1.75

each. But most nights it was fine and dry so we just unrolled our sleeping-bags in a field or some woods. It was marvellous sleeping out. We'd eat a pie and a doughnut and then natter for ages and sleep like logs until it grew light. The mornings were magic, soft and misty and no one about. That's when we used to talk about getting married — not because we actually wanted to be married (at least I didn't really) but because it seemed like the only way that we imagined we could make that kind of life go on for ever and ever.

We arrived in Bradford late at night. The last stages of the hitching were the worst — it took us about four different lifts to cover the last eight miles from outside the town to the other side.

We spent the next few days trying to find a room and fixing up for our dole. We did go through the motions first of looking for work, you had to do that before you could claim the dole. We went to the Job Centre — but it was a farce really. There was terrific unemployment in that area. There was nothing in Steve's line — motor mechanics — and I hadn't got a line anyway. So we went with clear consciences to the Social Security office.

Steve knew all the ropes. He also knew most of the staff at the DHSS office, and they knew him; they called him Steve and were quite matter of fact and uninquisitive. All they wanted was to have everything straight and according to the rules. I was put down as his dependant and between us we collected £17 a week.

Finding a home wasn't nearly so easy as getting the money. We went all round the area that Steve knew, the little streets surrounding his home, where his parents still lived. Whole rows of houses had been bought or rented by Pakistanis. Steve and I started by combing the ads in shop windows — just postcards with *Room to Let* written on them and the address, never the rent. We'd go straight along to the address and Steve would knock on the door while I hovered on the pavement. Sometimes I'd go up to the door with him. It was nearly always a man who answered; a lot of them didn't seem to have any jobs, except being landlords. The rent was always ridiculous — often £8 a week for one tiny room. And often we never got as far as asking what the rent was — the man who opened the door would just take one look and say 'No'. They never gave a reason. It was no use arguing with them. One said, 'We don't want your sort'. I don't know whether it was because we were white, or young or what. I'd never been looked over and turned down like this before; I felt awful but Steve was used to it — it didn't bother him. He just swore as we walked away and went on to the next address on our list.

In the end, a woman he'd known all his life offered us a room in her council house that had been condemned for about four years and was due to be pulled down 'next week'. It was in what's called a 'clearance area' but is actually a slum. This woman was hardly ever in her house now; she'd moved in with a sister further down the street whose house was in slightly better shape.

We both got jobs in a café, Steve washing-up and me serving and clearing the tables. We were there from twelve in the morning until seven in the evening, every day of the week except Mondays and at weekends. I was glad of something to do, but Steve hated it. It was the regularity of it that got him down. He wasn't used to it.

Although he'd been banned from driving, he still lived and dreamed motorbikes. He'd bought an old one which he was doing up in the yard beside the house. And our room was always full of bits of metal and engine parts. He used to spend a lot of time just banging them about and stroking them with a greasy rag. Most of the time I was in a daze, not understanding what I was doing there or why. The novelty of living with the boy I was in love with wore off very quickly. In fact, the bliss of having our own place and jobs only lasted a couple of days. The trouble was that I was the one who was doing all the changing. Steve wasn't adapting at all — he was still the restless, jumpy man with no goals except to keep me with him.

He began to resent the differences in me too. I used to read poetry aloud to myself in the room when he was there; I was trying to learn chunks off by heart, mostly Shakespeare's sonnets. He'd get mad and start picking objects up and dumping them down very heavily. When he got in a temper he never actually threw anything — he'd pick it up and bang it down very hard. He broke a radio once, doing that. He was getting more and more nervy, chain-smoking his roll-ups and flicking the ash viciously towards the fireplace. Often, out of sheer moodiness, he'd eat about two mouthfuls of a meal and then push the rest away. I began to feel, inside, more like his mother every day. I was always humouring him and cheering him up and letting him talk about himself. At the same time, things were getting me down and I used to get depressed sometimes and burst into tears.

I was getting homesick too. My mother was sending me letters with news of home and photos of my dog and always a pound note in the envelope. She never asked me to come back or asked questions about what was happening or what my plans were; she just kept asking me to ring. And I kept putting it off because I didn't know what to say. I knew she only wanted to know if I was happy — she was always saying, 'Nothing matters as long as you're happy and know what you're doing'. But I didn't know how I felt or what my plans were or where I was going so I avoided ringing her up but I did write her a letter or two, telling her about the room and the job but nothing about Steve.

But it was a hopeless situation. Steve and I began to row, mostly about somewhere else to live. Once, when I felt really fed up, I told him how I longed to visit Italy. I meant on my own, but he immediately started planning to go there, taking charge, working out how he'd raise the money by selling this and that. He couldn't bear me to have any wants or dreams of my own. We were in bed at the time and I suddenly felt trapped and got very angry and told him how stupid he was, the way he talked so much hot air about what he was going to do but never actually did anything.

While we were making it up after the row we decided to push off next day to my home. My parents might still prove something by accepting him. But I lay awake for ages that night. I suddenly felt lumbered. The truth is that I'd rather have been setting off on my own next day — free of him.

We hitched next day. Something made me take all my possessions with me but Steve only took his toothbrush and a change of clothes. It was winter now, just before Christmas and it was miserable hitching in the fog and rain;

we hardly spoke to each other. We managed to get about seven miles from my home at about six that night. We were so tired and cold we couldn't manage to walk that far and we tried to get a lift for about an hour with no luck. So I went to a phone box and rang home.

When the Daimler turned up, Steve took my arm quickly. I could feel his hackles rising, half-afraid, half-ready to defend himself. I did something then, without thinking, that I'm a bit ashamed of — but it told me how I felt deep down about taking Steve home. I moved my arm out of his and drew away a bit as Daddy drew up. It was fatal. Steve said angrily, 'Be like that then' . . . and stood there woodenly as I went up to the car.

I kissed Daddy through the window then I opened the back door and put my gear in. I beckoned to Steve to get in, he had to cross in front of the headlights. I saw my father stiffen as he saw Steve, he said 'Oh my God' under his breath. I whispered, 'Please understand — be nice to him. He's very unhappy and worried'. Daddy snorted. And then Steve was there, climbing in beside me and we drove off.

When we reached home, Steve stared at the house and said, 'Jeeze, that's a mansion like, isn't it? Must have cost a bomb' and I knew he was on his 'what's it all worth?' kick. He was intensely interested in the price of things, getting things cheaply, totting up what sum people's possessions amounted to. He often used to add up the price of everything we had in that grotty room in Bradford and say, 'Do you know, kid, we're worth £35 between us? That can't be bad'. He knew just what all his bike bits were worth, what he could flog them all for if he wanted to 'sell-up'.

My mother was sitting stiffly on the settee with a waiting look on her face. We hugged. She was bursting with questions, fluttery and anxious — 'Is everything all right? Are you happy, dear?' etc. But I said we'd talk later and went up to Honey, my dog, and she made such a fuss of me, jumping up and licking me and getting hysterical I nearly cried. She didn't give a damn who I brought home.

All through the meal I could feel the question hovering about how long I was staying and whether Steve was staying the night and what exactly was happening. They were steering clear of questions that would show, one way or another, if we were sleeping together. It must have been obvious that we were, but they didn't want it spelt out. As soon as we finished dinner, my father took Steve into the sitting room and Mummy and I went into the kitchen.

She came straight out with 'Now what are your plans for tonight? We've the spare room, as you know, dear'. So I said, 'Come off it, we wouldn't sleep in the same house without sleeping in the same bed' and, for the first time in my life, I saw my mother get really angry. 'How could you?' etc. 'He's not one of us' then she pulled herself together and seemed to remember that she was supposed to be the parent who 'understood' everything. She fell back on saying that, as far as she was concerned he could stay the night but that Daddy wouldn't allow it, she was sure of that. In a way, that made me feel relieved. I didn't realise it at the time, but I was looking for a way out from the whole Steve episode. But I couldn't end it myself.

I rushed into the sitting room where Daddy and Steve were both standing up, facing each other from opposite ends of the room. They were both bristling and my father was yelling about 'layabouts' and 'bums'. I felt almost hysterical and shouted at Daddy demanding, 'Why can't he stay here with me? We're lovers, you know, what else did you expect?'

My father hit the roof, there was disgust written all over him. He ranted on about 'Look at the boy, scruffy, uncouth', etc — all the stuff about bumming on the state, no standards, no principles, ending up with 'How do you think he could possibly keep a wife and raise a family?'

Then, before I knew it, I was yelling, 'But I'm not going to marry him'. Steve looked as if I'd shot him. There was a terrible silence. My father stared at us in turn, trying to work out how to react now. Then Steve came to the boil; until that moment he'd obviously gone on thinking we were together for keeps and that it was only a matter of time before we found a home and work and got married.

He started walking round the room very fast, touching the furniture, touching the lamps and ornaments. I got scared that he'd do what he used to do in Bradford when he was frustrated or angry — pick something up and crash it down into pieces. But he stopped still and rounded on me, 'A right c— you made of me then, didn't you?' and then a tirade about how he'd never have come here if he'd known he wasn't wanted, and he knew why, it was because of class-hatred and how I'd never given him a chance, nor had my parents, nor had *his* parents and nor had anyone else. It was all spat out aggressively but behind it was such awful self-pity and resentment that I didn't even feel sorry for him anymore, let alone loving. He felt sorry enough for himself. He seemed like a complete stranger to the boy I'd first seen on the beach, all cocky and confident.

Steve stopped talking. He said, 'Where's my gear then?' and stalked out to the hall. No one made a move to stop him, not even me. The front door slammed. My mother said, 'Well!' and then started plumping up the cushions. My father stared at me, lost for words for once. He pulled back the curtain and stared out of the window. He was full of questions but he wasn't going to ask them; he never did.

I've never been able to feel close to either of them since then. I can't talk to them really. And they can't talk to me — not properly. That was the end of my family life — the Steve episode. I go home for part of the holidays but mostly I stay with friends. And I've got a boyfriend here at Oxford. They'd approve of him all right but they haven't met him. There's no point. I've got my own life now. And my parents have no place in it.

'I felt at the time that Mum and Dad just didn't care. I thought they hated me. I don't know why. I think honestly it was the way I was behaving . . . they couldn't really fail to hate me.'

3   Kate and a family under stress

Kate is eighteen, bright as a button with dark violet black-lashed eyes like Elizabeth Taylor's. She is small and slim and talks very quickly. As she says herself she 'bubbles over'.
She works in Marks and Spencer's in the Berkshire town near her home. Her father is a retired executive with an oil firm. Her mother was an infant teacher until five years ago. She has a younger sister and they live, for the present, in a detached house in a commuter belt but they're soon to move further out. Kate and her parents went through a tough year or two starting when Kate was thirteen. Here is how Kate sees that time, why it began and how it ended.

We're a very close-knit family now. Well, I think we always were but we went through a very bad phase for the three months before we moved down here and for about a year to eighteen months afterwards.

It was all right until I met a boy and started going out with him and I suppose I knew all along he was completely wrong. He was terrible. I used to smoke then; he used to run out of cigarettes just as he met me, he used to manage to have only one left. He was earning more than I did but he used to be broke by Saturdays, I ended up paying for everything. He was a right sponger and he used to persuade me into things.

I suppose at the beginning I thought a lot of him but we used to row all the time, every time we saw each other we argued. His idea of a night out was drinking in the pub with me sitting there quite happy to stare at my drink all night while he was playing darts — and while I was paying for the drinks, of course. I think he was showing me off. He was very lower-class. I mean, that sounds rotten but he was. He couldn't think for himself.

It's amazing, the girls at work told me afterwards they always knew if I'd seen him the night before, I was so upset. I used to come into work nearly in tears, they all noticed it. A girl at work said, 'I've never met him but I've always wanted to hit him . . .' And they all said they could always tell when I was going to meet him, too. Round about four pm I'd start quietening down and I'd be dead silent. I was dreading seeing him yet I couldn't break with him. But one night we had a really flaming row because I turned up late.

We'd had a cocktail party at work for someone who was retiring and who was really good to me when I started. So I went; they were throwing champagne around everywhere, coming up and filling your glass or giving you another one if you already had a full one. I had a bit too much to drink — not all that much — I was a bit happy. So I rolled into the pub an hour late. But he didn't come for another hour, he was two hours late. I turned up at nine, he turned up at ten and he gave *me* a row for being late. We had a flaming row in a phone box. It really was bad. He started calling me nasty names. I've never told anybody this actually but he tried to strangle me. And I really thumped him — it was just fear. He had a lovely black eye actually.

Then we split up, but about a month later he said he wanted to go back with me and I did for about three weeks. And then I said, 'Oh for God's sake, I just don't want to know you. You're such a pain.' If I talked to anyone else and not him he used to say, 'Why are you ignoring me?' and he'd make a big scene and walk off and leave me. If I didn't run after him he'd come back and make another big scene. I got so fed up with it I thought, 'Right, you've made enough of a mess of my life. I'm going to get out and try and salvage something.'

Looking back it's one of those mysteries why I ever took up with him. We were getting on fairly badly at home and I think I wanted someone who would show their feelings. Someone who I could feel did care about me and I think that's what did it. And I know he thought the world of me and still does. His great sob-story to all the girls he asks out

now is about this girl he wanted to get engaged to and how
she turned him down and how he's never got over it — a
good line and they all fall for it. He's said to me several
times since we split up in March that he still wants to go out
with me but I just don't want to know now. I know what he
is. He used to drink and drink and drink, he never stopped.
He used to be in the pubs at opening time and for as long as
he could afterwards. That's one of the things that broke us
up, that he was getting to the stage where he'd get very
violent when he was drunk, and he was getting drunk
every night. I've got my standards now and I won't accept
less because I know I can keep them up and I don't see why
I shouldn't.

My parents met him and loathed him on sight. They
instinctively loathed him. And it caused a terrible rift at
home. I got so bad-tempered. I was really terrible actually. I
was very unhappy. I felt at the time that Mum and Dad just
didn't care, I thought they hated me, I don't know why. I
think, honestly, it was the way I was behaving — they
couldn't really fail to hate me. I was being so terrible at the
time, I really was. I still feel bad about it. But I can't
somehow say anything to them. That's why I want to get on
at my job as much as I can — because my Dad did, he
worked his way right up — and if I do, I can turn round and
say 'I couldn't have done it without you.' I can't actually say
'I'm sorry I was rotten.'

I was unbearable. I'd have shot me if I was my Dad,
locked me in my room or something. There was constant
arguing. Everything I said was wrong and everything they
said was wrong, and I used to scream at them and they
used to scream at me. I think Mum and I seeing so much of
each other when she was so strung-up, and I was so
strung-up too, we just ended up clashing in the worst way
possible. But I think what shocked everyone out of it was
Dad becoming so ill because of it. I know I had a lot to do
with that. I feel I did, because I was being so careless. He
got very worried, with the strain. But I'm not going to do
that again. I value my parents' love too much. I think I did
value it the whole time really. It was a vicious circle though.
I was so scared that they didn't care that I sort of went out to
be really nasty, to try and get them to say they did. But they

didn't say it, so I was even nastier, and all the time I was even more upset inside. I thought they didn't care about me at all.

We're not a demonstrative family, not with our loving feelings. We don't show them much. My sister went to France the other day and Mum and Dad were both very surprised that she gave them a kiss before she went off. It was surprising because she never shows feelings like that. I think we all hold back a lot. Mum, she was at boarding school and they were taught that it was immature to show your feelings. That was all wrong, they said, you should be hard. And I think that has sort of worn off on us. Mum hasn't shown much feeling but, well, the feeling's there. I think there is a big difference between having feelings and showing them.

I only realised all this fairly recently, in the last four or five months. I just sat down one night and thought everything out. I just thought and thought and thought and I came up with a few conclusions — that really you can't get away from it, family love is best. Because whatever you do, your family will always support you. It's something, you know. If I ever got into financial trouble or any other sort of trouble, Dad and Mum would always support me. I'd always have someone to turn to.

I think you need a mixture of this from parents with a bit of independence too. My mother's made me fairly independent. I do a lot of helping round the house. I have to. I know a lot of girls my age at work who don't even make their own beds or clean their own rooms or anything. My sister and I do our own rooms and we get nagged if we don't. I don't like seeing anything untidy now. I don't mind a sort of orderly mess but not so that you can't get into somewhere without falling over things.

Mum wouldn't help me with a job or anything. When I went for the interview, she took me there but apart from that she never actually pushed me. I did it myself. I knew I'd have to get a job sooner or later. It was lucky I picked Marks and Spencer's. I was only employed as a temporary seasonal. But they asked me to stay on and so I've stayed ever since. I'm in charge of the men's shirt department but I've applied for supervision. I've been told it's in the offing.

I'm going to help out at another branch and I think after I
come back from there I'll probably have a bit of training and
then be promoted to training supervisor. I want to go on to
management, you can get up the ladder quite quickly there.
One of our Department Managers is only twenty-six. Mum
and Dad have helped a lot to push me into supervision;
they kept saying, 'Well, look, you don't want to stay on the
sales floor all your life. If you don't tell them, they're not
going to know.' So I chased them up one day, rang up the
staff management and cornered them and said 'Right . . .'

I think you have to go through an arguing phase with
your parents to realise that what they're talking about is
right really. I mean, they do know. A lot of girls say, 'Well,
it was different when you were young, Mum' — but it
wasn't really. Mum said she was exactly the same yet you
always think your parents very strict and old-fashioned
and everything. But, you know, my parents weren't
married until a year after I was born. I didn't know this until
three weeks ago. They decided to tell me on my eighteenth
birthday because I'd be able to understand then. I've
always had my birth certificate. I've needed it for passport,
national insurance and everything. I've often wondered
why I was registered in 1959 when I was born in 1958. Once
I saw my sister's birth certificate and she was registered
three days after she was born. So I demanded to know. I
just said, 'I want to know why I was registered a year late.'
They said, 'We'll tell you about it tomorrow.' And Mum
told me all about it. That was the first time Dad ever got
emotional. After Mum told me he came in and said, 'So
Mum's told you . . .' and he was almost crying with
emotion. But to me it doesn't matter — OK, they weren't
married, but they're still together now. They cared enough
about each other to have children and stick with us, give us
the best. So it didn't matter.

It made me feel more stable really. Mum said she didn't
want to get married. She didn't see any point at first. But
then, when I was a year old, she did. It made them seem
more human. In my mother's family there are four girls and
only one of them conceived all her children in wedlock;
with one of them, their daughter was two years old when
they got married. And another had a rather premature

baby. It's amazing really but what counts is whether they stay together or not, as far as I'm concerned — and they have so that's all that matters.

I don't think it would have helped to have known earlier. When I was sixteen or seventeen, it was such a bad phase I'd have probably walked out or something. I would have felt then that I hadn't been wanted, that they had to get married just because I was there. I'd have twisted it round like that against them. But Mum said never was a child more wanted. I think it's so romantic. It's really nice. It's sad in a way that they had to go through all that, the worry of his divorce and everything. It's so romantic, like something that happens in books.

I don't want to get married until I'm absolutely sure that I and the person I want to marry are completely compatible, not so much that we're in love but that we share the same feelings about each other. I think that's the most important thing. If you're absolutely worshipping someone and they only feel lukewarm towards you it's doomed from the start. But if you share the same feeling, the same intensity, then I think it's a lot easier. Something equal is what I want. But so many of my friends at work are planning to get married the minute they're eighteen and they've been going out with their boyfriends for years and years and they never get separated from them. Their boyfriends pick them up from work every night and they phone them up every dinner time. They live in each other's pockets. You can't keep it up at that pace. One day you'll think, 'I know that person too well — I don't like him anymore.' I haven't really met anyone yet but I'd like to get married eventually. I'd like to have children, but not for a long time. I'd like to establish myself in a career first. You see so many broken marriages, especially among young people. I just don't think it's worth the risk. I think marriage should last a lifetime. I'm very much a romantic.

A lot of the men nowadays are very pushy, I think they put on an act just to keep up with the rest. But not the majority, there's a lot more politeness coming back — in dancing especially. I don't know whether you know Bailey's in Watford, it's a night club, and I was up there last night and the dancing is very much going back to the old

sort of waltzing, not grope, grope and you're forever trying
to avoid all the hands everywhere. It's a nice change and
they come up and say, 'Would you like to dance?' instead of
just 'dance?' They're getting a lot smarter as well. I think
there again you tend to find the polite ones are the ones
with a higher-class background. I know that in this day and
age class isn't supposed to exist, but it does. You notice it so
much when you see the middle classes, they're so much
better mannered and more intelligent. Even if they are out
for sex they do it so subtly that you don't quite realise
it — it suddenly dawns on you. But it makes all the
difference, being polite. And you can hold a conversation
with them. Whereas the other ones, all they talk about is
money and football. I like football but not every day of the
week. I like to talk about other things.

My main boyfriend is away at the moment. We get on
very well, he's a lot more mature than any other boys I
know. I look for maturity most of all. I like to be treated as a
person and not as a piece of china or a little rag doll or
something to be shown off; it gets a bit depressing when it's
like that. When I'm with people I find I'm a lot more
outgoing than most. I do tend to be the life and soul, not too
much, you know — I try to keep it down a bit, but if I'm
enjoying myself I show it and I really bubble over. A lot of
people aren't like that, they stick to their friends. I try and
make new friends, I love meeting people, I love going to
new places and trying out new fashions. At the same time I
believe in saving my money. My basic wage is £36.50 and I
take home roughly £26. I keep £7 a week in cash for going
out and for things like deodorants. I save £10 a week, half in
a building society and half in the bank. And the rest goes on
fares and food and my rent to Mum. So if I ever get a flat or
if I really want a holiday, or a car, the money's there. The £7
I'll spend as I want, I've earned it. If I want to pay out £4 for
a taxi from Watford, I will. If it's been a dull week I might
carry over £5 to the next week, If it's been an exciting week
I'll have about two pence left. It depends really what's
going on. But I find I can get by easily with £7 a week, so I
keep on saving.

I know I've not been a stay-at-home up to now. I have
tended to wander, I haven't stayed in one place long

enough to make best friends and feel settled but now my younger sister is sort of my best friend, I'm very fond of her. And I want to stay at home now, I couldn't bear the thought of being separated from home for any length of time. I feel uncomfortable even if I go away for an all-night party. I suppose it's a homing instinct but I feel I've got to get home to make sure everyone's all right. When I was twelve-and-a-half I went to Switzerland with my school and I think the best bit was when I had a letter from home. I kept that letter for years; I think it got thrown out when we moved down from Scotland, I threw out a lot of things then. But I do tend to miss home very much still. For the moment I wouldn't want to be living anywhere else.

I can go out four nights a week now. If there's something special on, Mum will let me out more, but she says it's for my own good and I know it is. If I do go out more than that I can't work and I get really tired so I stay in three nights a week and I enjoy it. Actually, I've only been out about five times in the last three or four weeks and I don't miss it at all. If I'm working the next day Mum would rather I was home at eleven or eleven-thirty so that I can get a good night's sleep. But if I'm not, I can stay out more or less as late as I like as long as she knows if I'm going to be later than twelve. So if I'm going to be very late I phone up and tell her and they won't lie awake but just leave the door open and I'll sneak in. And I can go anywhere as long as Mum knows where I am, or who I'm with. The other weekend I went up to an all-night party in London, and I was quite surprised, she didn't mind at all. She knew I went with Tim, my boyfriend and she thinks a lot of him. So she was very good about it.

I can understand how much my parents must worry about me because I worry about them. If I don't know where Mum and Dad are, if they're late home and they said they'd be home earlier, then I do worry. So I can understand it from their point of view. Like the other night they went up to a wedding and my sister and I went to a party. At least we tried to, but we'd been given the wrong address so we couldn't go and we came back home. That was at about half past ten and Mum and Dad weren't home. They left home at about four and said they wouldn't be late so we were a bit worried. We sat up and waited for them, made ourselves something to eat — fried egg sandwiches and things — and we waited until they got home. And until they came in the door about an hour later, I was worried.

Or if Mum just goes down to the village and she's gone for two or three hours, even though I know she's probably in the garden shop looking round all the vegetable produce and seeds and everything, I still think, 'Supposing she's not?' I never actually think what might happen, I just think *something* might, a vague fear. I think I'm a bit insecure. A lot of it is because we got on so badly and now we're getting on so well and I'm a bit scared I'm going to lose it all. But basically I suppose it's the same as they feel about me — I like to know where they are and what they're doing. I think a lot of people feel this way about their parents but can't admit it. I know lots of people whose parents have broken up, or a parent has died or they just don't get on. It's happening all over, families breaking down. It all makes me feel I've got something special, a stable family with two parents and with love there and I'm not going to risk losing it. But I nearly did, didn't I?

'I said to Kate's sister the other day, "Have I
got to go through all this with you?" And
she said, "You know you might not. I might
have learned quite a bit from what's been
going on".'

4 Kate's mother

*Kate's mother is grey-haired, slim and very energetic. She talks
very fast and high, with a Scots accent. Although she has rather
an anxious air and is seldom quite still, she comes over as a very
strong, philosophical sort of person. She speaks of a lot of family
troubles she's had to contend with, including her own depression.*

At thirteen Kate was very attractive, much older than her
years, very mature-looking. She got in with a terrible
Glasgow crowd. It was absolutely appalling. I used to think
they were going skating on Saturday evenings but they
weren't, they were going out drinking. Kate had always
drunk a little with us at home, always wine, never spirits
and stuff. She knows her limits and, in fact, drinks very
little. So that wasn't the problem. I wasn't worried about
that so much, I rather suspected something else. You know
how you get this sixth sense.
    She was always writing her diary when I went to say
goodnight to her. She'd say, 'Of course, you'd never read
this, would you? I'm writing this but it's absolutely private.
You'd never read it, would you?' A psychiatrist told me
later that this was an invitation to read it. Well, one day I
did. I read it. I wanted to know what was going on. I felt
desperate, It made my hair stand on end. I discovered that
when my husband and I had been out one evening to a
dance, and Kate had a friend to stay, they made a night of it.
They invited about half a dozen boys from Glasgow, one
had stayed the night. Now these two girls were only
thirteen and they'd involved Kate's young sister who was
only eleven; she'd had to tell lies and keep on telling lies. I

also learnt from the diary that she and her friend had been going down to Boots and nicking this and that.

Anyway I kept all this knowledge in reserve. I thought two can play at gamesmanship. I gradually brought things up that were in the diary — 'I knew that all along' I'd say, and she couldn't understand how I'd found out. She began to think she couldn't turn round without my knowing. I kept up this gamesmanship for a very long time — 'I wasn't born yesterday' type of thing.

Anyway she started having intercourse at fifteen after she'd been through several boyfriends. He was a nice, quiet boy and you wouldn't have thought he'd have done that. After all she was under age. He was quite dumb, I don't think he could even read, poor chap. This is what I can't understand, that they do like these awful herberts. She was very pleased when I found out actually. I just said, 'Well, I'm terribly sorry about it and it's a very sad thing but there you are.' She was on the pill because she had terrible trouble with the curse. She'd always been sick and fainted and things like that and the doctor had put her on the pill. It was some time before she found out it was the contraceptive pill and then she thought 'hurrah'. So I think this was partly the trouble. After that she's had no qualms about going and getting the pill regularly and she's been on it ever since. Sometimes I say, 'Now, look, you're not having a regular affair with anyone at the moment — why don't you come off it?' But no, she won't.

She had to part with this boy when we moved down South. She swore eternal love for him and that lasted about four weeks after we'd been down here. But she really wanted to spread her wings when we got down here. She started staying out very late at night and wanting to go out every night.

She was sixteen. Of course, she'd had to leave her school in Scotland and she didn't want to go to another school to take her A-levels, which was quite reasonable, so we said all right she could do them at college — and that was a disaster. She did not work at all and it wasn't until the last day of the first year that we got the report and found that she hadn't been attending lectures, not half of them. They hadn't let us know. They didn't haul her up or anything.

She went every day, but she was just with all the boys. The Headmistress of her last school said she was boy-mad. If she wrote an essay it was always about football or something to do with boys. She wasn't a tomboy — quite the opposite, she was simply interested in boys. You see, she'd been to a convent most of her life, and then to a girls' school — and no brothers. And then, at college, she was absolutely overwhelmed by boys.

So she threw up college and was unemployed for a long time. She was very surprised that everyone didn't want her because she had done very well with O-levels. As I say, she was staying out late and she'd got a frightful boyfriend who drank a tremendous amount. And it got to the stage where one night she rang up and said she was staying out the whole night because the boy's parents were putting her up and it would be perfectly all right. And I said, 'You're to come home now otherwise tomorrow you can go — you can leave home.' And this was when she was just seventeen. All she wanted to do at this time was sit in pubs with this boy. She didn't do anything healthy at all, not that you'd really expect them to, I suppose. I don't think we did at that age. If we'd had a choice of boozing in pubs or playing hockey I'm sure it would have been boozing in pubs — perfectly natural. Anyway she said she was staying out and I said, 'Then you can go tomorrow.'

So the next evening she came in and I said, 'Get all your things ready and I'll give you a lift down to the town.' I gave her a lift and said, 'Oh well, bye-bye. We're always here if you want us, and if you want to come back it's perfectly all right but it must be on our terms, and that is that you stay in for three nights a week and that you don't stay out all night.' And I thought, well, it would last a couple of days. My heart was breaking. But I was very casual about it. They don't care for it when you're casual. They prefer the drama. But I didn't go for her or anything. And off she went. And we went to bed miserably and locked the door. The dog started barking at one o'clock in the morning and after a while we went downstairs to find out why and there she was curled up on the doorstep absolutely crying her eyes out and saying, 'I'll never do it again' and this, that and the other.

And then next morning she turned round and said, 'Oh well, you can't turn me out anyway, not legally, not until I'm eighteen. You've got to give me a home till then.' Which is what I think is so stupid about whoever it is who makes these laws. They can do what they like from seventeen onwards and you have no say whatsoever over what they do, but you've got to provide them with a home. They can do exactly as they please from seventeen to eighteen and the parent has no come-back, nothing she can do. The police can bring them back and say, 'You've got to have them' and yet parents can't say, 'You've got to stay at home, or you've got to do this.' They have no rights at all except they've got to keep these little horrors. They can't even teach them a lesson really. So there's this awful year when they're at their worst when you can't do anything about it. Ever since that night I've reminded her, 'OK when you're eighteen, I can chuck you out.' But actually Kate's been much better since she was eighteen. And she's never stayed out again all night.

But to be fair to Kate, a lot of the trouble was because I went through an awful year of depression when we moved. I didn't want to leave Scotland. I didn't like this house. I didn't like anything. It was terribly difficult. Kate said to me the other day — it was the first time we talked about it as a matter of fact — 'You know, none of us knew what to say to you.' I was in a bad state. And I couldn't get any help for months and months. I saw doctors and they just said, 'It's your age, my dear.' And that's another thing, that girls become teenagers possibly when mothers are going through the change of life, and perhaps have aged parents to look after as well. In fact, you're right in the middle of it, a real pressurised time.

That depressive illness was a stress on Kate. And it *was* an illness. I realise that now. And I couldn't get any help anywhere. Moving down here we'd lost contact. When you move you lose contact with friends and you have no doctor who knows anything about you, your family or anything. At a point when I was going a bit berserk I rang up a social worker I'd been told was very helpful and said I was absolutely desperate. I thought Kate was going to get into police trouble, she and her friends were drinking and they were under age and they were drinking late in the pub. Anyway I left my name and they said, 'We'll contact you.' And about six weeks or two months went by and suddenly someone rang and said, 'Oh, you phoned us up.' I thought, 'Oh God, if that's the attitude, there's not much point.' I think they're hopeless. By that time things had smoothed out a bit with Kate but I was still going through my depression stage and I did want help from somebody. But I don't think I'd ring them now or ask anyone for help, because I can cope. I'm on top now.

I think what did get me out of the depression was facing the fact that I couldn't get any help anywhere. I knew I wasn't going to get any help so that made me do it myself. But then my husband was very ill and that dragged me down too. His illness was stress too and that may have been brought on by my depression to a certain extent. I wanted divorce, separation, everything — which was most unusual for us; we'd always been such a happy couple. He was very patient in his way, although I don't think men understand all these depressions and this, that and the other that women have. But he was going through terrible stress with his job, going up to London every day. And then he was just sick and sick and sick and he would be sick forty times a day for a fortnight. They couldn't find what was wrong and they decided it might be stress and tension. And, of course, all the trouble with Kate wasn't helping. She knew how to aggravate him. And we were aggravating each other. There was a time when we all thought he was going to die. It was dreadful. So finally he retired from ill-health and he had one more attack after that, a few weeks later, and that's all. Since then he's been happy as a sand boy and he's so fit you wouldn't believe it — pleased as punch that he's retired, you see.

He gets quite a good pension but obviously we can't afford to stay in the commuter belt. We don't like it anyway, having lived in the wilds of Scotland. So we're going to move out, possibly to Suffolk, possibly to Hereford, Worcester or Somerset.

But I'm sure poor old Kate is thinking ahead and wondering what's going to happen to her. Funny how they go on needing their home, even into their twenties many of

them need it. But there are Marks and Spencers everywhere. She's hoping now to become a supervisor and then
to go on to management. I don't know whether she will or
not. I don't know whether she's got the character to do all
that. But that's up to her. If she had to get a flat of her own
— well, it might work. With Kate, everything depends on
the boyfriends she has.

But, because we're going to move, I think she feels
terribly insecure. I think she's a bit insecure anyway. Also
she's frightfully emotional. And so am I, so we fly at each
other. You can start off an academic discussion with her,
say, about how Leslie Whittle's mother felt about the Black
Panther and 'Wouldn't you go and kill him?' Kate asked
me. I said, 'No, I wouldn't. I wouldn't want to go near him.
I'd much rather the law took its course.'

Then she relates it to herself — 'There, if I was found
murdered in a ditch you wouldn't care. You wouldn't care
if I died. You just don't care' and all this with tears falling
down her cheeks. She seems to want constant evidence
that we care. She says, 'You don't care for me because you
never cuddle me or hug me or anything.' But if you so much
as touched her actually it would be 'No, go away.'

You can tell in the morning when she gets up that it's
going to be one of those days that whatever you say is
utterly wrong. She'll twist everything and the whole house
shuts up. It seems that she must go up into the air now and
then. We think that every week she has got to have an
outburst and then the chemistry seems to settle down
again. She was like that as a child, but also desperately shy.
She wouldn't speak to you. She was demanding though.
She'd yell until she got attention, but then the moment she
saw an outsider she retreated into her shell.

I've never hit Kate but her father has. I'd come back from
London with Kate's sister and we'd had a lovely day and
there was chaos at home. Kate had been cheeking her
father and he'd hit her. This was the first time he'd hit her in
the whole of her life. Obviously she deserved it, but he'd
lost his temper. He just slapped her face. And the hate she
had for him for ages afterwards was appalling. It had
dented her dignity. A psychiatrist we know maintained
that whatever you do to teenagers you mustn't ever let

them lose their dignity. I've been tempted to hit her very frequently. But I think it's a teaching thing. I taught infants and I never smacked them either. You learn the habit of holding back, which I think probably helped. But I don't blame my husband and I don't blame Kate for being terribly upset. She gets on with him pretty well now. They do go for each other but I always seem to be brought in between them.

I think Kate thought I adored my schoolchildren as much if not more than her. She was a bit jealous. I did actually; I did love them almost as much, oddly enough. And I suppose I was always talking about them. But I have this feeling, as a teacher, that there are an awful lot of teenagers who have no relationship with any adult. Very few have parents they can go to with their problems. I think an awful lot of parents are fed up to the back teeth with their children by the time they're fifteen, you can't blame them. So they've suddenly lost their parents and they have not got one grown-up: they no longer have the minister, not that they ever did very much; no doctor has time to talk to them for more than one minute. I think that in the secondary and comprehensive schools they ought to go back to the close relationship between teacher and pupil that we have with the infants. They'd have one person who they would feel is interested in them and knows them. Some teachers don't even know their names. There's nothing between their age group and anyone with any wisdom. Schools have counsellors and this, that and the other, but they never know the children well enough.

Kate has been lucky and had one person she does relate to, a widow who has a daughter born on the same day as Kate. When she was at college she saw her every day. She is the one person she would go and talk to. But she gets on very well with her sister now, they're really good friends. I don't think her sister has anything like the pressures that Kate had. Admittedly there are still the sexual pressures to some extent, especially on TV. We've always let them watch anything on the grounds that if they understood it, it was all right and if they didn't understand it, it didn't matter. But I do think that television makes it seem clever to be swinging, the more sex you have the more clever you are. But I've read that these single girls now are getting a bit fed up with having flats and shacking up with young men because they're finding that they're really getting the thin end of the wedge, paying their whack and yet they're doing all the work as well. All the chores of marriage and none of the security. So it's no longer a status symbol to be shacked up with somebody by the time you're twenty. They're coming home to Mum because it's more convenient.

But it's funny actually that we seem to have none of these problems with Kate's sister. I said to her the other day, 'Have I got to go through all this with you?' And she said, 'You know you might not. I might have learnt quite a bit from what's been going on.'

There is one thing that's important, perhaps the most important thing because it was a kind of turning point for us and Kate. My husband John and I lived together for years before we were married. He'd been married before. We were not married until Kate was about a year old. So there has always been this awful business for the whole of these eighteen years that one of these days I'd have to tell her. Her birth certificate was all perfectly correct, of course, because she was legitimised when we married. But the year on it is 1959, the year after she was born. She'd asked me several times, 'Why is it dated 1959? I was born in 1958, wasn't I?' So at first I said, 'That's just a mistake.' Perhaps it was the wrong thing to say but you've got to choose the right time for the truth.

Well it came up about three or four weeks ago when Kate was getting her passport and had to have her birth certificate. She said, 'I want to know why it's the wrong date.' And I said, 'OK, right. I'll tell you all about it tomorrow.' I didn't want John to be there because I had a feeling he might put his foot in it somehow — he'd be a bit too sentimental. So then I told her. I said, 'Well, when you were born we weren't married' and I told her the whole story. And instead of the sort of reaction I'd expected she thought it was frightfully romantic. She thought it was smashing. She said it made us not so square. I hadn't expected her to be condemning. But I thought she might hurl it at me, use it as a weapon, you know. And she still might of course. I wouldn't blame her if she did.

'Whenever I'm in Liz's company now I feel as if I'm with a polite stranger. Somebody who would never for one moment take a step to help any of us that didn't suit. Somebody who would never alter the course of her life at all for anybody. Perhaps for another meditator, but I doubt it. She's totally self-absorbed.'

5   Carol, mother of a meditator

Carol is a good-looking middle-aged woman with grey hair and blue eyes. She dresses with panache in long, bright skirts and talks very wittily. Her husband, Peter, is in stage design and they have two daughters and one son. The eldest daughter, Elizabeth, joined the movement for transcendental meditation when she was nineteen and has now made it her whole way of life. Carol describes how this distanced Elizabeth from her parents, both physically and emotionally.

I think meditation was first mentioned when Elizabeth came back from college for holidays or a weekend. I don't remember having any strong feelings about it. I probably thought it was quite a good thing then. But fairly soon afterwards she started giving us the spiel, which was very simplistic and you felt was designed for five-year-olds: this is a tree and this is a root, almost a diagrammatic sort of thing.

It wasn't particularly surprising that she'd latched onto it. By nature she's something of an extremist. Had she become a Catholic she'd have thought of becoming a nun — she's that sort of person who would take things to extremes, once she'd agreed to them. I don't think she'd been looking for anything like this, any source of inner strength or anything. The way she presented it to begin with was that it was a solution to the drug problem. We knew that at that time students were very hung up with the

whole pot scene so we thought this can't be bad. She had
very strong feelings against pot. Much stronger than I had.
I thought if she wants a bit of pot let her smoke a bit of pot. It
wouldn't have worried me a bit, but it worried her. She told
us that this was the entire reason for going in for
meditation, not because she was smoking pot — she wasn't
— but as a sort of crusade against the whole drug scene. But
I think in fact this wasn't true at all. I think she really went
in for it because she was madly in love with Simon. He was
a meditator and she had no interest in it before she met him.
He was very hung up with the meditators and that was her
link with them. We didn't know Simon then. We'd never
met him — we didn't meet him for years and years. But we
knew Liz was in love with him.

It started to make a barrier between us the more she was
into it. I felt at the time and I feel now that they don't want
people who won't join. And I wouldn't join. It had no
appeal for me at all. Early on, Liz tried very hard to make us
both join, especially Peter. He did try and nearly went
round the twist so that made me feel pretty anti too. But for
myself, it just wasn't my thing and it didn't grab me in any
way. I thought the Maharishi was a silly little man and I
thought it was a stupid idea. Still do. I think I'd feel the
same way about anything that had this inward-looking
purpose. I've always felt it's totally wrong to devote
yourself to something that is merely a 'me-thing'. I mean if
they ever did anything for anybody else I would certainly
have more respect for it. But I don't really believe in things
that are just there to improve 'me'. Meditators don't want
to have anything to do with anybody who doesn't belong,
only on the most superficial level — which, when you're
part of a family, is fairly destructive, I feel.

The barriers went up very subtly. They are still there, of
course. It was a growing lack of interest in the family and
everyone else; a lack of looking out, it was always looking
in. She became terribly introspective. Also I loathe this idea
they have that they're entitled to dabble with minds. There
was Peter's experience, for instance. For Liz's sake he tried
to join. He went for three days and did the full initiation. I
don't know quite what they do because it's a bit like the
freemasons, there's some sort of secret rite and they're

given their 'mantra' which is supposed to be a deadly secret. But it made him a fully-fledged meditator. After about three or four days he was home and as soon as he got back he really flipped for weeks.

Then there was another girl at Liz's college who joined the same time as Liz and she went completely round the twist. We found out afterwards that she had some history of mental illness and so therefore shouldn't have joined, because they don't take anybody with a history of mental illness; but it seems to me that if it's going to do something to a mind it's a jolly dangerous game.

There's no doubt that, Liz being away at college, it didn't have the strong effect on us it would have had if she'd been at home. But when she came home for weekends or holidays she'd get more and more fed up with us and our ways and push off back to London again. She was getting more and more switched-off. She would tend to sit in her room mostly when she was at home. At mealtimes she was always a bit edgy. She'd become a vegetarian and wasn't eating any meat but she didn't really like us eating meat either. None of them eat meat but they all say you don't have to be a vegetarian to be a meditator. But this is changing. They were much more rigid when Liz joined.

At this stage I still thought of it as a passing thing with Liz. I also thought it was only a part-thing for her. I still think that as a part-thing — like saying your prayers, which is the way some people use it — it would have been all right. I didn't ever foresee it becoming her way of life, which it is now.

She was doing it for two years as a student. During this time she broke with Simon but she continued with the meditation. All the meditators seemed a bit wet and dull, that's what I thought, what a wet crowd they were, a droopy lot.

When we went there for her twenty-first birthday she had a very weird guy who was the boyfriend at the time and a meditator. He was ghastly and apparently a complete failure as a meditator because he'd gone on having his shots. That's not done: he was one of her failures. Liz is a great one for always finding lame ducks. So you could see the attraction of meditation for her. If she could find a cure

for lame ducks then she could get more lame ducks. I don't
know which comes first . . .

Then she went to live in Simon's house. I don't quite
know how or why because she'd broken up with Simon
then. He was abroad and we'd still never met him. She'd
never brought him home and apparently he was frightfully
weird then and would never meet anybody.

Anyway she moved into his house which was also lived
in by a great crowd of meditators who came and went and
ran up phone bills and never paid the rent or anything else.
And Liz used to go nearly spare with all these meditators
because she was the official tenant, paying the rent, and
then the bills were coming and she couldn't pay them, bills
for months and years back. All this time Simon had been
out in Spain with the Maharishi, and all the meditators had
been using his pad and running up enormous bills.

She was working for her living then, she had quite a good
job in an advertising firm, but she suddenly chucked that
and said she was going on a month's course in order to
become a teacher of meditation. It was then that she said
she was going to give her whole life to meditation.

So she went off to Spain for this course. When she came
back she said, 'I was going to get married in Spain. To this
German fellow. We were madly in love and we were going
to get married.' Then he went into a week's silence —
which they have every now and again — and she said that
when he came out of it he wouldn't speak to her anymore.
And that was the day they were going to get married! And
also on this course, which we didn't know about until ages
later, she suddenly had a completely paralysed leg. She
just couldn't walk — a sort of hysterical paralysis. I didn't
know about this side of it but apparently this sort of thing
was quite common in meditation—these physical manifes-
tations, and also these complete changes of personality or
whatever it is that makes you want to marry somebody one
week and not speak to them the next week.

Next, I think, she went to Italy for another course. And it
was there that she met Simon again and they suddenly
realised, not that they were in love or anything like that, but
that they were friends. To Liz, this was absolutely
marvellous. From there they were moved to Austria and

she came home, leaving Simon there. It was the summer, about June, and Simon had promised that he'd be back for her birthday in October. She came home to learn a bit more about publicity so that she could work on all the literature they put out about meditation.

She started off being quite reasonable but as time went on she got more and more like a nut case. This was really a traumatic time we had with her, although it was several years after she'd joined, of course. She became just hysterical and suicidal. And Simon seldom wrote. Whenever she wrote to him she would obviously make hints about him coming back and he wouldn't ever reply directly to this. And then she got to the stage of just ripping up his letters when they came — 'He won't come back. He won't come back.' This hysteria got worse and worse. She really was suicidal. I said, 'Look, Liz, go out to Austria. If you don't want to be here, go out there.' She wasn't doing any work. She was just sitting and crying all the time — terrible withdrawal symptoms. Well, you see, it couldn't have been entirely about Simon because I said, 'Liz, I'll give you a cheque for a flight tomorrow. Go out and see him.' She said, 'I won't. I can't. I can't go out there again. I can't go back there again. I can't get mixed up with them again.' She was absolutely scared, terrified.

Finally, her birthday came and he hadn't come back and he hadn't mentioned coming back. She said, 'I'm not going to write to him anymore. There's no point in me living.' And one night I was frightened she was going to commit suicide and I got bloody furious with this damned Simon whom I'd never met. So unbeknown to her I phoned his parents and told them I thought Liz was suicidal and I just wanted Simon at least to make some move to phone, or something or other, to see if he could be of any help at all. So they got in touch with him and he phoned, I think, the following night. Peter and I were out but Liz's brother and sister were there and apparently Liz had a complete hysterical breakdown and threw the phone down. I suppose he said that he wasn't going to come back right away. This period is a bit confused, but there was quite a long time of this sort of drama but the end result was that he did finally come back at the end of November. He stayed for about a month and then they went off to Spain to see the Maharishi. Simon could make no move of any sort without seeing the Maharishi. And the Maharishi said yes, they should get engaged. So they came back from Spain to say they were engaged and then they went off to Austria and Switzerland together and that was the way it stayed until they came back to get married the following October.

Then, after the wedding, it was really terrible because Liz had almost forcibly to be put on the boat to go back. She was so against going back. There was all the to-do about being pregnant as well and not really wanting a baby and not knowing whether to have an abortion. Everybody was going right through the hoop. It was the only time I ever felt sorry for Simon. In retrospect, I think it was misplaced, but at the time I did feel sorry for him.

The next time I saw her was when she had had a miscarriage out in Switzerland. And that was absolutely heartrending because she was so schizophrenic. Not about losing the baby. Again it was about meditation. She couldn't bear it. She said, 'I can't bear living here. I can't bear living anywhere else. I feel there's no point in me living at all.' She said, 'I feel I never want to see Maharishi again.'

But a week after I left her she was sent off by herself, away from Simon. I think it was for two months. She went to one of the other meditation places over the other side of the lake. She didn't see Simon at all. She was in seclusion of some sort and given the works. I think they have to keep people in the movement when they've reached this position in the hierarchy. They don't let them go. They're getting phone calls from Switzerland all the time, 'Come back'.

Since then we just don't communicate anymore about meditation. She has a sort of veneer on the whole subject. I don't think we get anywhere below the surface at all, on any subject. I don't think she wants to go below my surface either. She doesn't want to understand me and I've given up trying to understand her. I suppose you could say that we get on better than we ever did because we don't have any heights or depths anymore, we just go along on one level. But the result of it all is that whenever I'm in her company now I feel as if I'm with a polite stranger. Somebody who would never for one moment take a step to help any of us that didn't suit. Somebody who would never alter the course of her life at all for anybody. Perhaps for another meditator, but I doubt it. She's totally self-absorbed. They all are.

Out there in Weggis they have tape machines playing various tapes of the Maharishi talking — and that's all they have. They never tune their radios in or anything. They've no idea what day of the week it is. They know nothing at all about what's going on in the world. Not one thing. Except they collect horror stories from people who have come back from England. They tend to denigrate England all the time because the Maharishi doesn't like England. He's never had a good reception here so it's 'that rotten little island'. This is all they know. They love to hear people who come back and talk about the economic depression and unemployment and things like that. I expect they've been going through this summer living on drought stories.

But what appalled me most when I was out there was this complete uninvolvement between people. They are all switched off from each other. And from everyone else. Liz has no interest now in what Peter and I do or think or feel. And she has no interest whatever in people she used to know. She used to be so outgoing. She spent several years living a normal hell-raising, fun-time — lots of fellers and so forth. I occasionally see flashes of the real Liz. She's still just as short tempered as she ever was. I don't think people change their spots very much. Underneath, she's still really what she always was. That's why I think this living she's doing is so alien to her nature. She always liked the heights and depths. She's such a black and white person that this constant greyness she has now . . . it's not really Liz.

I don't really think I mind very much about any of this now. I think I'd mind if she was the only one. But I feel I've got a good rapport with my other children, so I don't have to feel that I've just made a terrible mistake with Liz. I don't have to ask, 'Where did we go wrong?', I don't feel 'What else have I got?' because I've got something else.

But I feel that because it all started when she was at college that she was gone anyway then. You know really when they leave home, for college or whatever, you've sort of given them up anyway. Certainly the mental break is made. Right until the day they leave you worry if they're late home — 'Where are they? Have they had a car crash?' From the moment they leave you don't think like that, you don't think 'I wonder where they are and what they are doing.' You never think in this way again. It's strange. While they're at home you are always conscious of them, always thinking about them. Then they go and this mental tie is broken.

I suppose there must be a reason for Liz getting so deeply into TM. But I'm at a loss finally to know why. I've wondered if she needed it as an anchor or a prop. But she seems to me to have tried to cast it off too often to want it for that reason. I know there have been psychological moments when I should have taken her out. I should have taken her away after the miscarriage. I should have said, 'We're going home now' and she would have come. But I think she would have needed psychiatric treatment. She would have had to be unpicked.

'I think that if transcendental meditation hadn't worked I would have gone on to find something else. Because I suddenly thought, 'Well, maybe I can do something about these failures in myself rather than always ending up fighting with my parents about them.'

6   Carol's daughter

Carol's eldest daughter, Elizabeth, lives and works in the Swiss town of Weggis where the Maharishi Mahesh Yogi (the Beatles' ex-guru) has set up one of his centres for teaching and promoting transcendental meditation. She is married to another meditator, Simon. The movement is Elizabeth's whole life now. Here she explains why. She also describes how her involvement with meditation estranged her from her parents.
Elizabeth is very, very attractive and the picture of health and happiness. She talks very easily and confidently and laughs and smiles a good deal. But, of all the people I've talked with during the writing of this book, she was the only one with whom I felt I'd had no real communication. It wasn't that I did not experience her as a real person, for I know that I did. It was rather that, in her presence, I no longer felt like a real person myself. It was very curious.

It was in my first year at college when I was just nineteen and I saw a poster advertising a talk about transcendental meditation. I don't remember any particular motives then. Nothing like 'Oh, I need that' or 'I must do that.' I just decided to go to this talk.

I can't remember anything about the talk. I was just impressed with the feeling of it. The people giving the talk impressed me and I was attracted to them. There was a sort of warm feeling about them. They seemed very easy and confident. But I suppose there must have been a seeking in some way for me to have been attracted in the first place. So

I started meditating and I found that the effects were very good and I felt a lot more relaxed. I used to get a lot of depressions and they seemed to be much less. I was happier and my work went better. And because of these things I got more involved with the movement itself. I enjoyed going to the local centre a lot. And then I felt the need to teach other people to meditate because I felt that it had helped me such a lot.

In a subconscious way I must have been seeking something. If I hadn't started meditating I would probably have gone into drugs at that stage. I had left home, in a way, by going to college but I didn't know what I was or what I had left. It did help me to find myself I realise now — but that came later.

I went home about every month or so and for most of the holidays. As soon as I went to college my relationship with my parents was much better and easier, seeing them for a shorter time, but until then it had always been a bit difficult. I had actually been longing to leave home but it never got to the point where I packed my bags and left of my own accord.

It was very much sex and those sorts of problems. They would worry that I was out at night and basic problems like that. The problems now are due to something very different — because I'm meditating and they don't and our values are different. I think my values were the same as theirs then. I would go out to pubs and get drunk and have a good time and go to parties, which is similar to what they do now.

But then I wouldn't say that practising TM actually makes you non-materialistic. I have gone a few steps into being more involved with the movement and with Maharishi. He's a monk and in his mode of life it's very difficult to be materialistic. One hasn't a home and is always moving. Simon and I live in hotels and usually for not more than about six months in one place. Therefore one can't accumulate things even if one had the money to do so because you can't carry them round with you. And we don't get paid. We just get a small amount of pocket money.

In fact, if I was living in England I would probably be as

materialistic as the next person but hopefully with a more spiritual viewpoint behind it. I can't say I'm not a material person but at the same time I'm not hung-up about not having a house or two cars or whatever. At college, for instance, I'd go round jumble sales for my clothes rather than to a shop, so I didn't mind that I couldn't afford a smart dress because I'd be quite happy rooting around in a jumble sale.

But I was not 'thinking' enough or old enough to be consciously rejecting anything by taking up meditation. If I'd started five years later I'd have had a much more intellectual reason. As it was, I had just an emotional reason for starting. I felt maybe a little lost and depressed and I was looking for some stability, something to involve me, more of a purpose. I wasn't satisfied with myself. It wasn't to knock against my parents or the way they lived. I was always ashamed of having tantrums and depressions, and being bad tempered. This seemed to be a way of not having to live with these things anymore. I think that if TM hadn't worked I would have then gone on to find something else. Because I suddenly thought, 'Well, maybe I can do something about these failures in myself rather than always ending up fighting with my parents about them.'

I don't know why I used to get so depressed and bad tempered. I would just feel miserable a lot, and for a long time. I think it might be hereditary or something. My mother gets depressed a lot and I don't know that she would have any particular reason for it — just living you know, and perhaps pressures. I remember not going out for months and months when I was living at home. I'd stay in deliberately and I'd think, 'If I don't go out for a long time, when I do go out I'll be prettier and more attractive and all right.' And I'd get deeper and deeper into this depression. People would ring me up and say, 'Aren't you coming to the pub?' and I'd say, 'No, I'm madly dieting, I'm madly doing this and that.'

And eventually I'd suddenly feel 'I'm thinner and I'm happier and the sun's shining' and I'd go out again and then I'd find that everything was just the same. No one had seemed to miss me and I found it terribly hard to make an impression. After two months of not going out, they'd just say, 'Oh hullo. Do you want a drink?' Nobody would notice and I'd probably go back into my depression. I never felt terribly adequate socially. But I'm sure now that no one does, or not many people. Maybe with age one feels more adequate, or you have props or just learn not to show it.

I don't get depressed much now. At least, I know when I'm depressed now whereas before I'd go for weeks not knowing I was depressed. And it only lasts an hour or so now — or maybe a day. But a day would be a terribly long depression for me now. So that's the main outward benefit of meditation for me — the lessening of depression. And this gave me more energy and my work improved a lot.

I also felt a lot more confident. At first this made me a bit intolerant of other people — I was doing meditation and I was better than them, I knew what I was doing and they didn't know what they were doing — a snobby thing. So I cut myself off from non-meditators and was more involved with other meditators. But I think that went. I always hope I can now fit in with any situation even if it's not the ideal for me.

So socially I wasn't nervous anymore and I didn't put on an act. Perhaps I was rather dull. I think perhaps my parents thought I was rather dull. They probably still do. I find it rather difficult to enjoy some of their conversations and the things they talk about because it just isn't a reality to me. I find it rather boring and they find my life rather boring. But I can't just sit and talk about wine and food — I'm not really interested in their food, being a vegetarian, and my life just isn't involved in drinking or smoking or any of these things and it doesn't appeal to me.

When I'm in Weggis we're with people doing the same kind of work and naturally one talks about one's work. One talks shop as one would in any situation. But someone who didn't know — my parents, say — would say it's not shop, it's being brainwashed and why are you always talking about meditation or the Maharishi or the latest pamphlet or whatever? But that's shop to us. We talk a lot about the Maharishi's teaching because we are living through meditation. And there is a deep philosophy behind his teaching which one believes in if you're making it your way of life.

And everything is discussed in terms of Maharishi's philosophy and this gives you different values from the way my parents discuss things.

But it's not just their generation. I know lots of young people who are just younger editions of my parents and I really feel as apart from them in outlook as I do with my parents. I don't like to feel that I'm cutting myself off from them, but perhaps I am.

Maharishi's goal is really enlightenment. Which could mean a lot of things. It's self-realisation really. How he would put it to the layman in terms of society today is 'a state of no stress'. A state of using one's full potential and one's full mind and one's full energy. And when you start using a little bit more of your potential then you realise how much more there must be. A higher level of consciousness is what one's seeking. That's the crux of it — that we are trying to achieve a higher level of consciousness and perhaps our parents and families and friends aren't seeking it. It's not that we've attained a higher level but are beginning to. I don't even want to say 'higher' or 'lower' in this context really — we're talking about *different* values, a different way of looking at things.

My parents will always look at what we do from their way of looking at life. I don't try to explain anymore and they don't really ask anymore. They think they know it all, you see. And from their level of consciousness they do know it all. Maybe I'd never understand what they are trying to do either, but the point is that they are *not* trying to do anything and that's what I don't understand.

I know I'd be no good as a social worker or doctor or nurse. Those are very valuable but I feel perhaps we're getting more to the roots of problems, spreading meditation. The more people who meditate, the less problems there will be in the world. I don't think my parents understand that. They feel it has taken me away from them. They don't think I've improved. I believe they think I'm worse. They still see me as someone who has depressions and tantrums and bad tempers. I probably still do to a certain extent although I'd very much disagree that I have them as much as they think I do. Sometimes they say, 'Oh well, we'd better not say anything about that to you or you'll storm out of the room and slam the door and sulk for two weeks.' And I think, 'Who are they talking about? They are talking about me! I haven't done that for years.' But they still think of me like that. I'm still as I was to them, not improved, not changed. They don't see inside. Especially they don't want to think that meditation could change me because they don't want to admit it's of any value. I think they're content. They're just involved in their day-to-day living, making money and spending it, worrying about not having enough and then making some more.

I can shrug off opposition now. I mean, the technique is too simple to be called brainwashing. Anyone can do it. And anyone can try it and decide not to do it. You're not forced in any way. You make a donation when you start and then you're free to carry on on your own or go to a centre whenever you like. It's up to you.

But opposition upsets me when it upsets other people. I can see people getting upset about what I'm doing and not understanding it. In the case of my parents or any of my family, it upsets me not being able to explain it to their satisfaction. They don't believe it does any good and therefore they can't think why I'm giving my life to it.

Yet I'm sure they feel that they have overthrown the values of *their* parents. My mother's parents were very Methodist and very proper and didn't drink and didn't smoke and were narrow-minded. Now my parents would see themselves as liberal-minded, artistic and forward-looking, which they are. But it's all on a material level. And a lot of people like me are seeking something else because we've had all that. Life revolving round parties and drinking and acquiring possessions and making money. Why do they have to have drinks and lots of people for stimulation? I think it's especially this need of stimulation that I don't feel as they do. It's not just drinking in itself. Meditation doesn't stop you drinking, or doing anything in particular. It permeates at all levels. It can enhance the values you already have. I know lots of meditators who still drink. They go and meditate and then come down and have their whisky — but they meditate first and perhaps they enjoy their whisky more.

Meditation should be regarded just as a part of society, a

part of the community. The TM centre should be like the doctor's surgery or the church, part of everyday life. Some people might start for religious reasons, some for medical reasons, some for psychological reasons. It should just be like that and I hope it will be. And, if it's like that, perhaps there wouldn't be so much estrangement between families. It would be more acceptable rather than something peculiar.

There was a certain amount of interest from them, my parents, at first. Later, when I was more involved, and I think they saw me moving away from them, that's when the knocking started. Now it's quite bitter at times. It's just not spoken about because it's a sort of dirty word to them really. I think the reason they still can't see that it's the important thing in my life is that there was about a year when I didn't completely enjoy it.

When I first became a teacher of meditation I was living a very material life as well. I was earning money and I enjoyed that. So when we first went abroad to a meditation centre I didn't like not having any money and not having any material life and I wanted to come back. Simon wanted to stay working for Maharishi and we had a sort of battle about it for about a year.

Eventually we saw Maharishi and he said we should be in Switzerland where he was going to set up everything more permanently. I was still very reluctant and I wasn't very happy for the first year. Throughout my student life I'd always felt that the way to be happy, even when I was meditating — in fact, even more when I was meditating — was if a situation didn't suit me, then I would just get up and leave it. I'd say, 'Oh well, these people are being rotten to me. I'll go somewhere else.' I felt I was being very free. In retrospect, it had just been running away from situations whereas I thought I had just got out of situations into better ones and thought how clever I was.

So suddenly I was with Simon, who I wanted to be with, in this situation where I wasn't happy. I didn't have much work to do then. I didn't really enjoy the people. I missed having money, and the freedom that money brings you. It was as if my ego was being stamped on. It was horrible. I felt trapped and very unhappy and went through a year of battling with Simon — 'You said we'd go home in six months' and then, 'Six months is up now. Can we go back?' I sat twiddling my thumbs, making no attempt to enjoy life there because I wanted to run away. I'd never been made to stay in any situation before.

Then I started to come out of all that. It was like breaking-in a racehorse in a way. Eventually I was broken-in, so to speak, and now I feel that I could be happy in any situation.

I think in any situation there are good points and bad points. You have to enjoy the good ones and put up with the bad ones. It's one of Maharishi's sayings, 'Just enjoy the rose and take no notice of the thorns.' I'd always enjoyed the rose and hated the thorns and said, 'Oh, there's another rose that hasn't got a thorn' — and off I'd go. But now, you see, there are dozens of thorns but I am enjoying the rose.

PART TWO

Driven out

7 Controlling and the crisis of confidence

In most families a daughter is watched over and protected in a way that a boy is not. She is subject to more supervision, is more at the mercy of clocks and the calendar. To a certain extent, this is inevitable because it is an extension of the biological differences between the sexes. A girl is in reality at greater risk of becoming the passive victim of moral and physical exploitation.

But it seems that many parents cannot differentiate between the real dangers and those which are based on their own anxieties and defences. Instead of giving a daughter the knowledge and self-confidence to deal with risks in her own way from her own resources they attempt to ensure that the risks will never have to be faced. In short, the aim is to stop her becoming adult and complete. And because this is an utterly unconscious motive on the part of the parents, it takes subtle, controlling forms and has an element of double bind in it. The parents — usually conscientious and loving people — are steering a daughter towards the fulfilment of their needs for her, which are, of course, based on their needs for themselves, whilst acting as if these aims were in her interest, or 'for her own good' or even what she really wants herself.

This thread runs through many of the case-histories in this book — the 'gamesmanship' which Kate's mother describes as operating between her and her daughter is a minor example — but it could be said to be wholly responsible for the breakaways from home of Alison and

Pauline. They were both in a sense driven out by the impossibility of becoming adult and controlling their own lives whilst still living alongside their parents.

In these cases it's plain that the parents were not dictatorial ogres, nor were the girls themselves unduly rebellious. As you read their stories, no doubt you'll warm to them all, as I did when I met them. They are indeed typical of the ordinary, concerned, loving families in a million homes, of which a great number nevertheless produce this kind of conflict between a daughter's growth of confidence in herself and her parents' unwitting attempts to stunt that growth in the interests of safety and protection.

Family members are, of course, unaware of what is actually happening when these tugs-of-will go on, or even that any manipulation or counter-manipulation is taking place at all. So the parents' attempts to control, and also the daughter's way of evading this control, are likely to take symbolic forms. In a mild way this is what is happening in the familiar parent-child arguments about length of hair, being too fat or too thin, style of dress, the amount of make-up a girl uses. It gets down to these practical, physical matters because a youngster's body-image is the most vulnerable feature to accusations of inadequacy and also the one feature over which he or she has, in the end, more control than a parent does.

And nowhere is this symbolic form of protest more clearly highlighted than in that mysterious condition called anorexia nervosa, from which Alison suffered and which she and her mother tell us about. This is the condition whereby a girl starts off on a slimming kick and, for a variety of reasons, can't stop and will eventually, if she is not treated or if her environment is not changed, starve herself to death. Is it a reaction to parental pressures? Is it a reluctance to grow up? Is it a desperate breakaway from a too close, too loving relationship with mother?

All these theories have their adherents. Research into its causes and treatment is increasing, which is of more than academic interest since one recent estimate has it that as many as one girl in two hundred suffers from anorexia, and in girls over sixteen this rises to one anorexic in every hundred girls.

It's clear from Alison's experience that whatever it was that drove her to refuse food also drove her to leave home. She still has the feeling that 'there's something about me my parents can't approve of'. Whatever the reality, she *feels* unacceptable to them.

This matter of feeling acceptable and self-confident is of tremendous importance to both sexes in adolescence. But there is a difference between the way a boy acquires it and the way a girl acquires it. Some aspects of the campaign for sexual equality have so misled us into believing that both sexes are the same in this respect that it's worth exploring the point.

It has always been recognised that adolescent boys have the need to prove themselves in some way as they enter manhood. Those who are not able to do so go on trying to prove themselves all through their lives and get stuck in adolescence as a result. In other cultures initiation rites take care of this; in our own, initiation is unritualised but it takes place all the same.

The whole motorbike and car cult serves the masculine self-confidence problem for a start. Getting a bike or car and driving it competently and/or aggressively takes many males over the boundary between boy and man. Making money and making love stand in for prowess at hunting and can increase status and self-confidence, although the lack of structure in young adult society (which is discussed in Chapter 1) can bring as many problems in these activities as rewards.

But generally speaking a young man is assigned his place in the pecking order according to his achievements. His self-image and feelings of adequacy depend far more on what he can do and achieve, according to his own value-systems, than on how much he's loved and respected by others or on the presence or absence of satisfying relationships. By and large, boys tend to look for and find physical solutions to their confidence problems.

Now it's imagined that, in striving for and partially gaining equality with men in the world at large, girls are striving for the same achievements as men and also, therefore, for the same answers to the big questions of 'Am

I OK? How do I rate?' On the surface, there's plenty of evidence to point that way. Many girls now have the kind of dreams that used to spur men alone — they want to fly, free-fall by parachute, sail the Atlantic single-handed and climb the highest mountains. They dream of fame and fortune and far-away places; and they are achieving these dreams. But when they do it does not seem to me that it is from the same motives as men: they are not undertaken as an outlet for the age-old pressures on the male to prove that he's arrived and matters and, in a duel against hardship or physical stress or fear or the next man, he can be the conqueror. There is no such pressure on females. The things they 'do' are therefore peripheral to their self-confidence. For this very reason girls do not achieve as much as they could. In a recent study by an American professor of psychology it was found that girls are consistently held back from realising their true intellectual and creative potential because their tendency is to cooper-ate rather than compete — and in a competitive male-dominated society this means they're not even starters, let alone finishers.

So the pressure on females is not that of achievement or competition. Instead it is for qualities which we ought, if we could only get out of the pecking order mentality, rate as high if not higher than the 'masculine' values. As most girls experience it, the pressure on the female adolescent is to be lovable and loving, to matter enough to others to be cherished rather than exploited, to have some choice about what is fulfilling for her and a more or less free hand in pursuing that self-fulfilment. In other words, girls tend to look for emotional answers to their confidence problems.

I have already said how careful fathers have to be lest by a careless put-down they topple this fragile, emotionally charged self-image of a teenage daughter. But I think that both parents have to be sensitive to her feverish internal debate about how lovable and valued she is right now and how likely to be in the future.

This may sound rather obvious but, in fact, many parents believe that the best way to guide a daughter is to keep emphasising her negative qualities and play down the positive ones. Many a breakaway is a flight from constant reminders of 'what's wrong' to somewhere, anywhere, where a girl can find 'what's right' about her.

The great fear in many families is that their teenage daughters will get above themselves and grasp more of life than they're ready to handle. To avoid this, the tendency is to encourage a girl to keep a low profile, and to restrain her confidence in her looks, social abilities and sexuality and sometimes in her intellectual and practical skills as well. But in truth most teenage girls are only too likely to be 'below themselves'. They have lower aspirations than their brothers, though often higher IQs. The general idea is that she should be 'a good girl' rather than a great one, and that means soft-pedalling the qualities that might take her up and away to distant goals but perhaps also to dangers. We no longer lock up our daughters, not physically anyway, but we often lock out the world of experience from them.

This holding back is what Pauline's parents were doing, without realising it, when they did their best to prevent her from having any guilt-free expression of her sexual feelings. This paradoxically went hand in hand with their hope that she would be a wife and mother before very long.

But sex is a feature of so many family conflicts, and figures so largely in most, if not all, of the case-histories I listened to, that it merits a section to itself (Part Three).

'Before I left home I felt that anorexia was beginning to happen again. I was beginning to refuse potatoes and cake, and being awkward. I know I was. It was because of the whole situation at home. I was beginning to feel, "Oh why am I doing this? Why am I at home? Why am I going to college? Why am I doing anything?" '

8 Alison: a case of anorexia nervosa

Alison is attractive, tall, well-built and very amiable. She's twenty, a student teacher and lives with her boyfriend's parents in an East Anglian town. Her father has a senior position in a local commercial firm, and her mother has just started working in market research. Alison has three younger sisters who still live at home. Alison had anorexia nervosa when she was seventeen. It lasted, on and off, until she was nineteen and was told to leave home. She literally starved herself and ended up in hospital. She describes the effects of this illness and herself and the rest of the family.

I can't remember exactly when I got it. I would perhaps say the end of my first year in the lower sixth when I was seventeen. It sort of came on gradually during that year. I was dieting but I was really more depressed than anything — and bad-tempered.

I didn't mind school. I never found it difficult. I was always quite happy in school, with nice staff, so I never had any problems there. I never had to work myself particularly hard so I didn't get worried over work or anything like that.

So it was at home, I think, that it started. My parents didn't like my boyfriends, or late nights, or parties or anything like that. I had to be home by ten-thirty on Fridays and the same time on Saturdays, unless I was going anywhere particular. Then I could have half an hour extra. I had a boyfriend and my mother got so bad about it she wrote out a list of rules of what I was allowed to do and what I wasn't allowed to do: I had to do so many hours of schoolwork a week, I could only see my boyfriend on a Friday night and on a Saturday night, I couldn't see him on a Sunday. If my grandparents were coming round, or any far friends from Scotland or even from round the corner were coming to tea, I had to be there.

I reckon they were very strict. I'm the eldest. Maybe that's got a lot to do with it. I think about it now because I've got three younger sisters and my third sister is now fifteen, younger than I was then, and she's allowed out virtually when she likes. She doesn't even have to leave the city until eleven-thirty which makes it twelve o'clock before she gets home.

But I think perhaps you could say that with me, my parents were still learning. And looking back on it now I can see more clearly where it all comes from. I used to blame my mother, but it obviously wasn't my mother, it was my father. My father made the rules and my mother wrote them out. I've always tended to be my mother's favourite. She always did spoil me. I know she did. New clothes before the others and this sort of thing. Whereas I started to fall out with my father when I started to grow up. I never really did get on with him. That really caused a lot of arguments between my mother and my father and that, in the end, was the reason I left home.

I think I'm a bit too much like my father. We used to get a lot of conflict. I was not really supposed to voice an opinion, he wanted me to have *his* opinions. We could have a little discussion about something and as long as I came back to saying, 'yes, of course, you're right, that was all right. But I'm afraid I was never one to say, 'Yes, that's right, I agree' or let him think that I did. I used to stick to my own point of view.

So things were already a bit difficult when I started to lose weight. I always feel that, at the start, I didn't do it intentionally. I just didn't seem to put on weight. I was always very energetic as well. I was always playing hockey and tennis and horse-riding.

But my mother's a good cook and I was enjoying my food and I began to see a way of getting back at her by *not*

enjoying it. I refused my tea or something. Or she'd put a
meal out on the plate in front of me and I'd say 'I can't eat it'
or 'I'm not hungry'. So it just went on from there. I was
eating less and less and after a while you don't seem to miss
it. It's something that happens gradually. Mummy dragged
me to the doctor because she thought I was a bit under the
weather and he said, 'Oh, you've got to try and eat more.'
But then we moved and I had a change of doctor and he said
I was just depressed. That was for about three or four
weeks and I had drugs for it and then he changed his mind
and said it was anorexia.

So then I had one lot of drugs for depression and one lot,
so they say, to encourage my appetite. My mother did
absolutely everything. She went to the headmistress about
my school lunch. She was managing everything. But I was
managing not to be managed. After a while I said I couldn't
possibly eat my school dinners because the smell just put
me off and it was too revolting, so it would be much better if
I had a packed lunch. Then I could sit outside and eat it. So,
all right, she gave me a packed lunch and I walked out in
the road and threw it in the rubbish bin. Oh that was an
easy way out.

Then I would say things like 'I'm not hungry because I
had a big bar of chocolate or something half an hour ago.'
Eventually she caught on to it and knew it wasn't the
slightest bit true. She tried to force me and that was where
she started to make threats — 'Eat this or you can't go out'.
And I'd say, 'No, I'm not going to eat it and I don't want to
go out anyway.'

It was a tremendous battle. They tried begging me to eat
and they tried threats, they tried to talk to me reasonably.
Well, my mother used to beg more than anything else. My
father used to say, 'Well, if she won't eat that, let her starve.
Ignore her.' My mother would never ignore me — well, she
might do for half an hour then she'd change her mind and
start all over again.

I was miserable most of the time, terribly depressed.
There wasn't anything that I really looked forward to.
There didn't seem to be any future at all. I wasn't bothered
about my exams or anything. The only thing I was really
interested in was the horses. We'd got four ponies at that

time and that's why we moved to the country really. Well, I say I was miserable but at the same time I had a tremendous amount of energy. I'd always be doing something — although deep down you feel sort of hopeless. I think you're continually active and busy because you just have to do something, you can't sit still and do nothing. You feel restless — I couldn't sit down to watch television, I didn't feel like seeing a film, I'd prefer to go for a walk.

But there was no joy in it, it was just to keep my mind off things. Underneath, I was despairing. I'd always say to my mother, 'I don't care. I want to die anyway.' And I really did. I wasn't just saying that. My father would say, 'Oh, take no notice of her.' But I think my mother realised there was a bit more to it than that. She went so far as to remove all aspirins and anything like that from within my reach.

There wasn't anybody I could talk things out with. I tended to close up terribly with my friends. I didn't make any effort with them. I felt incredibly alone for some reason. I tended to keep myself to myself. I think that's why I turned to horses so much; they were company but without making any demands on me — such a difference from people.

But I did have a boyfriend all through that time — not the one I've got now. He was terribly good. And he got on well with my mother. I think my mother needed someone to turn to. My father is not a very communicative type, not exactly sympathetic. I think my mother turned to my boyfriend quite a bit really. That was very good. But I wasn't getting any better.

They had said for several months that I'd got to go into hospital. But I'd say, 'No, I'm all right'. Then I took my A-levels, I expected to get Bs but I got three Es. I must admit I was lazy and I didn't do a lot of work for them. I was taking so many drugs my eyes were completely glazed. I went to the doctor because I kept saying to my mother, 'I just can't see. I absolutely can't see.' So in the end I didn't do any revision. I just went into the exams.

Afterwards we went up to Scotland on holiday and I remember it was particularly cold, we wore jumpers all the week. And I ate nothing. I got much worse and for the first time I felt really ill. I went to see my doctor and I'd lost more than half a stone. My weight had been going down a pound every week up to then, this was much more of a loss. He said, 'Well, obviously, there's only one thing for it — you must go into hospital and if you keep on saying "No" I'll make you go.' But at that stage I just felt so exhausted and worn out that I gave in.

I was in hospital for a month. I was six-stone-twelve when I went in and I went up during that month. I didn't gain much at first and then I went up to about eight stone before I came out. I went up about another half-stone during the rest of the holiday and then I went to University. But I lost weight again there and I didn't stay at University. I went to teacher training college instead. I like college. I never really wanted to go to University. But that's one of the things that my father can never forgive me for — leaving University. He was cross about that. He had said to me, 'Oh well, you can do what you like. You're old enough to know what you want to do.' Then the minute I did it he turned sour. You come to expect it. You come to know what he's going to do.

Then my mother started to get these funny ideas that I would leap into bed with any Tom, Dick or Harry. We'd have these very heated discussions about it. It was beginning to wear me down. I'd try to avoid her. I used to think, 'I'm not going home for lunch because I'll find her there.' I used to creep in when I thought she was in the garden or something, and change and get out to the horses or something.

She wasn't trying to explain about contraception or anything like that. Her attitude was that it was all wrong; I just wasn't to, and that was that. That was the way I'd been brought up and all the rest of it. I think she just got things out of all proportion and however much I tried to explain she just seemed to pick up the wrong end of the stick all the time. Once she got set ideas in her mind about what I was doing, then if I'd sworn I wasn't doing it she would still think I was telling a white lie. So in the end I just said, 'Yes, yes, yes. . . .'

When I went on the pill that was just about it. My mother knows everything that happens. I don't know how she knows. But, however careful you are, she knows. I know

she reads my letters, she told me so. I never really thought
she'd do that, I thought that was something private. She
thinks she's justified — 'It's for your own good', she says.
There was hell to pay about going on the pill; my father
called me such names as 'a little slut' — that hurt.

Well, one Friday evening they went away for the
weekend and I thought they'd be home after lunch on
Sunday. My next sister, she's eighteen, and I had made
arrangements to go out about seven on the Saturday. I said
to her, 'We haven't been told what time to come home so
we'll please ourselves'. She said, 'All right'. I'm a bit bossy
and I said, 'You haven't got much choice, have you? I'm
driving the car'. And I must admit that I was half an hour
later picking her up than I intended to be. I knew she was all
right because she was at her boyfriend's house. I knew she
wasn't standing on the streets or anything.

In fact, my parents came home that evening while we
were out. So we got home and my father said my sister
could go in but I couldn't go in. So, of course, my mother
did let me in after I made a fuss on the doorstep. There was
a lot of shouting, a real scene. My father didn't even come
down, it was my mother who came down. My father
refused to speak to me; he refused to speak to anyone
except my mother, like he always has done and always will
do, I expect. And she said I wasn't to come in. So after a
great deal of shouting through the door she let me in — I
knew she would. But then, of course, my father said he was
going to go. It was either him or me. So I went — there was
no choice really.

I went to my grandmother's first of all. Then I had a
bed-sitter in the city. But I found I wasn't managing on my
grant. A few weeks ago I was down to £20. I was paying £10
a week just for accommodation, no food. The landlady was
putting the rent up another £2 a week so I owed her about
£20 and I said no, I just couldn't do it. So now I'm living
round at my boyfriend's with his parents, where I just pay
for my food.

I couldn't possibly go home again. I'm sure I couldn't.
I've moved away emotionally now. At first I found it very
difficult. I tend to be the sort of person who depends rather
heavily on other people, although they may not realise it. I

always like to feel I've got somewhere where I belong.
Security — I do like that — and that's something you have
with a home. Although I felt the break was coming on a
long time. In a way I think I was just waiting for something
like that big row to happen. Before I left home I felt that
anorexia was beginning to happen again. I was beginning
to refuse potatoes and cake, and being awkward. I know I
was. It was because of the whole situation at home. I was
beginning to feel, 'Oh, why am I doing this? Why am I at
home? Why am I going to college? Why am I doing
anything?'

The last straw now is the fact that I'm living with my
boyfriend, Bob. That's really done it. Although it's at his
parents, that doesn't make any difference. And that's why
I've given up trying to get things friendly with my father
again. Basically the trouble at the moment, with him too, is
my boyfriend. He doesn't like him. They never liked any of
my boyfriends in any case. I don't understand it this time
because Bob went out with my sister for a time. They liked
him then. But my mother said he was too old for her — he's
twenty-one now. And my sister was never very keen and
sort of got rid of him. We never started to go out until I'd left
home anyway.

We get on terribly well. But he's not what my parents call
my type. I think they mean class — education and
money-wise. They're relatively well-off and he sprays cars
for a living — which I think is a nice refreshing change. I'm
very happy with him and they can't understand that. I
haven't really tried to explain it to my mother. The truth of
the matter is that I never really get the time. Whenever I go
home it usually ends in an argument. The other day she
said, 'I don't know what you think you're doing going out
with him'. But I never seem to get the chance to explain, she
never invites us home for a meal. She could easily invite us
round for tea on a Sunday — but she doesn't. So I tend to go
home when I know she's not there, I just go when my
sisters are there.

I get on terribly well with my sisters, all of them. I go up
to see them and take them out. I suppose my mother's just
tending to follow my father again. But I see her at these
Wednesday meetings I go to, the anorexic group, and

sometimes Bob comes with me. My mother is nice and as charming as anything when there are other people about but I went home on the Thursday to pick something up, the day after I'd seen her at the meeting, and she was as horrible as anything and I hadn't done anything. I just went round.

I sometimes wonder if she's happy. I realise that that was why my father had got cooler with me lately, because of Bob. It couldn't possibly be anything else. But I thought my mother did like him. I don't understand it really. I think they hoped for sons. They say they wanted the last two children to be boys—that might be part of the problem. But I don't know, I think my mother is happy. She's always been one of those people who's been ill, there's always something the matter; she had bad migraine at one stage; my next sister was difficult when she was born — but still, she had two more after that. She's started to work now. To be honest, she strikes me as being happier since she's gone out a bit.

I'm beginning to feel independent now, I don't think quite so much and worry about my parents and home now. And I think they see me as independent now, with money anyway. They never think of giving me any money or helping me out with anything. There are no hand-outs. I'm independent. A good thing really. I get the full grant so I don't have to rely on them. It's better really. It would be embarrassing if I had to ask them for money.

But it still bothers me a bit, about my parents. I think a lot of my parents and they've been terribly good to me. But there's something not right, something that just wouldn't work if I lived at home. There's something that they can't approve of about me.

'She gradually went down and down until she was virtually eating nothing except black coffee and pieces of cheese. Her only explanation then was that she was slimming, nothing more. But I began to think there was more to it when she became very, very depressed and thoroughly bad-tempered, just not herself.'

9 Alison's mother

Alison's mother is a young-looking, fair-haired bundle of energy. She talks quickly, moves quickly and gives the impression of a busy, capable woman, but also a kindly one.
This is her side of the story of Alison's illness and how she left home.

It was during the summer period that it began. When the rest of the family were eating sandwiches and cream cakes and having a cup of tea outside in the garden, Alison would be delicately having two Ryvitas with no butter on them and a piece of cheese. And, of course, one tends to think, 'She's fit and well, this won't do any harm for a few weeks. She'll get over this urge to have slimming things and feel hungry and start to eat again.'

She was normal weight at that time, about nine and a half stone, as she is more or less now. She was normal build, not overweight. We as parents are not overweight. Grandparents are not overweight. In fact I come from a lean family. My grandfather was over six foot and never carried any weight. And she knew him and she had no fear of being overweight.

Then she was obviously deceiving me with school lunches. In fact, she said she didn't want a cooked lunch so I said, 'Fair enough, I'll pack you something.' And the packed lunches were obviously going in the bin. She wasn't eating them — which she admitted afterwards. I suspected this. Her evening meals I thought she was eating, but she was obviously feeding the dog. The dog got wider and Alison got thinner. Of course, he sat himself under the table and the habit's never gone. He now sits under the table all the time — not that he gets fed any more. Also her sisters said they saw her put food in a napkin and empty it in the bin afterwards. But when there's a lot of you round the table your eyes aren't on everybody. Obviously, she did it when my attention was distracted. I left her to serve her own vegetables and she would never take anything she felt was in any way fattening, like potatoes. She would possibly eat some very lean meat. She gradually went down and down until she was virtually eating nothing except black coffee and pieces of cheese. Her only explanation then was that she was slimming, nothing more.

But I began to think there was more to it when she became very, very depressed and thoroughly bad-tempered, just not herself. So we took her to the doctor for months and months to be treated for very deep depression. She was getting all sorts of anti-depressives and things like this. This went on for, I suppose, nearly six months and I kept saying to the doctor, 'There must be more wrong than that.' I knew nothing at all about anorexia. I read nothing in the paper. I'd heard nothing.

Eventually, when I was at the doctor's with Alison, he said to me, 'I would like to see your husband on his own, if you wouldn't mind'. My husband went down the next evening. He said, 'I'm sorry to tell you this but I think your daughter has got anorexia and if she doesn't pull herself together she'll die'.

We were then at the stage of moving house, therefore we had to move to another doctor. Our previous doctor wrote to the new doctor and said that he'd been looking after Alison and that was what was wrong with her. The new doctor said no, she was depressed, and he started the same treatment over again. So we lost about four months with Alison until I finally put my foot down with the doctor and said, 'Something must be done. Can't she see somebody else?' He said, 'Oh well, if you feel like that about it, yes'. Doctors are funny sometimes — terrible, in fact. He sent

her to see the psychiatrist and he, of course, said, 'Yes,
Alison has got anorexia' and the treatment started with
him.

There again we went week after week after week. No
treatment — he talked and talked and talked to her and
every week she said yes, she'd try harder, she'd go home
and she'd eat and she'd try. But, of course, they get past the
stage of being able to eat. It just makes them feel thoroughly
sick to look at food, unless it's something they keep taking
like black coffee. Alison would drink that and she could
usually manage to nibble a bit of cheese.

There were so many worries. She even threatened
suicide. Because we'd just moved, you see, we hadn't even
got cupboards and things. Our picnic hamper was still
packed with all the medical kit. And I found her one day
sitting in the middle of the floor with the medical kit, saying
to herself, 'How many of these would I have to take?'

It got so that I felt I couldn't let her out of my sight. I had
to let her go to school obviously, but I worried until she
came back. I also worried as soon as she turned the
door-handle, thinking, 'Oh dear, now what are we going to
have to face this evening?' I was so tense that, as soon as her
hand was on the door, I withdrew within myself. I think
perhaps I didn't help her because I'd also got to such a
pitch. I knew before the evening was out there'd be a row
over something.

My husband and I were having rows about it as well.
Men don't take quite the same attitude as women on the
whole. I don't think they feel quite the same. Well, if he did
I don't think he would have admitted it. But I've seen him
many times very depressed and worried about Alison. Still,
he had had business problems and when he came home he
didn't want to be met with friction.

And then eventually my husband said, 'I'm getting a bit
sick of this going on week after week after week. I will go
with you to see the psychiatrist.'

So he came with me to see Dr M— and told him, 'We
must do something more, this has just gone on too long.
Can't Alison go into hospital?' And the doctor said, 'Alison
says "No". She's over the age you see. And unless we get
people to your home and really commit her, we can't do

anything about it if she says "No".' Anyway, after a long talk with us, Alison got to the end of her tether, I think, as well as us. And she said 'Yes', she would go in and have treatment.

So she was whipped in almost immediately, before she had time to change her mind. He put her in an empty cubicle in hospital — no books, no phone calls, no letters or anything. She just had to lie in bed. She wasn't allowed out to go to the loo or wash her hands or anything. She was just given pencil and paper and told to list her priorities of the things she wanted back, like going to the loo and having a bath, having visitors and so on. We left her in an empty room and took her clothes away. It was heartbreaking, terrible. Worse than a prisoner.

So we left her and she wrote this list of priorities and the doctor came down and said, 'Right, as soon as you eat something, we will start with your priorities but we will start at the bottom of the list and work up.' And fortunately, this seemed to do the trick. She did start to eat. They were giving her all sorts of gruel and stuff to try and put some weight on. We were allowed to see her very quickly because she was so good. I don't think it was much over a week before they let us see her, because of the simple reason that she did eat, she did make the attempt to be good and help herself. And then, of course, we started taking in chocolate biscuits and cream cakes and she would sit with us and usually eat. As a matter of fact, she didn't seem to feel so guilty when she was in hospital and eating. I think perhaps it was because she wanted to get herself out. It wasn't a very pleasant place to be in — a psychiatric ward. She says now she wouldn't ever want to do it again because she wouldn't want to go back into hospital.

After the hospital stay, it wasn't completely better straightaway. She ate, but she was terribly guilty about it. Whenever she'd eaten, we'd get a very bad mood, irritability and bad temper. And this bad temper would get to such a pitch that she'd be blaspheming. You couldn't think that she belonged to you because of the language she was using. She'd always had a fear of being sick, or of seeing anyone else being sick, so that was a saving grace — I knew she wouldn't make herself sick as some girls do.

Once she'd eaten something, off she'd go — 'I have to go for a walk' or 'I have to ride the horse'. She obviously thought this would get rid of the food she'd just eaten. She had no difficulty eating salads and vegetables and cheese — still the slimming foods — but it's hard to think where the turning-point came of eating everything. Even now she says she sometimes feels guilty of eating too much. . . .

It was also a difficult time of decision then as to what university to go to and waiting for her A-level results — all a very strenuous time. You see she took her 'A's whilst she was at the worst state of anorexia. She used to sit and go to sleep. We expected her to get a B grade in most of her things but she didn't. She didn't get the results she wanted, which she should have got had she looked after herself.

She got her place at Warwick. But in my opinion she shouldn't have gone there. I sat up with Alison in the hospital and I said, 'Do wait a year, Alison, you're not fit. Wait a year, do anything, do what you like in that year, I don't mind, do exactly what you like, do a job if you want, do precisely what you like, only get better.' But — oh no! She'd be too old at university if she did that, so she was going that year. So I said to the psychiatrist, 'What is the best thing?' And he said, 'If she wants to go, let her.'

She'd only been there a month and we got a telephone call 'Oh Mummy, I'll have to come home. I don't like it here.' I said, 'Look, Alison, stay at least for the first term. You've hardly given yourself a chance after a month to know if you like it. Then, at the end of that term, if you're really adamant, then you can come home.' She came home at weekends but when I put her on the train to go back she cried and I cried. So it didn't stop you see, it went on and on. The effects of this anorexia, it didn't stop. Her being so depressed and me being so depressed.

It was nice to have her away because the house suddenly went quiet and there were no rows. On the other hand, I kept thinking, 'Oh dear, is she all right?' They knew about her at the university — the doctor told them — and her tutor used to phone me up every so often and say 'Don't worry, she's reasonably well'. She was tucked into a room next to one of the lady tutors. There was also a girl from Alison's school there and she was put in the same corridor, obviously in the hopes of getting Alison settled. But she didn't. She came home at Christmas and didn't go back.

So it was back to the bad temper and rebellion at home. The crux came when we went away for the weekend, my husband and I. Obviously, they're old enough to leave on their own. It was business anyway, not anything terribly exciting. And when we got back we found the youngest one in the house entirely alone. She was thirteen at the time. We've got dogs and the rest of it but we do live in the country and I thought it was rather bad of the others to go off and leave her on her own. She said it was her fault because she didn't want to go with them. But it had been left that the other three were going to go out when we got home. I'd said to Alison, who was going out with a young man I didn't know anything about — who he was, I hadn't even met him — I said, 'Now, please, Alison, be in by twelve.' 'I'm not going to be in by twelve,' she said. And I said, 'I'm sorry, Alison, but this has gone on far too long. If you're not in by twelve, the door will be locked.' 'Oh well,' she said, 'I don't care about that. I shall not be in by twelve.' So then I said to the next one down, 'Now, Sharon, you come home when we pick up Cathy, (the third one).' And she said, 'All right, fair enough.'

After we'd left for the weekend, they'd got their heads together and Alison had said to Sharon, 'You can come home with me. I must be in by twelve and therefore that's reasonable for you, at your age, to be in by twelve too, and Daddy can pick up Cathy.' So I found a little note to this effect when we got back. Well, unfortunately — I mean, I'm soft and I wouldn't have done anything about it — but I'd said to my husband, 'I've told Alison that if she's not in by twelve I'm locking the door'. And he said, 'If you said that, you're to do it. It's no good making these threats and not carrying them out.' And then, of course, when I found the note saying that Sharon was with her I thought 'Oh dear'.

Anyway at about a quarter to one the telephone rang and Sharon was in tears — 'Alison still hasn't picked me up. I'm waiting for Alison. What shall I do?' She was fortunately at her boyfriend's home with his parents and they'd even offered to put her up for the night because they saw she was upset. And I said, 'I don't know what to do,

Sharon. Because, if I come after you, Alison could well
come and pick you up within the next five minutes and
Daddy's saying that you're not to come in.' So it really put
Sharon on the spot and me on the spot but I said, 'I'm not
having Sharon out all night'. She shouldn't have been
persuaded by Alison but on the other hand you can't blame
her entirely because Alison is very persuasive when she
wants to be.

So, of course, when they got home I opened the door to
let Sharon in and Alison barged past me and that was it. My
husband said, 'It's no good. We can't have this disobedi-
ence. You must go.' He said, 'Either she goes or I go'. It was
awful for me. I was obviously divided — pig in the middle.
But in fairness to him we'd had a very traumatic time. But
my husband saying 'Her or me' really put me on the spot. I
said to Alison, 'Well, there's the other girls to think of. If
Daddy leaves me, what am I left with? I don't know how I'd
bring up your sisters. I'd have to sell the house, I couldn't
have a big house like this one. Everything would have to
go, through no fault of your sisters. So what do you think?'
'Oh,' she said, 'I only did it to make you kick me out. I knew
it was coming to that. This is the last straw, I know.'

And I know my husband would have left. Because
having said he's going to do something, he'll do it. I don't
think he would have stayed away. He might have done for
a time, just to show us that he really means what he says.
You see, he thought that I was aiding and abetting.

She went the next day. She came in that night and slept
in her own bedroom. The next day we were supposed to be
going, all of us, that Sunday, to my husband's parents. Of
course, I couldn't go because I was too upset. And my
husband refused to go. Fortunately, my second daughter
drives so I said to her 'Take your sisters and go. Leave your
Dad and I to see everything's all right.' And then Alison
went. I think I spent most of the day sleeping. I hadn't slept
that night. I went to bed and my husband then decided to
be very kind and got me an aspirin.

That was an unhappy time, after she'd gone. We'd
always got on very well really. She'd always talked to me. I
think we're very much alike. She's very much like my
husband's family to a large extent but deep down she's very

much like me. I was never rebellious, though, when I lived at home. I had no cause to be, I suppose. My parents were very sweet to me. Life was different then anyway, wasn't it? We didn't expect to stay out late. If you missed the last bus you were stranded. I mean, my father didn't have a car and I knew that the last bus was the time I had to come in.

I don't feel very happy about her now. In fact, I have to try and switch off from Alison. Oh, we get on well when we meet and have a coffee and she talks to me but I feel when I'm talking that she's not really listening. She's got a boyfriend at the moment who — well, we can't say we dislike, because he's not the sort of boy one can dislike. But Alison has been — I'm not being snobbish, but she's been brought up in a fairly good way. She's been used to carpets on the floor and a colour TV and a car to run around in. And I don't think her boy can give her all of this. He's just a mechanic and he's got no ambition. If he was studying, perhaps, with the prospect of having a garage of his own one day, well then, one would only encourage him along that way. But I don't think he has any ambitions at all. And I feel that basically Alison knows this but because I'm saying 'Don't do it, Alison' she's doing precisely that, in her rebellious way.

It's difficult really. She's living at his parents' house and she wants to get married. Now she hasn't told me she does but I was told by one of my other daughters that she'd had a talk with Bob, Alison's boyfriend, because she found him on his own. She said, 'What are you doing on your own, Bob?' and he said, 'Alison's gone off in a huff because she wants to get married. . . .'

So things are dragging on. And, I forget when it was now, I think it was Christmas or round about that period — they had a dinner dance and she'd been going out with Bob for some time then. But she didn't take him to the dinner dance. She elected to take this son of a friend of ours who's also been used to a very good life and who has an evening suit. She elected to invite him and take him to the dinner. Now this, to me shows that she's rather ashamed of Bob. I think she's being just a little selfish because I feel she's using him. It's his car she's running around in, he takes her everywhere; she runs the Guides and he chases around doing things for her in that connection.

It is a worry. I feel if she could meet someone nice and get married perhaps my worries would be over. I'm sure if she married Bob it wouldn't work out. He's too easy-going to some extent, and will let her bully him around and push him around, which is her way with him. On the other hand, just at times, he gets very, very sultry. And I think the two temperaments clash something horrible. . . . She needs a strong character, she needs someone like my husband — someone really strong enough to cope with her bouts of bad temperament. Or, on the other hand, someone completely opposite — someone easy-going who doesn't mind the way she treats him. It's not going to be a very easy marriage, is it, whoever she marries? Deep down, as far as her conscience is concerned she's a bit like me. But the domineering bit, that doesn't come from me, that comes from my husband. He's very Victorian, he's got to be — life isn't very easy with four daughters.

Obviously I as a mother thought it was all my fault, the anorexia and all the trouble. I thought it's something I'd done — 'Where have I gone wrong? What have I done?' On the other hand you look at the other three who are growing up reasonably happy, healthy young ladies, and you think well I can't feel it's my fault. If I hadn't got the other three I would have been heartbroken. Well, I was. But it would have had a terrible, disastrous effect on me if I hadn't got the other three, if she'd been an only daughter. In fact, my second daughter is a real joy to have, she's a lovely girl. . . .

There are lots of things I think might be the reason. Alison being the eldest, for example. I had the three others to look after, therefore Alison had to grow up and perhaps she had to grow up too quickly. When I look at my fourteen-year-old now, being allowed to grow up in her own sweet way, and I think how Alison was having to help me to a large extent at that age, I think we pushed her too far, too quickly, and she didn't want to grow up so quickly. In fact, I think for many years she hasn't really wanted to grow up. I don't think I gave her an awful lot of responsibility but I think the eldest one always has to make a path to a large extent.

I often think of when she was fifteen, that was when she

last fitted into the family. I'd like to have that time over again, knowing what I know now. I think I'm handling my other three better because of what has happened to Alison. I think it's difficult with the first one, you're more worried. You start, at ten o'clock at night, thinking, 'What is she up to? Who is she with? Is anybody taking her away, kidnapping her?' All these things go through your mind. And Alison's the sort of girl who, if someone made a fuss of her, showing her a lot of love, I'm sure she would have gone. I don't think she sees through people. If someone gave her a bit of affection she'd be away.

I think there again, I suppose one shouldn't blame one's husband, but he doesn't show her much affection. He does in material ways. He always does a lot for them in that respect. But as for putting his arm round her and showing affection — never. He's not that kind of person. He doesn't show me any either, not in public.

Even now I think, 'If only she'd come home. . . .' I'd like her to be one of the family again — behaving like the rest of the family, of course. I mean they're not angels. You don't expect children to be angels. But they're quiet. I talked to them about it. I said, 'Sharon, do you feel we've been hard on you?' And she says, 'No, no, of course not.' She sees now the way Alison's living and behaving and she says, 'It wouldn't be right for Alison to come back. There'd only be trouble.'

'To Mum and Dad, I realise now, sex is
something that other people do, people who
aren't very nice. Or it's something that
happens to nice people if they're not careful.
I don't know how I or my brothers came to
be born, I really don't . . .'

10   Pauline, the pregnant runaway

*Pauline is an 18-year-old student nurse. Her home is a council
house in Northampton. Her father is a cabinet maker. When she
left school she started work in a supermarket on the tills and had
just been promoted when she suddenly left home and hitched to
London. Unknown to her parents she was five and a half months
pregnant.*

*She has great big brown eyes and medium-length dark hair.
She's quite short and plumpish, but not fat. She has a kind, nice
face which looks almost beautiful when it lights up. But most of
the time she has rather a 'closed' look and keeps her head down.
She has a very quiet voice and a shy manner.*

They've got this council house in Northampton still. I often
think of it because although I couldn't possibly live there
anymore after what's happened it was very cosy and
homey and for all her faults Mum was good at looking after
people. It was all she was good at, to be honest. It must
have been great for both of them when we were kids. They
loved all that, the bedtime stories and the picnics and
things. It's funny, Mum's favourite book, to read to us, was
Peter Pan and Wendy — you know, the boy who never
grew up. She thought that family, Wendy's family, were
marvellous. They were so nice — nice parents and nice kids
with nice manners. That's how she liked everything to be
really — nice. Everything soft and pink and romantic and
nothing nasty like arguments and scenes and, well,
growing-up too. That's it really — neither she nor Dad
wanted us to grow up, I don't think. Like for example, she

never told me anything about periods — not a thing. I heard a bit, of course, at school. But when they started I was still a bit shaken, as well as pleased. It was a Saturday morning, I remember and I wanted to tell someone. But no school and I wasn't allowed out visiting at all then, so I couldn't. It's interesting that I didn't even think about telling Mum. I don't think she'd have known what to say.

Still, to be fair, when she finally knew about the baby she was all over me and very comforting just when I needed it. A bit sloppy and sentimental but never mind. The point was that she could cope with the idea of an actual baby because she loved babies and was good with them and she understood about being a mother and that. It was all the business before a baby — sex and getting pregnant — that she didn't want to know about. So you can see why I couldn't stay at home when I got pregnant. She'd have flipped, and so would my father. Getting accustomed to it afterwards is a different matter, especially if the baby's not there to remind them. I think they've kidded themselves now that it never happened. But I still couldn't go back and live there. They're just the same but I'm different.

The whole trouble was that they just didn't want to know about any of the problems people have nowadays. Nothing about divorce or abortion or poofs or lezzies. If the paper had anything they wouldn't read it. If there was something on the telly they'd switch off. They didn't believe in any sex education at school, but they didn't think it was their job either. God knows what they thought about how I was supposed to learn — of course, you do learn a lot from other girls and the women's mags. Perhaps nobody learns much from their parents, I don't know, but you do need to be able to talk about it all like an ordinary subject of conversation and get it sussed out for yourself, what you'd do if something did happen and how they'd react and so on.

They stopped going to the cinema years ago, when, according to Dad, they started showing nothing but 'filth'. When I was fourteen I did a paper round and the newsagents changed hands and they got in a lot of mags with titles like 'Spanking Hot' and Dad saw them on display there and stopped me doing the round. He had no idea what they were really like, of course. In fact, they were very funny, a big joke. He was absolutely ignorant really about anything to do with sex. I think he wanted me to stay ignorant. I think he thought that was the same as being good.

When I started at the supermarket, he was still at the stage of getting uptight about my make-up. I was seventeen and he was treating me more like thirteen. I was expected to be in by ten-thirty every night and I was never allowed to spend the night with friends. 'Safer under your own roof' he was always saying, but they'd never mention or talk about what I was supposed to be kept safe *from*. The worst thing he used to do is to sometimes come and meet me from work. He'd usually pretend it was just by chance or it was on his way home — but it wasn't. The girls at work teased me and teased me all the time. They thought I was such a kid, even though I was older than some of them and even when I became a supervisor.

Most of their talk, of course, was about sex. They acted as if they knew it all and they all had boyfriends to talk about, though I think some of them were imaginary. But I couldn't talk about a real one because I didn't have one and I couldn't invent one because I knew nothing about boys at all, not to be with on your own. Mum and Dad seemed to think you could end up with a husband one fine morning without ever having had a boyfriend. They wanted me to be married, 'safe and sound' they called it, but they were against me meeting any men. I could see it was crazy but I hadn't got the guts to do anything about it. That's another thing that all this no-sex thing does for you — it makes you feel so put-down and such a kid that you just believe everything you're told and go along like a lamb wherever anyone leads you.

And that's what happened when the van driver chatted me up that came to the supermarket. I thought he was marvellous. It wasn't just that he noticed me and talked to me and asked me out — what was marvellous was that all the other girls saw this happening and he was older and good-looking and it all made me feel at last I was getting somewhere and I was grown up.

I had to lie about going out with him. I had to pretend I was going to a firm's dance. I felt very guilty about it because they got so excited for me and Mum lent me her best brooch and Dad was so chuffed about the manager asking me, which is what I said.

I never knew the van driver's surname or anything about him. After that night I never saw him again. I suppose he stopped coming to the store. I had no feeling for him or for anyone after that night. I just went sort of numb. It all seemed unreal.

I had a lot to drink very quickly. For all I know he spiked them. But if he did he needn't have bothered — I mean I was so daft then I'd have done anything he suggested without a single drink. Half of the sexy talk he was giving me I never even understood. We got into the back of his van after the pubs closed and that was it. I hardly remember anything except how silent it all was — no loving words or anything like that. I didn't enjoy it. I was sickened really. And when I got home Mum and Dad went moaning on about me being late.

There was a terrible time before I actually knew I was pregnant when I was going on hoping I wasn't. It's horrible. You keep on going to the toilet to see if your period's come. You start praying and touching wood and you hardly think of anything else. I didn't know anything about pregnancy tests. I was about three weeks overdue before I saw an ad where you could get it done by post for £3. So I did that then rang them up and the woman said, 'It's positive' and I still wasn't sure and I had to say, 'Does that mean I'm pregnant?' And she said, 'yes, that's right.' And in a way, it was a relief not to have to go on hoping anymore or looking for signs or anything.

I didn't tell anyone I knew. I couldn't. Anyway all my worrying had taken up all my time and girls at work were accusing me of being standoffish. There was one girl I was friendly with — life was a great big joke to her and although she'd have probably known all the answers I somehow just couldn't bring myself to tell her. She'd have made it the joke of the year. Anyway, she helped without knowing it because it was in one of her mags that I saw about abortions and how it's dangerous after twelve weeks and where you could go for help.

So I took a day off work and went to the BPAS, their

branch in Bedford. I didn't actually want an abortion. I just
wanted to find out if I did. It said in the mag that these
people could help you find out. BPAS is the British
Pregnancy Advisory Service so I suppose it's to help
pregnant girls. They arrange abortions if you're legally
entitled and it's cheaper than going private. Anyway, there
was a nice woman and we chatted but I heard myself
saying, well amost shouting, 'I don't want it taken away'
and she was very nice about it and said, 'I don't think you
really want an abortion, do you?' and I said, 'no'. And we
talked about me perhaps having it adopted or keeping it
and she gave me some names and addresses of people to
help me. But, of course, those were at home in Northampton and I already knew I couldn't possibly stay there once
the baby showed.

The awful thing was that around that time there seemed
to be nothing but baby-stuff all round me. My brother's
baby was always in our house, my Dad was always taking
pictures of it and my Mum cooing all over it. I used to think
well, they couldn't possibly feel like that about my baby
and I used to picture various scenes where I told them
about my baby and every time the end of it was always
them having hysterics and shoving me out of the house.
They couldn't go on loving me, that was certain. To Mum
and Dad, I realise now sex is something that other people
do, people who aren't very nice. Or it's something that
happens to nice people if they're not careful. I don't know
how I or my brothers came to be born, I really don't. It just
seemed to me I couldn't have had sex and be a nice person,
a member of the no-sex Wells family, at the same time. So I
had to leave the family.

It's funny how trouble makes you strong. I surprised
myself. One day Mum said I was putting on weight and I
thought, 'It's time to go.' I pretended I had a cold, stayed
home from work and while Mum was out shopping I just
packed one suitcase and left. I didn't leave a note — what
could I have said? That was a bit cruel I suppose, because
they did worry when I'd gone, I know. But I couldn't really
think about anyone else then, only me and the baby. And
all I knew was that we had to get right away.

I got onto the M1 spur and hitched to London. I nearly

turned back home; a lorry driver made a pass and then when I told him I was pregnant he went like an uncle and tried to persuade me to go back home. He dropped me at Watford, on the Northampton line and I really thought I was going to go back but I let the Northampton train go and I went across the bridge and got the next train to Euston. By that time it wasn't like me making the decisions at all. I was in a kind of daze. I didn't really get out of it until the baby was born.

I felt terrible at Euston. I cried in that big hall. I saw the notice about GALS, Girls Alone in London Service, and it was just across the street so I went there. But there's not all that they can do. They can tell you all about what money you can get, and they can get you an emergency bed for the night but there aren't many places you can stay for long. I was ignorant about all of that too. I thought it would be pretty easy to find a room or a flat and get a job even. But it isn't. It's nearly impossible, especially if you're pregnant. So the woman there spent a long time trying to persuade me to go back home and then trying to persuade me to let them know where I was. So the next day I did ring Mum, but I couldn't say much and I didn't tell her about the baby and I just made out I had to get away for a bit, hinting at being overworked or something.

Anyway GALS put me onto One-Parent Families, that used to be the Unmarried Mother and Her Child. You don't realise, till you get into a mess like this, what a lot of people there are who'll help, or try to. The social worker there was quite young. I went and saw her the next day. I spent the night in a hostel in Islington before that but I still hadn't anywhere to go for the next night. So the first thing she did was fix me up in another hostel but she had a terrible job finding any room for me, she was almost on her knees to people on the phone. And she, like the woman at GALS, did her best to get me to go back home. It's all tied up with money you see. When you go to a mother and baby home it costs from about £17 a week to £50 a week to keep you there. You stay six weeks before the baby's born and then six weeks after. And the council where you live, back home, they're asked to pay most of it. And they, of course, don't see why you shouldn't stay within their area, where

they can kind of keep an eye on you, get your family to help
and, most of all, try and trace the father. But I didn't want
any of that so I was still determined to stay in London.

Looking back I wish I hadn't now. I was desperately
lonely. I had about two months to go before I could go into a
mother and baby home. One-Parent Families found me a
single parent who was working and wanted someone to
look after the baby — they said I was terribly lucky. That
kind of job doesn't happen much. I liked the girl but she
was quite tough and made the whole thing look really
terrible, bringing up a baby on your own. So that was
another thing that made me decide on adoption. I don't
think she was right, mind you. I mean, that was only one
side of it. Other single mothers are very happy. Perhaps I
would have been. But it's too late now.

I was also very homesick. I'd ring home but I still
wouldn't say where I was or what I was doing, just that I
was all right. And naturally, this meant that whether it was
Dad or Mum on the phone, there wasn't much to say.
They'd given up trying to make me go back and yet they
didn't know why I'd gone — it was horrid on the phone,
very tense. But in a way I did long to tell her and talk about
the clothes for the baby and things like that. If we'd done
that, I'd have kept it, I think; somehow I'd have managed.
They might even have had me back there with the baby.
That's what I think, looking back now. But at the time that
seemed impossible, something out of a storybook.

So, in the end, I didn't tell Mum anything until I'd had
the baby (a boy) and the arrangements about adoption had
begun. I didn't want to see it at all. I thought that would be
easier. I had an easy time, that's being young, I expect —
and one thing about having a baby is that all those worries
about your body, you know, being seen with nothing on
and being examined — all that goes. With most people it
does anyway. But my mother's had three and she's still
very prudish. We never ever saw her or Dad with no
clothes on or even half-dressed; I never saw my brothers
nude, actually. And we never burped or blew off the way
some families do among themselves. It sounds daft but I
wish we had. I think all that is much more real and more
free. If I ever have a family again I'll bring them up like that

— more free.

So they took the baby to the hospital nursery and after a week he apparently went to a foster home and I went back for a while to the girl I'd stayed with before the baby was born.

I thought then I'd better tell Mum what had happened. And I did badly want to see them. I'd been away nearly five months and that's a long time if you've never been away from home before. So I did the same thing as when I came up to London — I hitched back and when I got near our street I rang up from a phone box and that was all a bit spoilt because there was no answer.

So I went round there and I waited outside. They always lock the house up. And I did begin to wonder if they were away but the cat was there and they'd never leave her alone for long. So they came back after a bit and it was a big let-down really because everything was so awkward. We didn't know what to say, any of us, and I suddenly got the feeling, when we were having tea, that they were worried in case I'd come back to stay, come back for good. So I got that out of the way quickly and said I'd got somewhere to live in London — which wasn't true and that I was thinking of taking up nursing, which was true, only I'd half thought of doing it locally.

Eventually, I got Mum on her own and told her about the baby and that was a bit of a let-down too. She said she thought as much and she didn't say anything about whether she'd have looked after it if I'd kept it. Well, she had already got a grandson so I suppose that made a difference. But she was, as I said, very comforting about me giving up the baby. She was very weepy, in fact, this was just the sort of thing she used to cry about on the telly. I knew she'd have another cry with Dad about it when and if she told him.

It wasn't hard to leave again. I felt miles apart from them. I've been back since and we never talk about it. They approve of me doing nursing and they know I'm all right living in the nurses' home. I can't say I pine for the baby. Perhaps if I'd loved the father I might have, or I might have kept it. But he didn't ever really feel a part of me. Only really when I was thinking about an abortion, then suddenly it did feel like a bit of me that I was going to get rid of. I know most girls don't feel like that. I wish I hadn't, then I would have had an abortion — one of those quick ones when you only go for the day — and I'd have just gone home and carried on normally. But there you are — something made me go on and have the baby.

Actually one thing that does cheer me up is that I keep reading about couples who can't have children and they want to adopt but there's a terrible shortage of babies — they say now you've only got a chance if you'll take an older child or a coloured one or one that's handicapped in some way. They said my baby was perfect. I don't know that because I never saw him, but I don't see any reason why not. I looked after myself properly before he was born. So whoever's got him now — I've made them happy.

'I wouldn't bring up a girl again for anything. Compared with boys they're nothing but trouble and you have to be watching them all the time . . . they're that deceitful.'

11   Pauline's mother

Pauline's mother is, like Pauline, quietly spoken and shy. She's middle-aged and neatly dressed. She sits with her arms held very tightly against her sides. Half-way through our talk she picked up a large piece of knitting and seemed more relaxed when she had this to occupy her. Her voice didn't betray what she felt – it's a one-note voice – but I noticed that whenever she did talk about feelings, and particularly when she mentioned the word 'baby' or 'babies', tears came to her eyes.

Pauline was a lovely daughter until the day she left home. She was bright at school. She kept her room tidy. She helped me in the house and she was a lovely cook. Assuming she wasn't telling lies — which, of course, I don't know anymore, not after these past months and all the lies — she just wasn't interested in boys and make-up and going to discos. She was a real home-loving girl and she adored her family — you could see that by the way she sat round the TV with us instead of going out. So there was nothing to tell us how she was going to turn out. I wouldn't bring up a girl again for anything. Compared with boys they're nothing but trouble and you have to be watching them all the time . . . they're that deceitful.

You know, of course, that here was a boy? I don't really know how she could refuse to see it but I suppose it's for the best. We don't talk about it — none of us do. No one else knows — the rest of the family, or the neighbours or our friends. No one. As regards Pauline, everyone thinks she went off suddenly with another girl to do nursing. She's been back since once or twice and everyone can see it's all normal so that's one blessing — no gossip. That would be terrible on top of everything else.

Arthur and I honestly can't see that we put a foot wrong. Pauline can't either — at least she doesn't say if she thinks we went wrong. All she says is that she was ignorant and that's why she got into trouble. I don't think it was that. If being ignorant about sex means being innocent and keeping sex for Mr Right and marriage — then she was innocent and Arthur and I did our best to keep her that way. She can't say we were the sort of parents not to care what she did. Some of them round here are like that — permissive. They let their girls plaster themselves with make-up at fourteen and stay out till all hours and they don't have any family life the way we do — the way we did. I believe it makes the girls think the parents don't care what they do. Pauline could never have thought that. She didn't, that's definite, otherwise, of course, she wouldn't have run off like that. She knew we cared and couldn't bear to let us down. But that still doesn't explain why she went with that man, and the lies about going to a dance — why she had sexual intercourse, I mean. As far as I know no boy had so much as laid a finger on her up to then.

And that wasn't because Pauline was in any way cold and standoffish. She was always very loving with us. She was a great one for a cuddle. She'd sit on her father's knee right up to the time she left school. They were always joking together, having talks in the shed. They were very close. He didn't like to go anywhere or do anything without his Pauly. We never went out together, Arthur and I, just the two of us. And we'd never had a holiday together, except for the honeymoon, until this last summer when Pauline was gone. So every cloud has a silver lining.

She showed no interest in going out with boys. She didn't do anything to get to know any. At school she was on the plump side and she used to worry about it and I think that stopped her from getting boyfriends. A blessing in disguise, I always thought. You hear about these schoolgirl mothers; there's so much talk now about everything — it's all sex, abortions, the pill. There's too much. It can't help the youngsters having it screamed at them all day long. It makes them want to try things. They think it's clever and grown-up. And what I can never understand is why they have so much of this stuff on the TV when it's supposed to be for entertainment. It gives me quite a shock sometimes when you're watching an ordinary sort of play and then suddenly a couple — not man and wife usually — are in bed. You see them taking their clothes off. It's all so unnecessary. If life is like that I don't want to see it on the TV and in the cinema.

But I don't think life is really like that — people having sex at the first opportunity they get. Arthur says it's all to do with business interests. People make a lot of money out of dirty magazines and books, he says, and out of X-films. So it stands to reason that business people will do their best to make sex look as if no one can live without it, and get people into the state where they buy more rubbishy books and see more rubbishy films. I think myself that girls have got to be a bit silly before they get sensible — fall in love and go dancing and perhaps a bit of what they call petting. I wish, in a way, Pauline had had a bit of that but somehow she didn't seem to want to. She preferred home. But if she had, then she'd have come up against all this pushing of sex and all the pushing of teenage rights. And whatever else Arthur says about Pauline, whatever else I think myself, she has, in a way, stayed innocent through all this. I know she's had a baby but she's not gone wild after it. She's dedicated to her nursing and I doubt if she has any boyfriends as such even now. I think she'll still do what we always hoped she'd do, find a steady, family-loving man and settle down. But, of course, I don't know whether this baby business has spoiled her chances. Or whether she'll tell people about it. We've brought her up to be honest — but on the other hand, she's got used to keeping secrets now.

That day she left was the worst day of my life. Naturally, my first thought was that something had happened to her. I don't know what — perhaps a man had come to the house and taken her off, I don't know. Or she'd gone out and been picked up in a car or she'd fallen for someone and run off with him unwillingly — someone with a hold over her. It didn't strike me that she'd just go off like that, of her own free will, no letter or anything. When Arthur came home he phoned the police. We'd never had them in the house before — it was like a bad dream. The policeman went to her room and he said had I checked her things — toothbrush, clothes and things? I hadn't — I was that much in a state. So I did and she'd taken her suitcase and a lot of clothes and all her night things and even her mascot, a big furry thing Dad gave her when he won it at a fairground. So then, as the policeman said, 'She's gone of her own accord. There's not much we can do about it.' She was seventeen, nearly eighteen, you see, and it was up to her, to go or come back, unless she got into trouble with the law or the police or anything. He said they'd check the hospitals and put her down as missing and everything else they do when this happens. But that was that. Anyway, the next day she rang up. And although she wouldn't say anything about why she'd gone or where she was — just London — at least we knew she was all right.

Our younger son was very good. He came round a lot during the next few days. He's a teacher and lives quite near. His wife came and their little boy, little Kevin. Colin's a good son. His brother Alan, we don't see so much of him. There was a bad time with him when he was about eighteen and he left home rather suddenly. He said he felt 'smothered'. All that came up again, unfortunately, when this trouble with Pauline started. I thought Arthur had forgotten all that — but when you're worried of course you do start to take it out of each other. We wanted to blame someone for Pauline going off. We had some nasty rows, those few days. We blamed each other. But it was soon forgotten. As I said, Colin and Margaret came round. Margaret can be very sharp. I've always been a bit frightened of her really. She never minces words. But this time I was quite grateful for the way she spoke out. It did a lot to clear the air. She was the first one to say that perhaps Pauline was pregnant. And she told us a lot about Pauline we didn't know — I mean, how she'd never even talk to Margaret about boys or anything. As Margaret said, she'd clam up if the word sex was mentioned, the way I do. I could see what Margaret meant.

Then I did start adding things up — or trying to. And it still didn't come out that she'd been pregnant. We rang up the manager at work, of course. He had nothing to go on. She hadn't confided in anyone there either. When I spoke to her on the phone it was like talking to a stranger; she sounded so different, very secretive. She didn't say anything that mattered — just she was all right and wouldn't be back for a bit. I thought she was very cruel. I still think so. It's the cruellest thing to do, that, leave a good home without a word and then not explain anything. She kept us guessing and worrying and that was very cruel. I don't think we deserved that, whatever we'd done or not done.

Sometimes now I worry about her state of mind. I wouldn't have thought you could have a baby and give it up and then just carry on the same. It must do something to you. You hear about young girls and women who've had babies and given them up — they snatch babies out of prams and take them off. Pauline seems all right — but she's very different. She's very aloof whenever we're together now. But she's nursing now and they don't let you into that unless you're all right. Or I expect they get you sorted out if there's anything wrong. The best thing that could happen to Pauline now, in my opinion, is to get married and have a baby straight off. I don't think I'll really stop worrying until she does.

PART THREE

Sex and the spin-offs

12 Status, sexual identity and the search for love

It's generally supposed that when a girl leaves home, or defies her parents for the sake of a sexual relationship, it's sexual activity for its own sake that she's after. Many parents and moralists genuinely believe that we've come to a sex-mad generation and that most young girls are only waiting to reach the age of consent — or not even waiting that long — to lose their virginity at the first chance they get and thereafter embark on a life of irresponsible and promiscuous sex relations out of sheer self-indulgence.

But everything I've heard from girls about their sexual feelings — and from those counsellors and helpers who listen between the words — convinces me that, if sex is the biggest problem for the girls themselves and the biggest point of conflict with their elders, it's because of what we might call the 'fringe benefits' of sexual relationships rather than for the rewards of sex itself.

Before I outline these fringe benefits, I must make one point in the endless debate between those who say that few adolescent girls are ready for the physical and emotional demands of sexual relationships, and those who say that, because of the continuing trend towards earlier and earlier puberty, most girls are sexually receptive, and most boys sexually active, so much sooner than their parents were, that earlier and earlier sex is inevitable.

But, in fact, the average age of puberty, which did indeed fall comparatively dramatically in the hundred years preceding 1955, is now slowing its downward trend, and has been doing so for the past twenty-five years. So that the parents of today's teenagers probably matured at the same rate as their children are maturing and there's very little argument for saying that the bodies of today's teenagers are clamouring for earlier and earlier sex, or that this clamour is biological and can't be denied. In any case, we are only talking about physical maturity. If there could be any research on emotional maturity, I doubt if it would show that this has kept pace with earlier physical maturity. It seems to me rather that many of the problems associated with adolescent sex are because of this dichotomy between the mature body and the immature emotions.

So if one wants to set an age at which girls or boys are 'ready' for sex, one can only work this out with the individual girl or boy who's in doubt and this working-out is likely to be more helpful if it concentrates on emotional factors rather than physical ones. Nevertheless, because of the pressures to have sex at an early age and because of the 'fringe benefits' (some of them unconsciously experienced) to be gained by premature sex, it's right, I believe, that we set the legal age of consent at a higher age than is appropriate for some teenagers.

The main fringe benefit of having sex is status. Status as defined by job, education, income, accent or dress has given way to status as defined by how you function sexually. And because what you actually do about sex is still private, status depends entirely on what you say you are doing. Yet there's a good deal of bluff going on here which accounts for the enormous pressure to gain adequate status in sexual terms. Sex blazons out from television and posters and book stalls and people get the idea that it's a completely open subject and that if they're not taking part they're the only ones who aren't. But most people are not open about their personal sex-lives — and a good thing too — and if they do talk about it, they lie. For if you're the kind of person who needs to tell people about your sexuality you're also the kind of person who needs to dress it up, a fear of being thought inadequate being the motive for both the telling and the exaggeration.

The greater escalation of hot air about sexual performance, however, has to be supported by an escalation of sexual activity — particularly by those who don't know that what they hear and read and see is largely fantasy. So the result is that, in order to be 'in' with sex, to gain status with their peers and to feel adequate, many young people who don't particularly want to be sexually active are driven into sexual encounters. Another pull is that our society tends to go for quantity rather than quality, in sex as in many other areas. So the race is on to have more sex — more partners, more orgasms, more games and tricks and variations — rather than better sex.

So that's one fringe benefit — although, of course, it's in no way beneficial. Another is the hidden benefit for the girl who gets pregnant. For schoolgirls, pregnancy is often a way of rejecting school life because it's not offering what they need. What seems to be an utterly irresponsible act may, in fact, be a way of gaining adult responsibilities that are withheld for too long. Some college girls who get pregnant choose this way of escaping from intolerable academic pressures or the demands of community life, rather as Service girls escaped this way from Forces life in the war. Whether the outcome is abortion, adoption or single parenthood, many girls choose pregnancy as a way out of untenable positions at home, in their work or in their relationships. In all these cases, sex is the means to an end and not the end in itself.

Emma, the unmarried mother, is an example of mother-hood chosen as an answer to relationship problems. Pauline, the pregnant runaway, was not led to have sex by her desire for the experience itself. It was simply that her parents' anti-sex attitudes put her into such a state of confusion and ignorance that she was utterly helpless in the company of the first predatory male who took a fancy to her. And on the psychological level, she was compelled into some such sexual encounter as a way of confirming that she had a sexual identity. That is something which her parents were anxious to deny her and in that they were not a bit unusual.

Many girls cannot, or are not permitted to, become sexual beings within the home. Sometimes this is because the parents' sexuality is unacknowledged and home is a place where sex simply doesn't exist. Sometimes it's because of the parents' sexual difficulties, and anti-sex

attitudes are subconsciously or openly passed on. Sometimes parents simply can't make the transition from 'our
little girl' to 'our adult daughter'. So the fringe benefit to be
gained from sexual adventuring while still at home, or a
breakaway from home into a sexual relationship, is the
girl's much needed view of herself as a sexual being and a
'whole' person. We should note that it's not necessary for
any young adult to have sex relations in order to have this
view of herself as sexual and 'whole'. It's only necessary for
her to acknowledge and, if needed, share, her developing
sexual feelings and attitudes without having to feel guilty
or 'bad' about them.

The greatest fringe benefit to be gained from adolescent
sexual activity, however, is love. And here we come to one
of the most extraordinary and grisly features of our society
— the way in which it keeps on trying to limit 'love' to its
sexual expression between one adult and another. Prefer-
ably, says society, it should be between opposite sexes but
we are increasingly tolerant if they're the same sex. Once
past the age to be cuddled and touched and treated
tenderly by mother and father, there is almost no way in
which a man or woman can find loving arms except in a
sexual context. We simply do not touch and hold and warm
to each other non-sexually anything like as much as human
nature needs. So at adolescence, there's a sudden drop in
the emotional temperature and the only warm place to be
found is in a sexual partner's arms. This, of course, is even
more avidly sought if the temperature at home has always
been on the chilly side.

Francesca's mother, who tells us of all the sex-based
escapades that her daughter got into, veers between being
mystified by her behaviour and putting her finger right on
it — 'She's a very affectionate child', she says, 'I think she's
longing for love.' And she adds, 'She still thinks I don't love
her.' All Fran's actions — all the destructive relationships
with drug-taking boys, getting pregnant, getting VD,
staying out all night and seeming not to care what befell her
— could be seen in the light of a desperate uncertainty
about being a lovable, OK, valued person.

In Kate's story too there are elements of this search for
love and emotional security through the medium of sexual

relationships. Kate says of the time that she was hanging about in pubs with the out-of-work youth who knocked her about 'I felt at the time that Mum and Dad just didn't care. I thought they hated me . . .' And Kate's mother comments at one point 'I think she's a bit insecure . . . she seems to want constant evidence that we care.' The main problem for today's parents seems to be to know exactly what *is* evidence that they care. Is it a firm control over their children? Is it letting them be? Or is it a combination of both? I explore this problem more fully in the discussion of choices in Part One.

So a great deal of sexual adventuring by girls is a disguised search for warmth and love rather than for a mate. Many girls fall for father figures, with whom sex plays as much a part as in the relationship with their real fathers — that is to say, quite a bit but not a major or explicit part. They fall for older men and married men and people in authority — teachers, lecturers, gurus, the GP or the boss.

Caring is also a big ingredient of the love that they're now expected to give to, as well as receive from, a sexual partner. Unless a girl with a strong streak of *carità* becomes a mother, a nurse, an infant teacher, a nanny or something of the sort it's hard for her to find some way of using it except in a sexual context. Many girls, therefore, have affairs with drop-outs, alcoholics and immature boys of all ages — men who appear to need what they want to give. The 'ministering angel' image and the idea that 'the love of a good woman' can reform the rake and the rogue are still very powerful and attractive influences on many a young girl's idealism. Unfortunately, this kind of loving more often pulls the woman down than it lifts the man up.

No one can talk about sex and the unmarried without mentioning the contraceptive pill. Fifteen years ago it was hailed as the answer to unwanted pregnancies and the universal agent of sexual freedom — and the people it was hailed as liberating most were the young and unmarried. Well, has it?

Figures for 1975 show that while effective contraception has played a big part in bringing about a decline in childbearing among married women and in pre-marital conceptions, the number of illegitimate births to women under twenty has not declined. Nor has the number of abortions to girls in this age group. Taking women of all ages, there were 55,000 live births outside marriage in the twelve months ending March 1976. In the same period there were 63,000 abortions to unmarried women.

So the Pill has hardly proved the agent of carefree sex. This failure begs the question whether the availability of effective contraception has all that much to do with accidental pregnancies — or, indeed, whether pregnancies are ever accidents at all. Emma's story reveals one of the motives for an 'unplanned' pregnancy outside marriage, and Pauline's experience raises a number of points about just how available any form of contraception is to the young girl whose parents don't acknowledge her as a sexual being and who therefore can't acknowledge it herself.

It was anticipated that the Pill would come to be the first choice of contraceptive method by both married and unmarried women. We loaded it with high expectations of freeing women not only from the fear of unwanted pregnancy, but from the clumsiness, the failure rate and aesthetically unsatisfactory features of other methods. There was even the bonus, in a breast-conscious age, that it sometimes increased bust size. And for men it sounded like a great cop-out from any responsibility for avoiding conception. If she wasn't on the Pill she'd surely say so — silence means consent.

But it not only increased bust size — it frequently put weight on all over. Doubts arose about side effects which have not effectively been spelt out or laid to rest. It was contra-indicated for women with histories of liver and kidney complaints, and of thrombosis. Older women, especially those in or coming up to the menopause were wary, or their doctors were. Many women found it reduced their libido or made them depressed. Many girls and women with lives and work that required them to be alert and active disliked the tendency of the Pill to alter their pace to a slower, more passive one. And there was a lot of resistance — and not all by fanatics of 'nature knows best' — to having one's body 'mucked about' by incomprehensible chemical changes. Finally, there have recently been some anxiety-provoking accounts of the long term effects of the Pill by women who have come off it after 10 to 15 years continuous use, ranging from infertility to a sudden onset of wrinkles and shapelessness.

So we cannot, I think, say either that the Pill is as popular as it's thought to be or that it has lived up to the hopes of bringing in a new dawn of responsible sexual freedom for women.

On the contrary, the evidence from young girls is that it has given them an additional burden in their struggles to have sex-with-responsibility. In so far as many men believe that the only argument against extra-marital sex is the risk of an unwanted pregnancy, the wide use of the Pill — which in itself is a good thing — makes it that more difficult for a girl to say 'no' when she'd like to say 'yes.' That is to say that she has fewer rational, articulate counter-arguments to reinforce her emotional ones in the difficult, ambivalent process of deciding to have sex or not to have it. That is, of course, if there is any process of decision-making at all. Often there isn't. Which is why emotional attitudes to sexuality will always be more powerful in the sexual liberation of both men and women than any contraceptive method. And the personal accounts in this book show very clearly, it seems to me, that those emotional attitudes are born and developed at home, in a girl's relationship with her parents and in the acceptance of her sexuality which they either help her to acquire or unhelpfully withhold from her.

Being dead set against any expression of her sexuality is not the only parental attitude to drive a daughter from home. Increasingly, children are affected by the liberalising of the laws and social attitudes relating to psycho-sexual minorities. Homosexuals of both sexes are 'coming out'. Transvestites are venturing into public places in the clothes of the opposite sex. Lesbian mothers are slowly gaining ground in disputed custody cases. Some lesbian couples are setting up conventional family structures, with mort-gages and babies. And many more transsexuals, like Margaret's father, are actually crossing over, as far as this is physically possible, from one gender to another. Also, like Margaret's father, a good proportion of the members of these minority groups are — or have been — married and are parents.

These changes towards a plural and more open society have tremendous implications for family life in a general way but especially where children are actually involved. The very terms 'mother' and 'father' have to be rethought out. Some parents can no longer be taken as complete models by their same-sex children, nor as learning sources by opposite-sex children. This may be to everyone's advantage in the long run — our bisexuality has been feared and repressed for too long. But meanwhile, as Margaret's story shows, it produces new pressures on a daughter when a parent makes the breakaway from the family and his accepted gender role in it.

In Jane's case too, it was sexual problems in the adults of the family that eventually drove her out, but not until she had spent five years — her entire adolescence — in a sexual relationship with her stepfather. Since it's generally agreed that the incidence of actual incest (sex between blood relations) is not declining, although one might expect that it would in a society which tolerates freer sexual behaviour outside marriage, it comes as no surprise that sex relations between step-parents and stepchildren are not declining either. Jane's experience is echoed in my post, in counselling centres and in psychiatrists' consulting rooms. And although one may share the Freudian view that sexual feelings for a father or father-substitute are a normal feature of any girl's development, actual sexual activity between them does raise questions of exploitation and inequality, even if the girl is a willing partner at the time. For Jane it certainly meant that she had to break away from her stepfather's relentless sexual domination before she could make contact with her real father and find a man — her husband, Sam — to love and be loved by in equality and freedom.

With the increase in divorce and remarriage, and the proliferation of step-relationships, there's good reason to expect more of the kind of breakaway problems that Jane faced and, to be fair, more of the kind of pressures that her stepfather faced when he married a woman whose sexuality was dormant but whose daughter's sexuality was just emerging. These are inevitable spin-off problems from the most far-reaching social change of our time — the increase in family breakdown. And that is the theme of the three breakaway stories in Part Four.

'At any family occasion Fran would be the
odd one missing or she'd be the one to spoil
it. She would sit at a meal and not speak.
The whole atmosphere would be absolutely
ghastly, she was so hostile. In the end we
never went anywhere, never saw anybody,
because she would spoil it.'

13   Francesca the tearaway: her mother's view

*I have not met Francesca. I have only met her mother and this is
her story of her daughter's boyfriends, drug taking, abortion, VD
and other experiences between the ages of thirteen and nineteen.
Francesca's mother is very pretty; she has short dark hair with
goldish streaks in it, such expert make-up that you think she isn't
wearing any, and the figure and fashionable clothes of a
30-year-old.*
*She calls herself a 'typical Home Counties Mum'. She and her
businessman husband live very comfortably in a Buckinghamshire
'dormitory town' in a Georgian-type house up a tree-lined road.
She does a lot of voluntary work in the town – with the Citizens
Advice Bureau, Family Planning Clinic and so on. She also runs a
small employment agency.*

Fran's problems started when she began her periods. This
made her prematurely sexy in my opinion. And once
they're sexy they're not interested in anything except boys.
They don't pay any attention to their studies and they don't
do awfully well at school. Yet they can't cope with boys.

Fran is a very pretty child. She's always been the centre
of attraction and she hasn't been able to cope with it. And
she's attracted the sleaziest creatures I've ever seen in my
life. They've come round like bees round a honeypot but
she's never been able to say 'no'. Also I don't think she's
had any confidence in herself. So the only people she can

feel superior to are these awful ones. And they do like to feel superior, these girls, don't they? They want power over someone, to feel confident.

Another reason for all the trouble with Fran is that I always had a terrific social life, an awful lot of fun in my life and she does envy me that. I've talked about the fun I used to have. I had a lot more fun than she does. It was more romantic. It wasn't just 'go out for the evening and get your knickers off, girl' — which is what it is now. We were more restricted. Up to about sixteen I was definitely playing 'kick the can' and 'hide and seek'. But my daughter missed out on being a child. I didn't know the facts of life until I was eighteen, but I made up for it very quickly. I was pretty awful actually. I talk about my child now but . . . Well, it does mean that I also know the pitfalls she can fall into. We were always frightened of getting pregnant but it doesn't mean a thing to them now, which is a pity.

She started playing up at thirteen. It was terrible. She used to go out at night and I didn't know where she was. She wouldn't tell me. 'I'm with my friends', that's all she'd say. She didn't get one O-level — she didn't want to. She was smoking at school and I had to go and see the headmistress because I found out they were importing drugs. She doesn't know that I split on them but I had to. Two girls were expelled actually, which was rather awful. But I thought I had to do something.

At sixteen she got pregnant. It was dreadful when she told me — like a Thunderbird going right through the top of my head. The father was the filthiest, down-and-out, lying, scruffiest man. She'd been going out with him for months — he'd bring her home at two o'clock in the morning. He was druggy too — he'd been in prison and sold drugs — and he was the father; I could have killed him.

Our doctor told me this was the most terrific age for getting pregnant. She swears to me — and I believe her — that she never actually had intercourse at all. It was one of those nonsense petting things.

She had an abortion. I took her myself into women's surgical. It was absolutely ghastly: they kept her hanging around all day with these older women — and there was Fran, just sixteen. Of course, she was very anti-me all

through this. But I took her up there and I banned the boy
from the hospital, I wouldn't allow him to go and see her. I
was there when she came round and it was awful. That's
partly my own pride though, because I knew the surgeon
socially. He knew who I was and who Fran was and it was
beastly really.

Anyway she got over that and she stayed in for a week at
home and was all right for about a month. I think in a
romantic way she'd hoped to keep the baby and form a
family with this awful boy. But on the other hand she knew
darn well that at that age she simply couldn't cope. And I
said I was *not* going to look after it, which she couldn't
understand. I said, 'I don't want to go through all that
again, thank you very much. No point in that.'

I think now she's got over it. We've talked about it. This
chap's completely disappeared now. I've heard he's squat-
ting in Hampstead. But he did come backwards and
forwards over these past three years. I was always trying to
lead him out of the back door. Soon after the abortion he
was in court again. I went into court to let him out on bail. I
thought if I'm nice to him perhaps we can get through to
him that way to keep away from Fran. But it didn't work.
He was sentenced to six months; I went and saw him in
prison which was quite horrific.

Then he went abroad and was peddling drugs and he
had an accident and broke his leg and he was in hospital for
ages. He came out and did exactly the same thing again so
he was more than a year in hospital. But Fran had met him
after the abortion and I had a telephone call from
Pentonville saying, 'Would your daughter please go and
see her doctor because we believe she's got VD — he's got
it.' And she had. So we had all that nonsense, sitting
outside the VD clinic. It was a bit shattering. But we got all
that cleared up. She's a bit frightened now though — she's
going through the twitch that perhaps she won't be able to
have any children.

Then she met a boy called Pat who was always giving her
speed and all sorts of peculiar things. She used to miss
work. She used to disappear for four or five days at a time.
She was taking drugs all the time and it was a helluva mess.
It all worried me terribly. It's awful waiting until five o'clock

in the morning for kids to come in.

Anyway, once after four days away she phoned me and said, 'Mum, can you ring up and say I can't get into work today?' And I said, 'No. Where are you?' And after a long argy-bargy, I found she was at Tufnell Park and she'd had an overdose. So I had to go up there by tube and get her back. I got hold of a mirror and I said, 'Just look at yourself. Look what you're doing to yourself.' She said, 'Do I really look as bad as that?' I told her 'Yes, you do.' She looked absolutely frightful, yellow and old. And she'd got these hard lines around her mouth. And she wasn't quite with us. She wasn't like Fran at all. In fact, I began to wonder if she was schizo. I'm still wondering about that actually.

The doctor said she could go for treatment — mass therapy. Fran simply wouldn't entertain that. She hated him. She hated everybody medical — it wouldn't have helped at all. The only doctor she ever liked was the girl in the VD clinic. Fran thought she was super because she was black and she was going through a pro-black period. I was always frightened she'd go off with a black man but she hasn't done that yet. She might, but I don't think so.

Pat was an absolute menace and he was evil. He used to beat her up. So did the first boyfriend. I began to wonder whether she enjoyed it. She used to come home black and blue, and scratches all down her back, which absolutely appalled me. You couldn't ask her about it because she wouldn't tell you. But she was terrified of him.

Pat took an overdose and he nearly kicked the bucket but was saved by a friend. The friend told us but Fran was on one of her disappearances and oh, the telephone bills chasing her round the country. Eventually I traced her. It goes round on the grapevine and someone tells her, 'Your mother's been on the phone and you'd better contact the old bag because she's worried.' So she phoned back and I said, 'Get home at once' and she said, 'What's happened?' I said 'I'll tell you when you're back.' When she got home I said, 'Pat's taken an overdose and he's very ill indeed. Now either you love him and you'll go to him now, or finish and you don't see him again — you leave the boy alone.' She chose not to go to him. We took her out to the races. It was the most ghastly day, but we took her. And I think that was

almost the end of him, although she sees him sometimes, I
think.

Last year she went to a party with a very nice boy who's
been hanging around for years. He's still number one at the
moment — I'm just hoping . . . The next morning, after the
party, there was no Fran. She wasn't in her bed. I asked the
boyfriend, 'Where's Fran?' He said, 'I don't know. She
walked out of the party and I haven't seen her since.' I rang
up other friends of hers — 'Where's Fran?' 'Don't know',
they said, 'Don't know where she is. Suppose she must be
with somebody somewhere . . .' I thought, 'Oh God in
Heaven, where is she?' My son and his girlfriend came
home and I asked them, 'Where's Fran?' They said, 'We've
phoned up everybody at the party and she's completely
disappeared.' I thought 'Oh my God! She's in a grave in the
middle of Epping Forest.' I said I'll just sit tight until twelve
o'clock and then I'll phone the police and we'll have to start
a search. We had the most ghastly morning. I was sitting in
the hall. I don't know why.

The phone went actually at ten to twelve, 'Mum, I'm
somewhere north of London — I don't know where . . .'
Eventually I got her to find out where she was and ring
back. I said, 'All right, stay there. I'll come and fetch you.'

And to cut a long story short I drove to this little cottage
way out in Hertfordshire and she hurtled out of the door
and got in the car, looking terrible and shaking like a leaf.
'How did you get here?' I said. 'Well,' she said, 'these two
chaps picked me up. I was walking along the road. I don't
know why I was walking. I was just walking.' I said, 'You
just can't walk around in the middle of the night in a white
suit. You could be murdered.' And there again it was drink
and drugs. She simply wouldn't realise that they don't mix.
And these chaps had taken off all her clothes and they had
tormented her and stripped her and everything else. And
anyway they decided it wasn't much fun and they left her
alone. And she stayed downstairs and got herself dressed
again. And I said, 'You know, you do realise you were let
off jolly lightly, something awful could have happened.'

So we got home and at that point she collapsed into her
father's arms and cried and cried. She shut herself in her
room next day and she was frightful for about a week but

then she picked up again and she was all right. But she used to do these stupid things. We always kept saying 'Can't you ever learn?' But she couldn't. Still, I think she is learning now. We're coming out of it. We couldn't stand it much longer, always waiting for the next thing to happen. Every time we went away — that was the time she'd do something stupid. She crashed the car twice.

I think that one of the things that caused the trouble was that everything I've done, I've done efficiently and made a success of it. She always said about everything 'I can't do it as well as Mummy.' The only thing she did better was the piano and she gave it up. She could never live up to what I was doing. I suddenly realised this. A friend pointed it out to me too. She said, 'Let Fran go into something that you can't do, and don't have anything to do with it.'

First of all I put her in for a typing course but that was a mistake because it came from me. She was soon back home, doing nothing. One day she waltzed in and said, 'I'm going to look at the crocuses in Regent's Park' and I said, 'You're not. You're going to sit down and write some letters and get yourself a job.' So fortunately she did write those letters, and one of the people she wrote to had just sacked someone so Fran was engaged on the spot. She's doing hairdressing and she's done very well and I have nothing to do with it whatsoever. And we've been on much better terms since we made her go in for it.

She's 20 now and supposed to be sharing a flat with a cousin. But she hates it and the whole thing is a disaster and she's home now more than she's away. And she does appreciate it. In fact, she almost says, 'Can I come back?' And I've said, 'Well, you know, on our terms . . .' But we've also got an aged grandmother and to cope with both of them . . . I don't think I could do it anymore. Fran says I've changed though. Over the weekend she said, 'Oh Mummy, I can't think why you're not a crabby old bitch — you usually are.' And I said, 'Well, I'm not now.' It's given me a new slant on things having my work to do, building up a business. She wouldn't have anything to do with me from the age of thirteen — no days out with the family or anything like that. She didn't want to know. She'd rather go out with her friends. So I'd sit at home and wait for her in

the holidays and think, 'God! Everyone's going out and
doing nice things except me.' That's why I started the
business.

But I was round the twist at the abortion period and it
broke her father's heart. It shocked her rigid too. She just
wanted something to love; I think she felt we didn't love
her. At any family occasion Fran would be the odd one
missing or she'd be the one to spoil it. She would sit at a
meal and not speak. The whole atmosphere would be
absolutely ghastly; she was so hostile. In the end we never
went anywhere, never saw anybody, because she would
always spoil it. When she was on the drugs and things I
caught her at it several times and I said, 'We know you take
it, so why don't you roll it in front of us? I'd love to see what
it looks like. It won't bother me. If you want to smoke
yourself to death, then smoke yourself to death.' That
rather de-winded her. She said, 'I don't like it when you
know too much.'

I think the sexual pressures are enormous. They all
expect to leap in and out of bed with each other at the drop
of a hat. This is a tremendous pressure because half of them
don't want to. Mentally, they can't cope. They've been
hammered and hammered and hammered to do it. I know
this has been the trouble with Fran. She was absolutely
frigid after the abortion. She didn't want to sleep around
and yet there was this constant bullying from the boys. She
had a terrific hang-up about ever having full satisfaction. I
said, 'It's extraordinary, at your age, that you worry about a
thing like that. I think there are very few women who are
completely satisfied. They're damn lucky and they have to
work jolly hard at it.' And she said, 'Well, you know, do
you and daddy . . .?' And I said, 'Yes, fortunately we have
a fantastic sexual relationship, but don't think it happened
overnight because it didn't. You've got to work at it with
one particular person that you love.'

It must be very frustrating for them if they don't get
anything out of it and the boys do. They ask themselves,
'Do I go on trying? He's no good. He's not doing it to me.
Perhaps someone else will.' And I think it's a hell of a strain
on the boys too because they've got to be spot-on every
time. The girls expect too much. It all cuts both ways. There

are so many magazines now telling you how to do it, what positions etc, etc and it's stupid. I just wish they'd shut up about sex.

I think marriage is the best answer, especially for Fran. She's awfully fond of animals and small things. I think she would make a very good housewife as long as I don't interfere. She's a very affectionate child. I think she's longing for love. She gets it from her boyfriend but she still thinks I don't love her. How could I anyway? She thinks, because she's always tried her hardest to make me hate her. 'I hate you', she'd say, 'and you loathe me, don't you?' So often I almost said, 'Yes, and I'm going to strangle you at any minute.' But I never said it, never. We always impressed on her that home was there and it was a place to run to. I think home is a great anchor to these kids, you know.

She did admit last year, 'You were always there and I could always come and kick you because you always took it.' I said, 'Yes, you can kick me, slosh me as much as you like because we do love you. I don't know how much I can take but I can go on for a bit longer.' She's had her hand round my throat and nearly strangled me, and all I would say is, 'Have you finished?'

Her friends used to put her against us. They were so anti-parents, that was the trouble. She'd come home all steamed up with hate. I think we're over it now. But it has been awfully trying — I couldn't possibly go through it again. What kept me and my husband going through it all was that we loved each other. We had been very much apart but we came back again. We had to pull ourselves together.

'I think he waited very carefully until I was
16. I'm quite sure he was as deliberate as this
all along. By that time he was saying he was
in love with me . . . It went to my head a bit,
I was flattered but I didn't want him, I
wasn't interested in a physical
relationship.'

14   Jane and her stepfather

*Jane is married to a college lecturer. They live in a bright, colourful
semi-detached house in a cathedral town. She trained as an actress
but gave it up when she married. She is thin and rather waif-like
with large pale blue eyes and long ash-coloured hair. She has a
very warm personality. From the age of sixteen to twenty-one she
had a sexual relationship with her stepfather from which she was
only able to break away when she met her husband-to-be. She told
me about it in a slow, deliberate voice — 'finding it quite painful',
she said later. She also said that talking about it had helped to put it
to rest.*

There was a divorce when I was, I don't know, very young
— two or three. And my mother cut me off completely from
my real father. I never saw him. Not until last year when I
met him again. I was so lucky — it was a fantastically good
meeting. I think lots of people find it's nothing, re-meeting
a parent. It was fantastically exciting. I'd no recollection of
him at all. And my mother wouldn't even talk about him.
So I knew nothing about him. I only knew he was a
musician and that was it — little bits in the paper and things
like that. He's quite well-known. He's also married again
and has children.

I asked my mother very few questions about him. I had a
bias about asking some questions — about sex, about my
father. So I never did. I used to ask relatives later, but it took
me an awful long time to get round to it. They were very

evasive about why the divorce took place and I realised they didn't know either. It was one of those war-time marriages and neither of them was very articulate at the time. I still think to this day that my mother isn't really sure why the divorce took place.

I'm an only child. I was living with my aunt from the age of two. My mother kind of left me there more or less permanently. During holidays I used to see my mother, stay there for some of the time and found she was living with this man. He was introduced to me as this great professor who musn't be disturbed He had a very shy exterior, very awkward, no kind of communication with a child whatsoever. And my mother very much in awe of him and a bit frightened. And then one holiday when I was there, I was left with somebody and they went off all dressed-up. They came back and said, 'You know, we got married this afternoon.' Just like that. They said, 'What do you think of that?' I remember my stepfather laughed nervously. They had no idea how to handle this sort of thing. I was about eight at this stage and I'd never had men around me. My uncle was dead and my aunt lived with two sisters, it was very much a house of women. I guess this is fairly pertinent to how things turned out, that I'd never had any contact with men, always and only with women.

So this sort of odd situation went on, where I'd go home for holidays and my stepfather was a complete shadow. He had nothing to do with me. He was there, of course, at meal-times, but he was quite unable to talk to a child. He's the kind of man who works in the evenings anyway so that I was with my mother most of the time. I think you're very aware of emotions when you're an only child and things haven't been normal around you and I knew she was rather frightened of him, not completely at her ease with him. Although I think they were quite happy.

Then at ten I went to live with them permanently which was fairly disastrous for us all. This was in Scotland, they'd moved to a new house about the same time I went to live with them. Of course, my mother found it very difficult being presented with a ten-year-old child in a fairly honeymoon situation. They were obviously very physically in love at this stage. I was full of past resentments against

my mother and suddenly things were expected of me
whereas before nothing had been expected of me. My aunt
never expected anything of anybody except to be as you
were, be yourself. But now I was in an academic household. My stepfather expected you, if you weren't academic,
to play an instrument or do something. I wasn't academic at
all. I was expected to be an achiever, a doer in some other
way, to be seen to be doing something. I'd always made
things and painted but as soon as I felt pressure on me I
never touched a thing. I knew my mother wanted me to be
something other than this shy, unprepossessing little girl.
He'd been married before and had three children. My
mother was very uptight about the previous wife. Most
women spend a long time settling into the idea of a
previous wife but I guess that my mother was a lot younger
and more insecure than some. I'd argue with her a lot.
There was a lot of 'Why don't you go out and find friends?'
Being an only child and brought up on my own, I found this
impossible to do. So I hung about the house not knowing
what to do, and she didn't know what to do with a child
either. And gradually my stepfather began to be aware of
me.

I remember the first inkling of any kind of approach, any
kind of relationship at all, when I overheard him saying to
my mother, 'Try to be nice to Jane today'. And gradually I
started to go to him. After school I'd kind of play-fight with
him, horse-play; I was at a boisterous age and he joined in. I
think he was doing very well at this time, he was at the top
of his profession and he was opening out a great deal. At
the beginning I believe he thought he ought consciously to
do something about me. He hadn't had an awful lot to do
with his own children, they were all under ten when his
divorce took place. I believe it was a messy divorce, a lot of
conflict and bad feeling. I think his children felt he was in
the wrong.

So there was this horse-play. I was about fourteen. I
started to see one or two boys. I began to be aware that his
horse-play and his reactions to my boyfriends were, well —
there was something more there. My mother knew he was
jealous and it was a vaguely laughed-at thing. But the
horse-play was turning somewhat. Then he started to come

to my bedroom every evening, to talk to me or something, say goodnight to me, taking over a role, doing the parental thing. He started to touch my breasts. I was taken aback. And he kissed me — just a straight kind of kissing. But all these experiences were presented as something rather fun, all a joke. I was terribly innocent then, I disliked any sexual talk at school. But I was aware of something different creeping into our relationship.

At this time I was also desperately worried that my mother was going to become pregnant. She was traipsing round to doctors, wanting more children. The fact that I was there must have been an even greater niggle. But she never produced any more children. That was probably why he turned towards me.

We moved house to London and then it just escalated. He touched me more and more. And, you know, at fifteen I was excited by it. I'd go often into his study. My mother was encouraging me because by this time I was their kind of go-between. Things had become difficult. She hadn't become pregnant. Perhaps their sexual life was getting difficult too. And I think I was being accepted. It was obvious that I was not academic but I was being accepted more as the feminine young daughter around the house whom they both wanted to flatter and please.

And then I was sixteen. I think he waited very carefully until I was sixteen. I'm quite sure he was as deliberate as this all along. By this time he was saying he was in love with me and that kind of thing. It went to my head a bit, I was flattered but I didn't want him, I wasn't interested in a physical relationship. I was happy about how far it went then — I was obviously aware that it would start to go further but I never for one moment dreamed that it really would. It just never occurred to me that he'd encroach like that. I'm sure I played skittish games, and he'd buy me small presents and do things to please me. It was a Lolita kind of thing. He'd joke about it. My mother was still encouraging it — why I'll never know, except that she has a capacity for switching off unpleasant things. She was innocent herself in many ways. She may have thought she was encouraging good family relationships.

So when I was sixteen he crudely de-flowered me. I think

he would put it like that too, just getting it over with. He called me into the bedroom and said, 'Come and sit here.' I was as stupid as anything. Right to the moment I never thought he'd go through with it or do anything which might harm me. I drew away but I think he took that as me being worried about the first time. He took no precautions. I'd started my periods, of course, but he always knew when I had a period. He would have timed it to be safe, I'm quite sure of that. He always did that, he was meticulous. I felt very shattered afterwards. I went out of the house, just not knowing what to think or what to do or anything. It wasn't in any way a loving thing. I discovered later that he was just an extremely bad lover — just completely 'bang' within about a minute. I don't remember now — or perhaps I never did know — but I suppose my main feeling was shock. I don't think I felt fear. I think I found it slightly repulsive. I told nobody. There was no one to tell. I couldn't tell my mother.

After that he would never leave me alone. I could never be in the house by myself — I'd know he'd be coming to find me. It was always as brusque as the first time. He thought he was a reasonable lover but he never was. It became absurd because after a while he'd pick me up from school and take me off somewhere. He was always pushing, always the pressure on and so in the end I thought, 'What the hell, maybe it'll be pleasanter next time.' About twice I really wanted the experience and then I realised there was nothing, there was to be no pleasure at all. So he'd meet me from school, come and find me at home. I was constantly thinking, 'Where is he?', 'What's he doing?', 'Is he coming after me?' I had to start the subterfuge with my mother, lying about where I'd been or what I'd been doing while she was out. I was constantly trying to dodge him — but where could I go?

My bedroom was next to his bedroom and he would come in many nights, with my mother in the next room. I completely acquiesced and just lay still. It all had to be quiet. I was completely turned-off. As far as I was concerned it was the easiest way of getting it over. He was buying me presents and making a big fuss of me, but I knew he was the kind of person you could not fall out with. I'd seen very unpleasant tempers coming on. My mother never dared cross him and I certainly wouldn't because what was left for me if I did? I was insecure and wanting a family and now I had a family of sorts — so I couldn't cross him. I'd been brought up in a sheltered existence, boarding school and so on and you don't just go away from home or think you're going to go out and work in Woolworth's or something. I thought, 'Well, what do other girls of my age do?' They would have maybe told him to stuff it and left. He never showed bad temper but he was the kind of person who makes you aware of undertones that you just wouldn't want to disturb. I'd seen him with one of my boyfriends, the only time I'd really seen him lose his cool. I'd been out; he was furious, he snatched the car keys out of the car because I hadn't come in earlier. He was shaking with rage and jealousy. He couldn't lose his temper deliberately, a cross word was never spoken. If he ever said anything approaching anger you could see the tremors and contortions it meant for him to keep it back. So it was impossible for me to say anything. I knew I couldn't.

He was very good at pretence, keeping up polite conversations at meals for instance. He would take more and more risks, almost as though he liked the risk. When we were out at a dance he'd dance extremely close. It must have been very obvious to other people.

He was in his early fifties at that time. I had more in common with him, very much more than with my mother. We shared more things — we still do — and I was the only person who stood up to him. He was the great white wonder for everyone, for all his colleagues and for my mother. I remember him once flouncing into the room when we were having a party and saying, 'It's much too hot in here. Open all the windows.' And I said, 'Why don't you take your pullover off?' and everyone went 'aaah' in amazement that someone had actually said something like this to him, because he had such a formidable manner.

And I knew I was the only person close to him. He had no friends, no friends coming to the house. They entertained a lot but it was purely superficial. But I really was the only one he talked to or had any feeling for. I felt desperately sorry for him in many ways. I was never in love with him.

Well, I think you love someone if you know them very well. And I did know him extremely well, much better than my mother did, I'm quite sure, much better than anybody knew him. And so this was another reason why I couldn't tell him to go and get lost. Because I was aware of just how fragile he was at an emotional level. He couldn't cope. He was very much a child at coping, no personal confidence, with an awful family background which he obviously carried with him. He was considered the dull one. He knew he was a very good plodder but he didn't have the brilliance and he knew this. Emotionally, he was absolutely deprived. He'd loved his mother, who was a very gay lady. His father didn't care much for him and thought he was spoilt. I had complete sway over him, in that way, emotionally. What could I have done? I had his security and he had mine. So it was quite unbreakable.

I went to drama school when I was eighteen and for a while I stopped actually sleeping with him. But he was constantly waiting up for me, kind of going over me and wanting to all the time. There were times when he'd rush into my bedroom and say, 'Oh, let's tell your mother.' He even tried to be tender but I was as cold as anything by now. So it stopped for a while and during that time I thought I was pregnant by a boyfriend. He'd kept asking, 'Are you sleeping with anyone?' and I'd say 'No' because it was easier and when I told him I thought I was pregnant he was flattened by this. But it shows the double-side of him that he immediately said, 'Oh, one way to bring your period on is to make love.' You know, he was so clever in many ways, waiting until I was sixteen and using the 'safe period'. I was in such a panic about thinking I was pregnant that I did sleep with him again.

So it went on. He played the jealous lover all the time. It was a complete juggling. It was just getting worse and worse and I was still fairly close with a boyfriend, and also clinging to some kind of security, some kind of link with the outside world through him. My stepfather knew about the relationship with the boy. He didn't care for it but he wasn't out to fight it. For stretches, it was all right. But then I'd get into terrible states.

Once I had a very bad nervous rash. He didn't do

anything until I was absolutely covered and then he said, 'You ought to go to the doctor' and made big scenes at the doctor and got me to a specialist. It was all very unpleasant and he was wary of it all because the specialist said it was obviously emotional troubles. They both kept away from me and during this time I used often to be very depressed. My mother took me for a check to another Harley Street doctor and there again he asked about emotional problems. All through this time both of them ignored the fact that I was obviously very unhappy.

I used to think if I'd had any guts I'd get up and walk out of the situation but I still felt, 'But what do I do?' And by this time, at drama school, I suddenly discovered I was good. It was a very exciting time that first year. I discovered I was better than I thought. It really was something I was very much at home in, the whole field. It became more difficult though, after the first flush. You needed to fall back on yourself more, to put more into your work. But I was in such a turmoil, juggling with the situation at home. In fact, I began to find it very difficult to work at all. I didnt' know which direction to go, not surprisingly. I was aware that girls going to drama school find a style very easily; they seem to have a greater natural facility than men. And I desperately didn't want to be an actress who got stuck in trivial parts.

I realise I didn't think of the future very much, nothing concrete, because the present was always too pressing. I never managed to look ahead. I was so tired in the house; I could never relax because it was always, 'Where's your mother? Is she still in the house?' and, if not, it would be 'Let's go upstairs'. And even if I said 'No' it was still an encroachment. Whichever way it went it was an encroachment each time he wanted it. It was a constant kind of mooning after me. If I said 'No' he'd press a little and be very pleasant about it and say, 'Oh well, next time'. He'd never be cross or show anger. But I felt it just as much. It was so constant, so pressing. If I went out he was still up whatever time I got in. I don't know whether my mother had an inkling. She certainly played the game as if she didn't know. She didn't want to know. She blocked off. I think she was very unhappy then. I don't think she had any relationship with him at that time. Keeping me there was the only thing that kept her coping.

Then I went to France. This was my twenty-first birthday present. And I think he knew in his heart that it was a dangerous thing to give me — freedom. I went for six weeks and he gave me a lot of money. I joined a drama workshop in Paris for a month. Nothing really happened and then I started to meet people and suddenly one evening I realised I didn't have to go back. It was a fantastic thought — I didn't have to go home, I could get a job and stay there. And that's what I did. I stayed there after the six weeks was over. And I met Sam a little while afterwards. It was the first time I'd had any freedom to be myself. I'd been deprived of my youth. From sixteen to twenty-one I always felt middle-aged, always aware of everything. I wore jeans to drama school but I had three or four cocktail dresses at home which were for 'fitting in'. I was very good at that. I think if you're insecure you can be very good at fitting in to people's images of you. I know I was. I think my parents had given up any idea of academic success. They were grooming me for being the charming hostess with an up-and-coming young man. It was one of my stepfather's ideas to buy me a flat nearby when I came back from France. He saw no reason why things shouldn't continue as they were, no reason why it should ever end.

I stayed in France for six months and I got married out there. In a way it was a stupid thing to do, so we did it. But I didn't really view marriage as a lifelong bond. With divorced parents, I don't think you do. It was the first time I'd had a really good sexual relationship. I don't know why I hadn't been put off it, but I hadn't. The thing is that I was so sexually motivated. My sex had been plugged away since I was fourteen, been developed, so I did many things from a very sexual angle, always very sexually aware. And because of my stepfather I was always waiting, I guess, for it to be really good. With my boyfriend, too, it had never really been satisfactory. We pretended it had, but it hadn't. I had the opportunity in France to become very promiscuous. But I drew back from that. I was afraid I'd go overboard and become a raving whore. I have the potentiality there, very much geared that way, so I always drew back at the last minute — except with Sam and that was very good and

I think our relationship at the beginning was based on that.

I'd missed so many opportunities. I'd never been young and ridiculous. And I thought this time here was an opportunity to give and get something I wanted and I was darn well going to grab it, regardless of the consequences.

I went to France in July and we stayed on until Christmas. I should have been home in September. And at first there were a lot of hurt letters. And not until about three weeks before I went back did I tell them about being married. So then there were very hurt, desperate letters. Very cold letters from my stepfather because he'd been writing me outrageous love letters. He always had, even at home if he ever went away on trips. He was so indiscreet. He played it so near the mark. Why my mother never found those letters . . . well perhaps she did, I don't know. Really flagrant love letters, very physical. He must have liked the danger. Because he got nothing much out of sex as such, these bits and pieces must have made up for it.

We got back at Christmas. My mother was very pale. Everything was cold and miserable, I think she purposely gave us cold food. Everything was a kind of reproach, it was really awful. I knew they weren't going to like Sam — he hadn't gone to public school, he hadn't got a job, he was years older than I was. If I'd come back to England and said I was going to marry him I don't think I could have withstood them. They'd have made it difficult. Not outright, because they'd be the first to say that they had no snobbish tendencies, you know, everything very correct, never put anything in your way — of course, if you *want* to marry him. . . . Everything about Sam was distasteful to them.

The really odd thing was that Sam and my father — when I met him — looked so alike, and are so alike. My real father, that is. They've got the same build and that same warmth, an odd memory that lurked from my childhood. Sam comes from a Jewish family, it was the warmth that attracted me to him, it was the involvement. Whereas there's the cold and non-involvement of my mother's side. My father's not Jewish but he's warm and cuddly and it's so different. Oh, it was nice meeting him because it filled a gap for me. Obviously I fit into that side much better than my mother's side. The meeting was good for my father too. The idea came from Sam. I wondered about trying to see my father because I knew he'd got another wife and family. But Sam said, 'Oh, for goodness' sake, why don't you get in contact?' So I told my aunt and she gave him my phone number and then he rang up.

When I told my mother I was going to see my father she came out within about two or three minutes with the utmost poisonous theatrical things about him that she'd obviously built up over the years — saying that he was a handsome cad, 'Don't let him take you in like he did me', and, 'I hear he's deserted this wife' — all this kind of thing, complete fantasy. I must say I felt she'd done very well not to have said anything before. But I never mentioned his name again.

I see her and my stepfather very little now. I cannot have any relationship with my stepfather because as soon as I'm remotely friendly or give an inch, wham, he's there. It's absurd. Back to sex. My mother out of the house and he says, 'Well, what about it?' He doesn't say anything about that long, long time when we were having sex. It's just come to meaningful glances, deep sighs, looking mournful, ridiculous things like that.

For a while I thought that there'd been no harm done, that it had given me an interesting upbringing, given me quite an experience. Then I felt more bitter. I felt it had taken so much time away from me. I spent an awful long time thinking about it, talking about it to Sam, getting it out of my system. So now it's just a memory, whereas before it was dominant. And it's helped in a way that when I do go back there I'm treated like a perfect stranger instead of the daughter of the house. I'm asked if I take sugar in my tea, 'Do you know where the bathroom is?' This is the way they've dealt with it — no wedding present, my mother doesn't remember my birthdays, it's as if she doesn't remember I exist. Sometimes she mutters about bad blood, putting it all down to being my father's daughter and that's all there is to it. But she's happier. They look incredibly successful, a well-groomed, happy, prosperous-looking couple. Only since I left home did they begin to drag themselves up, get something back into their relationship.

If my mother did but know, it was the best service I ever did her, leaving home.

But a great deal more of this kind of thing goes on now. I think it's inevitable, with more step-parents. And it's happening with real fathers too, of course — always has. I think it's very damaging. It depends a lot on how people come through it. But the damaging aspect is that, as with me, there's often nothing spoken, it's all non-verbal. So you can have this powerful experience but be left with no comprehension of it.

Looking back on it I see it as an awful encroachment, an exploiting. It's a taking away of something he had no right to take away. It was wasted years. I wish I'd been able to do other things, get on with my acting and been myself as a person. My energies should have been into outside things. But it turns you in. It deprives you of growth. It deprives you of your adolescence, the exploring, the adventure and the discovering.

'I can't say, "Hullo, this is my father." I have
to say, "This is a friend of mine." Or "my
aunt" or something!'

15 Margaret, whose father changed sex

*Margaret is separated from her husband, whom she married four
years ago when she was nineteen. She lives in a smart flat in
Chelsea with her son and a female lodger. She's vivacious and
rather beautiful, with one of those mobile, alive faces that actresses
often have. In fact, she's a dancer and she also earns money
illustrating books.*

*When Margaret was eighteen her father changed sex – which is
convenient shorthand for saying that he underwent a series of
operations that enabled him to dress, look, speak and behave as if
he was no longer a man but a woman.*

*Margaret describes what her father's sex-change meant to her and
what difference it made to her life.*

It's hard to say when I first knew my father wanted to be a
woman. A lot of it is coloured with hindsight. It's a case of
knowing now how to explain certain things which before I
thought had no particular meaning. For instance, finding a
box of coloured slides of my father dressed in my mother's
clothes. He had a camera that you can set up and run round
and take photographs of yourself. I saw all these photographs and I didn't really think anything of it. I thought
somebody was having a game or a joke or something. That
was when I was about ten or twelve and I never really
thought any more about it.

But my elder brother knew more than I did. One of my
aunts rumbled and said something to him about it so I got a
few bits from him. He just mentioned it to me when I was
about fifteen – he just said, 'Dad has always wanted to be a
lady', and I sort of pooh-poohed the idea.

My mother knew about his wish all the time I think but

she never said anything to me about it. I think it was very loyal of her not to bring it up at all. It must have been a tremendous strain for her to go through this emotional trauma and not be able to explain to us why she was doing it. My parents used to row a lot. My mother was the warring one – shouting and screaming and that type of thing – for obvious reasons I can see now, but I couldn't then. I suppose if you fall in love and marry somebody and then find out they're not all that you thought they were, it would be rather a shock.

But, before his operation, there was never anything very different from usual about my father. You see, he was always rather effeminate anyway. He was very young-looking and of very slight build and dedicated to the theatre – lots of men dedicated to the arts tend to be effeminate in that sort of way. I used to notice little things like never wearing men's socks. He would always wear thin, silk ones – like what we call pop-socks now. And all my friends' fathers wore great thick socks. There were a few things like that, nothing more. He was always a very quiet, very gentle person – so that's the kind of father he was too.

Then my mother died. She committed suicide – not directly as a result of my father's nature, but obviously that had been a build-up throughout their marriage. I think it was just the whole picture, everything generally got too much for her. She was just very, very low and depressed and in a bad way. She ended up on drugs. I don't think she really meant to do it.

So there was my brother and myself and my father living together. And gradually little things started to come to light. I had a friend then called Diana – she was much older than me, but we were working together. I'd just started as a dancer and she'd been in the theatre for some time. We'd have dinner parties at home and she used to come round a lot to make up the numbers. She and my father struck up a relationship. It seemed to be going very well and then, for some reason, my father suddenly broke it off and I couldn't understand why. It was a mystery to Di too.

And then he started up with another friend of the family who was divorced and who, in fact, was the spitting image of my mother, which was strange. And that went along for a while and it looked like they were aiming to get married. But that broke up, and then he went back with Di – the friend who's now my stepmother. And when they went back together my father was able to explain why he had broken it off before: because he really wanted to have the operation to change his sex, and he couldn't quite face up to a relationship with somebody who didn't know anything about it. They talked it out and as far as I can understand they agreed to get married on the basis that they would go and get this operation done for my father.

So he married Di and they went to Casablanca on their honeymoon and he had the operation done there the day after they arrived. There's a clinic there, the high-class place to go to for this operation. I remember Di saying she felt terrified all the time they were there because of her responsibility to my brother and me – if anything had gone wrong. . . . Because my father wasn't a young man, he was about fortyish, early forties. It could have been dicey. She was terrified of having to come home and explain what they'd done.

But at the time I still didn't know anything about it. When he remarried I just thought he'd given up all those ideas, as little as I knew about them. But I was upset at him remarrying even though it was to a friend. I suppose I had the same reaction as any teenager has to a parent remarrying, but especially after a death that had come about by suicide and all that had gone before – the rows between my parents and so on. There had been so many upsets. And my mother and I weren't getting on very well at the time of her death, the way teenage daughters and their mothers usually go through a bad patch anyway. I think she was fantastic not to have betrayed the pressure she was under. I just remember her saying, 'Do you love me? Do you love me? Do you love me?' And it's impossible to say you love somebody when they ask in that way.

After the operation, I still didn't know anything about it because my father went on dressing as a man in public. He only dressed as a woman when he and Di were very private. They moved to the country in order to live the life they wanted. But as far as anyone else was concerned, and at work, he still used to dress as a man. I had noticed the fingernails being very long and the hair very long but that didn't seem to have made much impression on me.

Then, about a year or eighteen months after the operation, I was speaking on the phone to him one day and he said to me, 'I've got something very shattering to tell you but I won't tell you on the phone.' And in my brain, I went straight to the truth. Immediately I thought, 'God, he must have done something like that.' It was a sort of intuition, based on all the little signs adding up, I suppose.

Diana and I were still working together and we were going to work one day and I mentioned this conversation to her and I just wormed it all out of her. So, in fact, it was she who told me in the end. My main reaction was, 'I thought as much.' But at certain points afterwards I felt, because of my mother's death as well, like an orphan. I no longer had any parent figure. But I don't know how much of that was sort of self-pity about not having a normal family. I'd never had a conventional set-up really. I remember as a child always craving convention. I went to boarding school and everybody else there had neat little families, Sunday joints, going to dances at Christmas and that sort of thing. I never had anything like that – life was full of theatre people everywhere I went. So when I knew about my father, a lot of reaction was this same feeling of self-pity – 'Hell, what have I done to deserve all this?'

I'm not even sure I still needed my father as an identity point or a parent figure. After all I still had him as a person. But the image was topsy-turvy in a way. Certainly I can't now say, when I'm with my father and we meet someone I know, 'Hullo, this is my father.' I have to say, 'This is a friend of mine,' or 'my aunt' or something. One thing I feel is that I could never say, 'This is my mother', I've never been able to say that. He could never slip into the role of mother instead; I don't think anyone could do that. Apart from anything else, no matter what his gender is, there's the question of personality. It's like my not being able to say that Di is my mother – she's not, she's my stepmother. Perhaps if I'd been very young I would have been able to see him as 'mother'. But the *person* just isn't that. Still I've often found it quite curious that I couldn't transfer my father into my mother. . . .

After I'd been told all about it by Di, there was still a while when my father was dressed as a man whenever I saw him. I can remember being relieved not to find her in women's clothing. I was a bit awkward with her then – but not now, not anymore, not at all. The first time I did encounter her in women's clothing was quite amusing. I'd got a steady boyfriend then (he's now my husband) and Di had suggested all four of us meet up for a meal in a rather smart restaurant in the West End. He and I went there and we were waiting and talking because the others were a bit late and I suddenly said, 'Oh Christ, you know what's going to happen don't you? As it's a social evening, she's going to appear as a lady.' We both rushed to the bar and had two large Scotches. It was so funny when we suddenly looked at each other and realised. But it was good actually that we had; if she'd just walked in without us realising beforehand how she'd be dressed, it could have been difficult. As it was, the evening went off very easily.

At first, I was very conscious of looking at the make-up and clothes and everything. I already knew about two things my father had gone through, but seeing him as a woman for the first time made me more aware of them. Firstly, he'd had electrolysis to get rid of the beard. This left his skin much tireder-looking and very dry. I think perhaps if it was done with a younger person it wouldn't have shown in quite the same way. And then there was wearing powder on top of it. In fact, I think my father looks older as a woman than he ever did as a man, because of mucking around with his skin so much.

And the other operation that he had done was a nose job. He used to have quite a sort of Roman nose and it was turned into a retroussé nose. The trouble with that, though, is that it does give you black eyes when you have the operation and if you're older you lose the elasticity of your skin. So it leaves you rather baggy round the eyes. She's gone through a helluva lot to achieve her end – an enormous amount. Mostly, I approve of her dress but she does wear some peculiar things sometimes. Actually, one of the most disturbing things is to see her in a trouser suit. Of course, a woman in a trouser suit can look very feminine, but if you're used to someone wearing men's clothes anyway and suddenly they're in trousers as a woman. . . it seemed very strange at first even though she was always such an effeminate-looking man. Somehow just the fact of wearing trousers made her look more masculine and therefore more like someone in drag. But I don't react that way so much now. It was only at first.

There wasn't an enormous difference in her mannerisms and general behaviour–as I said, these were on the effeminate side anyway, before the operation. OK, there were little things like more hand movements, but she began to use red nail varnish and I think you just notice hands a bit more when they've got red tips to them. I did notice that when she spoke she was trying to lighten her voice so that it wasn't such a masculine voice. In fact, that was another operation she had after the main one; she had an operation on her vocal chords. That was the last of them, the throat one. It does work as an operation provided you do the speech therapy with it. I was amazed once, hearing her practise on a tape. I don't think my father knew I was in the house. I was passing by his study door and I could hear this voice, it sounded exactly like a woman talking. No trace of a masculine note. I thought to myself, 'There's a lady in there.' But it was my father's practice tape. You know, she'd practise with a feminine voice and record it. But she could never put it into practice socially. On the tape it sounded absolutely feminine but once with people she'd lose it. Very strange. . . .

When people found out about the operation there were quite a lot of close friends–or we thought they were–who wouldn't see her again. The men who knew her were shocked. I've always thought this about men's reaction to transsexuals or homosexuals or transvestites or anything, they're always much more shocked than the women–their own manhood is threatened by it. And I think you find that most women are more squeamish about lesbians than men are. So it was mostly men who made the nasty comments. I heard quite a few.

I suppose one of the biggest threats to me was that people were wondering about *my* sexuality. Once Diana and I were going off for a drink with a man we both worked with–and everyone knew that Di was married to my father – and another guy said to the man, 'You want to watch those two, they're funny.' I felt very sensitive about it and quite embarrassed about the whole thing at work. I'd walk in and they'd whisper, 'That's the daughter' and things like that. It must have made me very anxious to prove I was feminine. I got married quite soon after his operation had become common knowledge. And almost immediately I was married I became pregnant. I think that subconsciously the gossip was probably one of the reasons for this – just to prove there wasn't anything peculiar about *me*.

Mostly we get on very well with each other now, my father and I. We're still very close, we talk every day on the phone. But one of the things that's unlike a normal parent-child relationship is that I won't allow him to criticise me. I tell him, 'I'm more or less a product of what you've done. You mustn't criticise me because you don't really have any right to.' I don't mean that in an unsympathetic way. For instance, there was a time when I had a lot of work, a lot of dancing jobs coming up, and so my son was with my in-laws quite a lot and he'd say things like, 'Don't you think you ought to be with your son at home instead of working?' and I'd say, 'I just don't think you've got the right to say things like that.'

What's interesting is that actually I still think she's rather a male chauvinist pig. Because it's like she still wants to be father, organise my life and give me advice and all that sort of thing. At her home, with Di, there's still this scene of who does the washing-up at night. She never does it. Di is the one who cooks and shops and takes the dog out and does the washing-up and everything – very chauvinistic. That's fine when my father's working and shuts herself up in the studio. But it's the same when she's just around the house. If Di is out for the day and I'm there it's me who does the cooking and shopping and washing-up. She'll do just the odd little things like wash up a teacup. It's quite amusing – the best of both worlds. It's a major event if she even makes a bed.

She was here last weekend. I was rather down and depressed and so she came over to see me. She got my son, who's three, to show her over the house – she hadn't been here before. I do all the visiting, lots of weekends I go to her home and sometimes go and stay there for a week. Anyway, she came downstairs and she said, 'I've made your bed for you.' And I said 'Thank you very much. That's kind of you.' Two hours later I went upstairs and you'd never have thought the bed had been made. It was absolutely terrible, just thrown together.

So she's become female but she hasn't taken the feminine role really. There's not a great deal of her character that's changed. She's more or less the same as he was. But living in the country has changed her life-style and that's reflected on her. She's become less active in some ways. Before the operation we were living in London and there were always people dropping round and she was always very lively and a very easy raconteur. But now it has to be by invitation only because it's such a long way for most people to go. It's become more humdrum and dull and I don't think she enjoys that very much. She does something that she never used to do and that's sit and watch television in the evening, any programme that's on, and it's very hard to get it turned off. I go down there and say, 'Come on, let's play scrabble or something. . . .' It's getting a bit better but there was a time when they just sat and sat. Quite a lot of the time she and Di are just on their own. In a way, she's opting out.

Something I haven't tackled yet is my son's relationship to my father. He just calls her 'Granny' and we leave it at that. I don't know if he'll ever query it when he gets older. I can't really bring myself to say to him that she's his 'grandmother', anymore than I can think of her as my 'mother'. There's just a block about it. I don't know why. I do wonder if it will be easy for him if I just say, 'This is your grandmother' and leave it at that for ever, or if I should one day, say, 'This is your grandma but she was once your granddad.' I don't know whether it will confuse him. I'm just leaving it. It's going to be quite a while before he's going to query it at all, if he ever does.

They adore each other. My son loves men, whenever there are blokes around he really enjoys himself; I think he sees women as a nagging sort of thing. And when we go down to my father's it's interesting how he wants to spend

more time with Granny than he does with Di so he's
responding to her as a male. I may be imagining that but I
don't think so.

In some ways I'm conscious of having something in the
family that's a kind of secret – something to be kept slightly
under wraps. It depends who I'm with. Mostly I'm very
open about it and if, say, I'm going to take a friend down
there for the day I just say, 'By the way, I'd better tell you
this so that you won't misunderstand.' If they come and
they meet her and they don't understand, well, I don't
mean it unsympathetically, but that's their problem. It's
more or less a thing that somebody's got to accept. There's
nothing you can do to change it. I've had to be realistic
about it.

But I've often felt resentful about what he's done. I've
certainly often thought, 'Why couldn't he just stay as a
man?', especially with my mother having died. I resented,
in a sense, my mother dying without me ever understanding her. I was always terrified of her as well. She was very
dominating but I don't know that she ever meant to be. On
the other hand, she could be the most generous and gentle
person. But when she demanded, she demanded in a way
that frightened me. I knew that if I put a foot out of line,
there would be a row and I hate rows. And I suppose that's
why my father and I are quite close because my father hates
rows as well. So I resented not being given the chance to
understand my mother. That's what I resent most now,
more than just my father becoming a woman. I think at the
time my mother died I felt a sort of relief. That was one
thing over and done with. No more rows – not between my
parents, and not between her and me. Most of the rows
were about stupid things like how late I'd stayed out at
night – the usual things with a teenager. But on occasions
there was, 'You don't love me, you love your father.' She
obviously resented me being close to my father, knowing
what my father had done to her. In a way I wish she'd told
me about it. I don't know why she didn't; I suppose she just
thought I wouldn't understand.

Well, I understand now – both what she must have gone
through and why my father had to have the operation. I'm
not sure whether a transsexual is born or is made that way by

conditioning. One thing my father does remember is that his mother always wanted a daughter. She found it slightly repugnant to have a son, as though boys were dirty or something like that. Perhaps that was to do with her own sexuality. I don't know. Therefore she dressed my father as a girl until he was about four years old. He had ringlets and wore dresses and she put rouge on his lips. I don't know whether that's programming or not. But I'd imagine that basically it's a hormone thing that you're born with. I don't really know how it comes about.

I suppose I must have been fairly positive about everything but there are still black times. Even now I get a fit of the dismals sometimes thinking, 'What did I do to deserve it?' I've been through a low patch with the break-up of my marriage. I suppose I'd like my own private life to be more secure—but it's hard to be sure of that. Everything's been so upside down for such a long time that I can't imagine what it would be like to have a smooth, ordinary life—boring, I expect. But I wouldn't want life to be ordinary as far as my father is concerned. I've got so used to that change now that I can't imagine him any other way. I wouldn't wish him back as a man.

PART FOUR

Broken homes

16 After the breakaway, what next?

It was remarkable how often, without any previous knowledge of the family backgrounds of the girls I interviewed, I learnt that there had been some form of break-up in the family – a divorce in most cases. In the personal stories reproduced in this book, Emma, the single parent, and Jane, who didn't know her father at all but knew her stepfather too well, are both the products of divorce. Cheryl's mother deserted the family and Tracy grew up in a Home, Margaret's mother committed suicide and Susan, who grew up happily in a stable adoptive family, was nonetheless driven by her illegitimate entry into the world to search for her 'real' mother.

In addition, a number of the stories feature a remarriage by the divorced parents, with its attendant stepfathers, stepmothers, half-siblings and step-siblings. This means that as well as coping with the results of family breakdown, many children of divorced parents have to cope with a re-alignment of relationships in order to take in new ones. A teenage girl may be so split by these pressures from divided loyalties, and by confusion and jealousy, that she may have to get shot of the whole lot for a time before she can be certain of her own identity.

There's no refuge in imagining that these girls are unrepresentative. Latest figures for a complete year show that there were 120,000 divorces in 1975 – the all-time high. These divorces involved 180,000 children under sixteen. The latest figures available on remarriage are for 1974 and show that, in that year, one in every four marriages involved a divorced bride or groom. It's estimated that if present levels of marriage and divorce rates continue, twenty-two per cent of all females would divorce at least once by the age of forty-five. And as far as children are concerned, the trends are a decline in the proportion of childless couples among those getting divorced and an increase in the average family size of those divorcing couples who have children.

So, all in all, we can expect more of the kind of shake-up of old relationships and reorientation to new ones that is required of children when their parents divorce and remarry. At present, as the stories here indicate, many children of divorce find their own desperate solutions to the emotional problems of family breakdown. But there is perhaps an indication of the need for more counselling help – or of the willingness to seek it – for these casualties of what some people, including me, see as a transitional phase between the one marriage tradition and the possibility of second and third marriages becoming the acceptable norm.

But I still think we need to be wary about believing that the prime cause of protest and problems among adolescents is the break-up of the family, either in the form of divorce, desertion and death, or in the form of mothers out at work instead of keeping the home fires burning twenty-four hours a day. Certainly the figures for various forms of social breakdown among young people – girls held in custody, runaways, vandalism, venereal diseases, illegitimate births, violence inflicted on self and on others, etc – continue to keep pace with the upward trend in divorce. But parents and their children live in the same world and are subject to similar pressures. Perhaps both marital breakdown and the anti-social or self-destructive situations that some young people get into are all symptoms of the same malaise. There may be less cause and effect between the problems of the two generations, more a case of us all being in the same boat.

There's one big disadvantage the breakaway girl faces that is not quite so bad for a boy – the difficulty of finding somewhere else to go.

A boy or man on his own can doss down anywhere for a

while. True, he might be moved on if he's in a public place but then again he might not. Few girls can adapt to sleeping rough and society tends to regard them as weirdos if they do. A boy or man can shack up more easily with single or married friends and he's more welcome at bed-and-breakfast places than a girl. As floating visitors and lodgers, males are considered 'no trouble'. Landladies, friends and girlfriends expect to tend to their food and comfort and the demarcation lines between his territory and theirs are relatively clear. But females, as short stay visitors or lodgers, are 'trouble'. They want to hang their tights and pants all over the bathroom, they want to entertain boyfriends, they are nearly always in, and frequently on the phone. They bring their nesting instinct with them; they want to make 'home' out of wherever they are and centre their lives on it, whereas a man will use the essential facilities and carry on his main life outside. For him, home is the place he's left behind or the place he's going to settle down in later on.

This offers some explanation for a girl's difficulty in finding alternative accommodation if she leaves the family. But the major explanation is that single girls and women are a part – and a disadvantaged part – of the enormous national housing need. Of the seven million unmarried adults in this country of working age, only one in five has a place of their own. The rest live in other people's households, which in many cases are their own parents' homes.

Some, perhaps, are content to do so if they envisage getting married young. But for those whose jobs or enquiring natures take them far from home or who want independence without getting married, there's virtually only the dwindling supply of furnished tenancies and the squats to turn to; and for these the young single girl is the last in the queue.

This means that a girl who leaves home on impulse, or is pressurised to leave, will invariably fall into the 'homeless' category straightaway. She may get a few nights in emergency accommodation or, if she's lucky, a few weeks in a hostel. But June Lightfoot of CHAR points out that a girl has less chance than a boy of getting to one of the various projects in the big cities for accommodating the homeless. She's more likely to get picked up first and start living with a man or drifting into amateur prostitution, just for the sake of a roof.

There is still the belief that what girls need most is moral protection. Yet, as the stories of Tracy and Cheryl show, the reasons for a girl leaving home are often far from anti-social ones that make her especially vulnerable to moral danger. It's the *homelessness*, in fact, that makes her vulnerable. Many of the hostels for girls have strict curfews and limits on visitors etc; some girls find this safer, particularly the girls who've been in care or who come from violent homes. But many homeless girls are like Tracy and Cheryl: in that situation because of poor relationships in the home – they have had to break away in order to survive and what they need most is simply somewhere safe. Would Emma have become pregnant if she had had somewhere to go, free for a while of both her parents and of unstable companions?

So there is a growing need for straight accommodation with less policing, for the ordinary, law-abiding girl who has made the break with home or whose home has broken under her. It does seem that the very absence of this safe alternative accommodation for a daughter who has out-grown day-in day-out family life is responsible for many of the breakaways into inappropriate situations, and for many hasty sexual liaisons.

'I'll never have kids – too much arguing.
Every new generation always thinks they're
going to make better parents – they never
do. It's always the same – too much arguing,
too many arguments. I'd be just as bad.'

17   Cheryl and family strife

*Cheryl ran away at sixteen. A month before, her mother had
walked out of the family home, leaving her father, who's a
milkman, her younger brother and herself.*
*She's seventeen now and works eighty-three hours a week for the
Turkish owner of a restaurant. The owner's wife relies on Cheryl
to do all the ordering of food and wine for the business because she
and her husband speak little English. They think a lot of her.
Cheryl is heavily built and sultry-looking. She has dark untidy
hair and pretty green eyes. She chain-smoked Turkish cigarettes
while she talked to me.*

My Mum and Dad were always rowing, they rowed all the
time. I don't know what about, not about another man. I
used to think my Mum was right, I don't now. I hate her.
They rowed about her housekeeping, when he put it down,
to keep her in at nights. I don't know where she went, she
just went out. My brother always sided with my Dad, they
were always close – I stuck up for Mum. She was always
saying she'd go but she always said she'd take me with her.
The night she went, a Friday, they had a flaming row and
she packed up and she went. I was crying on the kitchen
floor. She wouldn't take me with her. She only wanted me
for what she could get out of me. I hadn't got a job and she
wanted my money, so she wouldn't take me without a job.
   I stayed at home with my brother and Dad, then a few
months later I met her in the town. She said I only had to
ring her if I wanted to go with her, to pack my case and ring
her. One night I went to a girl friend's engagement party

and I rang her. She said meet her in town at eleven o'clock. I
had my case and I waited for her and she never come. It was
half-past-eleven, I was terrified, on my own in town at
eleven o'clock at night. I went back to the party and stayed
with my girlfriend. I couldn't go home, my Dad's got a
terrible temper when he's up.

Next day I came down here to the caff and they said I
could have my meals here if I worked in here all day. In the
evening I met the kid from the pub opposite, he come in
here, nine he is, just a kid this high, and he took me by the
hand and he said, 'You come and sleep in my house'. So I
stayed at the pub, nights, and worked in here all day for my
food. Fantastic, it was. They was nice, his parents.

Then I met a Lebanese bloke in the caff and he said, come
and live with me. A student he was and he'd spent all his
grant. I had a job in a canteen by then, £4 a day I got; he
wanted my money. I stayed with the Lebanese bloke a
week, then we had a flaming row in the middle of the road
because he wanted thirteen quid off me because I'd worked
four days. I said 'not likely' and we had this row and that
was the end of that.

Then I met a mini-cab chap and he offered me a job taking
his calls at night. I did that for three days. Then I went into a
pub up the road, and the bloke behind the bar said, 'I hear
you're looking for somewhere to live.' I thought, amazing,
isn't it, how news gets around? Well he says, 'Would you
like to move in with me and I'll give you money and you can
cook for me?' I said, 'all right' and wondered what I'd let
myself in for.

Well that was a laugh: he was queer, I was as safe as
houses. He had a nice room, a sort of flatlet. I gets in with
him in his bed, then it turns out he's queer; he never
touched me. He was a nice chap, really. He worked up at
the RAF, he enjoys his work. He used to bring his friends in
and I'd go out.

Then I was in the caff one day when someone said, 'Why
don't you go and stay with Mrs Castle?' I didn't know about
her before. She runs a place for homeless girls. So I went up
to see her but she said she couldn't take me unless I came
through the police or probation. So she said, 'You go and
ring the ambulance service and say you're homeless and

they'll fix it up so you can stay here.' So I rang the ambulance service and by the time I got back they arranged with Mrs Castle and I moved in with her.

It was good, I liked it. It was £7 a week or £1.50 a night. I hadn't got no papers or cards, nothing at all. But she sent me down to the unemployment people and I got the dole and signed on.

Two weeks later she closed the house down because she was going on holiday and she doesn't keep the house open when she goes away. By then I'd got myself a job in a factory.

I left Mrs Castle's on the Friday and I spent the whole day in a department store trying to pluck up the courage to ring my Dad. I phoned in the end at four o'clock, I said, 'Hallo Dad, this is Cheryl. Can I come home? I've got a job.' He said, 'Oh all right then.' I went home and the place was in a shambles. I cleared it up and he got me my dinner.

I lost the job in the factory because I was swearing. There was a Christian woman worked there, and she kept complaining and complaining and in the end, they chucked me out.

So I came back to work in the caff again and I didn't like walking home at eleven o'clock at night, so I stay here now. I've left home again but it's different. I've got an Egyptian boyfriend, he used to be my girlfriend's fiancé but he chucked her because she went out with another boy, he's twenty-five. He's waiting for his mother to come over and take him home; he doesn't do anything while he's waiting – he just waits. I'm definitely going to Egypt next year. I save £20 a week and just keep about £7 for cigarettes and things. I've been up to the Consulate place and they've got me a hotel in Egypt – that's a laugh, *got me a hotel*, – I've got a job as a receptionist. All I have to do is speak and write English. They seem to like English girls.

My Mum and Dad's marriage, if that's what you call it, has definitely put me clean off marriage. My Mum didn't like me. That's it. She'd never have anyone in the house. She said they'd make the house dirty. Everyone else seemed to have loving parents, they could have friends in, we were never allowed to.

I'll never have kids – too much arguing. Every new

generation always thinks they're going to make better parents – they never do. It's always the same – too much arguing, too many arguments. I'd be just as bad.

I sent my Mum a bouquet on Mother's Day. I suppose I did it for the ceremony. She rang me up. She said, 'What's this for?' I said, 'Well what was yesterday?' 'Oh yes,' she said. She never said 'thank you', she said, 'Well what do you want for your birthday?' That's how she said it and I said 'a gold signet ring'. I'll screw as much out of her as I can.

'There were times when I wanted somebody to talk to about all the things that had gone wrong before I became pregnant but being pregnant and having the baby, I was a lot happier doing that on my own. I wouldn't have liked sharing that.'

18 Emma, unmarried mother

Emma is nineteen and has a four-month-old son. She not so much broke away from home as had her home break away from her when her parents separated. She was fourteen then. They were divorced when she was sixteen and she left home to live with her father until he remarried a year later. She and her son are now living with her mother in the Hertfordshire countryside. She talks about the break-up of her family, about being a single parent and how she sees life ahead for herself and her son Michael.
Emma is tall and well-rounded – the traditional ultra-feminine type. She moves gracefully and wears both her hair and her skirts long and full. She looks very young and vulnerable but talks in a forthright, determined way.

I don't think I could have done anything else but keep Michael. There was a time while I was pregnant when none of the rest of the family had definitely accepted that I was going to keep him. And if my mother, and sister, who was living at home at the time, had been totally against it then obviously I couldn't have kept him. It would have made life unbearable trying to bring him up in the house with people who didn't like him or refused to have anything to do with him.

I suppose I probably could have found somewhere else to live and, with social security and everything, kept him in some other way, but if that had been the case I would have ended up in a flat in a big town or something. That wouldn't have been fair on him and I couldn't have given him anything I wanted to give him. One of the reasons for keeping him was because we live in the country and there were all the animals and the rest of the family around to be part of his life, a good part of his life.

The rest of the family took a while to decide how they felt about having the baby at home. Quite reasonably, they felt it was going to make enormous inroads into their lives. This was something they didn't really want so they thought, for a while, that adoption was best. I'd totally ruled out having an abortion; this was suggested by various people at the beginning. Before I was actually pregnant myself I'd felt that abortion might be an answer for some people in that situation. But once you're pregnant and you've already started to think of this thing as part of you, then it's as bad as cutting off your own hand or something. I still do feel that maybe it's an answer for some people – for medical reasons, of course, and for anyone who would be really miserable actually having a child – but I wouldn't personally.

Anyway, the baby was wanted from the start. I'd always been rather the opposite of most young girls who go through the stage of having dolls and liking babies. Well, I didn't when I was younger; I couldn't stand babies, they made me feel sick. But then I began to have this longing, not so much for a baby, but for a fellow human being who I could teach things to and help to build, a person I could have contact with and who would communicate with me. I'd been living with a bloke for a few months and he also said he'd like to have a child; at the time we believed we were going to be together for good. Admittedly I don't think an enormous amount of thought went into it. I was pretty upset over my parents getting a divorce and everything else that had happened so I went straight into it without really thinking.

I was nipping on and off the Pill anyway because I hated being on it. It was all a bit badly organised. He'd been married and had three kids and he was in the process of getting a divorce. He wanted to marry me after he got his divorce. I was a bit half-hearted about it. I was very happy to be engaged, I enjoyed that. That was very nice, you know, without making a definite decision about your future life. So we were thinking about having a child for quite a while. I didn't get pregnant so I got rather relaxed about the whole thing. And I also began to think that perhaps I *couldn't* have one.

But by that time things were starting to go a bit wrong: Joe was turning out not to have any desire to get a permanent job and there was a different note creeping slowly into the relationship. When I met him he struck me as an amazingly nice bloke. He was kind and nice and had a very gentle way. But then he gradually became, I don't know, more dominating. He just couldn't understand when I wanted to do anything off my own bat, anything that I enjoyed doing and he didn't. It wasn't possessiveness exactly – I don't mind that. I was just there, I wasn't a person to him. For example, he used to walk ahead of me in the street, never beside me.

So when I got pregnant and found that he wasn't being responsible about it, I said I was going to sort things out by myself and that I'd have to leave. I felt this was one thing that I was going to make a really good job of – if I was going to have this child, then I was going to do it properly and give it everything I could. In no way could I bring it up the way I wanted in a squat or in one of the rough old places we'd been living in.

I remember him saying once when we were having an argument – we seemed to have quite a lot – 'Well, now you're pregnant, you can't leave me, can you?'. That was more likely to make me leave than anything else, I'm always one for doing the opposite to whatever anybody says. If he said, 'Now you can't leave' then I would leave. He made a couple of mock attempts at suicide which by that time didn't really make any difference. It wouldn't have kept me there, nothing would have kept me there. He survived it all – and I left.

I went back to my mother's house; not because I thought of it as home, I didn't feel I had any home at that point. I'd felt as much at home in the rough old places in Birmingham with Joe as anywhere else. Home is where the most important person in your life is; at that time I think I was the most important person in my life so I didn't think of anywhere as home. My father's place was out of the

question, they had just announced to me that my stepmother was pregnant. This was at the same time that I was
a couple of months pregnant myself and was just leaving
Joe. I remember being a bit thrown by it. I suppose I felt
terribly guilty that I'd rather bummed up her pregnancy, so
I didn't tell them about me being pregnant. In fact, I might
not have told them for quite a while but Joe went to see
them and told them.

So going back to my mother was just a first move, the
most sensible place to go while things were being decided.
Then, gradually, I became very sure about how I felt about
the child and how I was going to manage. It was only other
people's feelings that were throwing me a bit. I knew how I
felt and how I was going to manage but there was still an
awful lot of discussion to go on about how my mother was
going to manage, and my sister. But I'd got it sorted out
quite soon; I was getting into my old swing of knowing
where I was going and getting on with doing it. I was
thinking ahead–I think you do that more when you're
pregnant. Everything went through my mind, how I could
earn a living, what I was going to tell him about his
father–all that. But I wasn't *worrying* about it, just getting
on with thinking about it.

There was no definite point at which the decision was
made to keep the baby, it was very gradual. I remember
going out and buying a few vests and things and thinking,
'Well, I'll buy them now anyway and even if he's adopted
he'll need something for the first few weeks and I can put
them by until I have kids that I do keep.' I had some money
I'd saved from the time that I was earning and now, for the
time being, I have social security money and I give my
mother £5. That seems to work out all right.

While I was pregnant and when I was in hospital having
the baby it seemed to me that people were a lot more
considerate to me than to a married woman. I suppose they
were over-compensating for the fact that I was alone. They
were extremely nice. I never once felt guilty about it or
whatever anyone's supposed to feel. I was having a child
the same as anyone else. The only difference was that it was
just me that was having it and not someone else as well. If
anything, you know, it can be a lot more enjoyable when

you're the only one taking pride in it and making the decisions – a lot easier.

There were times when I wanted somebody to share all the things that had gone wrong before I was pregnant, someone to talk it over with, but actually being pregnant and having the baby, I was a lot happier doing that on my own. I wouldn't have liked a bloke around then, I didn't miss that at all. When the baby was born, I had no longings to share that. It was me who'd done it – why should anyone else share that triumph with me? Blokes have very little to do with babies anyway – and it's so long beforehand. No, it was me who was having it and me who was putting all the effort into it. It's a bit selfish really. . . but the truth is I felt a lot more secure doing things on my own than I would have done with an insecure person sharing it all.

It's only very rarely that I wish now there was someone
el__ _____ ____ ____ ısibility. Sometimes I can get very
y about what would happen if I
over by a bus or something. I worry
ɔen to Michael. I just don't know, I
pose if I were ill my mother would
vas too busy then he'd go into care
I suppose he'd go up for adop-
n't make me very happy – but there
ı whether or not he's a member of
definitely is – at least of the small
mother here in this house – but it's
y mother would have to look after
ıg on her own. But I'm sure she
ıe. She obviously loves him a lot.
:he family thing – the business of
the more people who have close
he better. I'm not worried about
the more people you have contact
ı can turn to and, if somebody has
g at you, at least there are quite a
re being nice to you at the same
ıld end up with a lot more family
narried. A husband and wife and
closed shop. I don't believe that
of surviving as a larger family, an

extended family of grandparents and so on. Unfortunately
I think it's regarded as a bit old-fashioned to want your
grandmother around or whatever. I know families do move
about more and lose touch but I think if you wanted it that
much you could manage it. If people try hard enough they
can work life out the way they want it.

There are a lot of marvellous families of just husband and
wife and kids but I think they're missing out on a lot. I know
I'm missing out on a lot too because I haven't got a husband
but I welcome other people in my child's life and lots of
parents don't. I don't like the idea of communal living
because there's no connection between the people, they're
just a load of strangers together who've got to get on. It's
the family ties I feel strongly about and you can't make
those from odd people.

I don't think there's much chance of earning my own
living until Michael's at an age to go to some sort of nursery
school. I would put it off as long as possible or do a job at
home because I believe that mothers should be with their
children. I'm totally against the idea of mothers going off
and doing jobs and hardly seeing their kids but I realise
some mothers can't help it. I have pretty firm ideas about
bringing him up. I have a lot of trust in a child's own
feelings. I don't think they try to con you as much as people
make out or if they do, they've got a damned good reason
for doing so. If a child, for instance, is continually saying he
feels too ill to go to school then he has a good reason. He
may not be actually ill but he's got some other reason for not
wanting to go to school and I feel you should find out what
that is.

At the minute I don't feel that I ever want to get married,
when I'm older I might feel differently. I think it would be a
good thing for me to have somebody else in my life because
I might otherwise be a bit heavy with Michael, which would
be a bad thing. But I'm not all that interested in marriage.
I'm pretty bad at compromise really, I just like to be doing
things my own way. I've got quite strong feelings about life
and how I'd like to lead it and ideals and so on. I think
people would find it very difficult to live with me because I
go my own way.

I think it's very easy to get far too mixed up in

relationships, far too mixed up with other people's feelings; you're not quite sure which are your feelings and which are theirs. You can get life far too complicated to a point where you can't manage it any more. I wouldn't like to do that. It's different with a child because you can't mix up their feelings and your feelings. Any feelings or attitudes they have are very strong and straight and in no way could they be confused with mine. There's something direct between a mother and a child, or between two children, that you can't get in any other sort of relationship. Between adults there's a lot of games-playing but I don't think that matters – it's a part of human nature. What does matter, to me anyway, is that you have to spend a lot of your time avoiding confrontations and situations. If you're living with some-body, there's an awful lot of treading on eggs, watching out in case you suddenly upset them. I think I'm over-cautious about that in some ways, which is not necessarily a bad thing. I used to feel like that with my parents. I used to think it was up to me to keep things going. But there comes a point when you think, 'What the hell, they're going on with what they're doing so it's far better if I just get on with my life.'

I think obviously the people who are affected worse in a divorce are the children because they've got no say in the matter, they just have to wait and see what happens. But you still worry about your parents; you worry if they're quite far away and you don't know what they're doing and wonder if they are all right. You have to convince yourself that they are adult and that they can manage. But there was a time when they weren't being adult and they were being childish and it's too easy to miss out on a lot yourself because you're worrying too much about them. It wasn't a matter of trying to keep them together because they *were* together, and I didn't know they were going to separate until they actually did. It was an attempt to stop them arguing, because I don't like arguing. I seem to get into arguments a lot but I don't like them.

It got to the point when I just felt this is all a bit too much for me to take in and understand and fathom. Nobody really told me what was going on. I knew that things were beginning to go to pieces. But I hadn't thought they'd separate because I could still see all the close things in the family. I could feel that although the situation between my father and mother wasn't close, every other situation in the family was, between all the other members of the family. There was still a lot there between my parents and us even though *they* weren't close anymore.

I'd been at boarding school a couple of terms when this was happening. I went there by my own choice – I just felt it was time to do something on my own for a while. I got to the state where I felt I couldn't work any more and found myself incapable of doing anything. I couldn't even get up, I'd just lie there and cry solidly. So they'd cart me off to the sickroom and I'd lie there and cry instead of in my own room. I had a nice headmaster who said, 'Well you're not doing anything here at school. There's not much point in you being here. You might as well be at home and at least you'll know what's going on there.' So at fourteen I left school and went home and by that time my father had left. After a while I went to work in his business; he then moved the business far away from my family home and just my father and I went to live in a house together and run the business.

I couldn't say that the longing to have a baby actually began when my parents split up, or that it was caused by it. I can't remember really – I think I had the feeling before they were separated. That was the most traumatic time, when they actually separated. The divorce didn't mean much in feeling terms because it's just tidying up the loose ends. But I think it was more when I could see that both my father and my mother were just getting on with their own lives after they'd been divorced and I was left a bit in limbo between the two.

In fact, there were good feelings all round between my father and mother by that time, there hadn't been a lot of nastiness anyway. But my father, who I'd been living and working with, had remarried and it was pretty difficult to accept that there was another person who had such claims on my father. I did a lot of shifting about between the house I'd lived in with my father, where I stayed on my own after he'd married again, and my mother's house. And when I went there, to my mother, I was having less and less to do with the home and felt a bit of a guest there and my mother had various blokes around the house and so did my sister. Somehow I felt as if everyone was carrying on with their own lives and I was getting a bit left out in the cold. So I made friends with some people who were living in a squat in the place where I'd lived with my father – and that's how I eventually met Joe.

It would be too simple, perhaps, to say that what's happened is that I lost a family so I made another one – but maybe in a way I have. The baby isn't really taking the place of anything I've lost, he doesn't slot into a gap, he's a totally different thing. He's using up some of the feelings and skills and time and energy, some of everything that I have. He's obviously satisfying something that I felt I needed, and do still need, but I couldn't really say what that is.

Sometimes I have thought how I would like him to turn out but the world will be a totally different place by the time he's grown up, so I don't know – in the end all you can do is wait and see what your children are like. I hope he'll be intelligent because if you're intelligent you can work your way through most things. And I hope he's musical, I think that's terribly important – it's one of the best outlets there is.

It's also extremely important to me that he's got my surname, I can't think of a better name for him to have. I wouldn't have wanted him to have his father's, I couldn't anyway unless he'd agreed and by then I wasn't having any contact with him at all and there's been none since. I do worry sometimes about what to tell Michael about his father, I keep changing my mind about it. I've got to decide some time. I think you can only tell a child the truth because one day he's going to catch you out otherwise – it would be ten times as bad if he found out you'd been lying to him about it.

But that's the only worry about being an unmarried mother, it seems to me. I regretted having a baby when I had to get up in the middle of the night to feed him – what mother doesn't? – but I don't seriously regret having him. I might do, but I haven't yet. I think babies are a lot more work and effort than you think they're going to be and there's a lot of difference between the way you imagine holding a baby in your arms and the way it is when he's widdling all down you.

But there's no point at which I've felt I'd taken on more than I could handle. I still get out when I can but I had such an enormous amount of that – out every evening when I was living on my own or with Joe – that I've had enough of it for now. No doubt later on I'll start to feel I'd like more. I still like company, I like to have friends around and I like to have male friends around – I find men a lot easier to talk to than women. So I try to keep my friends to chat to – it keeps you with a balanced view of life.

Having Michael has changed me. I've gone back to being a home-loving person, having gone through stages when I wasn't. It's made me a lot more sensible and direct too. I'm having to think out what I'm going to do and how I'm going to do it. It's also made me think a lot more about what sort of relationships I get into. I used to get through relationships pretty fast but now I think it out because I've got to take the child into account. Although at this age he's not going to know any difference I must start as I mean to go on – you can't keep changing things over all the time.

I haven't come up against any prejudice. Nobody has anything against me or the child. I think people are embarrassed by it all more than anything else – and they're inquisitive. That seems understandable, I'd be interested in who the father was if somebody else unmarried had a baby. Mind you, I've had it a lot easier than many unmarried mothers because I wasn't chucked out.

I do think sometimes that it might have been easier to have had a girl purely because of the physical and mental understanding between females. But that's no worry. As long as it's human you don't really mind which it is really. As it is, I'm glad to have a boy. So there's nothing different I'd wish about him. Not yet anyway. Ask me in another twenty years and I'll tell you. . . .

'I don't think he's a poor little bastard
actually, I think he's incredibly lucky. He's
got a marvellous mother. You'd think Emma
had had six, the confident, loving way she
handles him.'

Chapter 19   Emma's mother

*Emma's mother, forty-eight, writes educational books and works
mostly at home — a three-bedroomed Victorian villa set in open
country. She and her ex-husband, who runs a printing business,
were divorced when Emma was sixteen and her sister, Kim, was
eighteen.*
*She's quick-moving, energetic and not very relaxed. Like
Emma, she's tall and dark-haired but is much more angular in
build. Their home is bursting with books, records, animals and,
now, with baby equipment.*

I knew straightaway, when Emma was pregnant, that it
was no accident; I knew that a baby was what she wanted.
She'd often talked about it but she'd stopped about a year
before she actually got pregnant and I did somehow think
that she'd dropped that longing. When she did speak about
it, I knew why she wanted a child so much. I understood
her reasons so it was quite impossible to say it was a rotten
idea and she mustn't feel like that. All I could say was that if
she could only wait a bit she'd find other ways of solving
her unhappiness and getting someone she could 'belong to'
again. I pointed out how muddly and difficult it was to
bring up an illegitimate child.

I believe it's difficult for the child, actually, more than for
its parent — emotionally, that is. But I'm glad I didn't
labour that point seeing that she now *has* an illegitimate
child. It's quite a job for her, or will be, working out how to
help him grow up without a father and how to give him a
good image of the father he'll never know in person. She

doesn't want me saying 'poor little bastard' all over the place.

I don't think he is poor actually, I think he's incredibly lucky. He's got a marvellous mother. You'd think Emma had had six, the confident, loving way she handles him. She doesn't over-do it, she's not besotted with him. She's had the same feelings that all mothers get — murderous when they go on crying and, in the first few weeks, she'd have been very happy to 'send him back' quite a few times. And at nineteen, when you've never really had to buckle down to any routine and boring little jobs that aren't strictly in your own interests — at least Emma never has — it must be very difficult to do all that sterilising and bottling, washing and nappy-changing day after day. She gets fed up with it sometimes, but she does it.

The divorce and the couple of years before it were very, very nasty for Emma. I think it was nasty for all of us, me and my other daughter too, but I had my work to help me cope and Kim, our eldest, had already gone through the break with her father. That was painful enough for her, I think, though Kim never shows her feelings the way Emma does, but at least the tie was broken already when her father left home.

For Emma the tie was strengthened because she went with him. At first she worked with him every day and came home for the nights and weekends. Then he moved his business over a hundred miles away and he and Emma set up home together there. She was only sixteen and she virtually became his 'wife'. She left all her friends and her dog and her sister and her mother and went to a town where she had to start all over again to find friends of her own age. He had friends there; in fact, he already had a girlfriend there and Emma was involved in their courtship. At the same time he hadn't a clue about helping her to find friends of her own age.

She has a fantastically strong caring streak. She felt somehow responsible for us both when we separated. Both her father and I became very sad after we'd parted, on and off; Emma would always make a cup of tea and talk things over and say things like, 'Well, it's best really, you couldn't get on together any more.' She looked after him when they worked together, before he moved. And when they'd moved and he had this girlfriend and so he was getting looked after, I think she was at a loss. When her father married his girlfriend and moved out, she got herself a puppy and some budgerigars but, of course, they weren't enough. She got in with the only people it was easy to mix with if you didn't go to school or college or have any family to produce friends, or if you didn't go to any classes or clubs or anything — and that was the drifters and squatters and the other lonely, lost people in the neighbourhood.

Honestly, I think life must have been awful for her at that stage. Well, I know it was. When she came home now and then for about five days at a time she was so mixed up and unhappy. There'd be huge scenes and rows with me or with her sister, or else she'd be terribly depressed. She used to cry at nights in bed and yet she was unable to talk about everything. I knew it would be hard to talk to me (she blamed me at that stage for the break-up of the family, now she realises it was both of us) but I kept suggesting counsellors or the Samaritans or other people we knew that I know she liked, but she couldn't. She had this thing that her father has about how you have to pull yourself out of your troubles and that you ought to be able to do it without help. He's a great person — and that's not just my view — but I think he'd be twice the person he is if he'd been able to sort out some of his emotional hang-ups. But he didn't want to know about himself, and Emma, although she could talk about herself pretty freely, didn't want to sort things out that way either.

Still, we did have lots of talks; usually they'd come after a big row and we'd be chewing things over at one o'clock in the morning. It was difficult for her sister, Kim. Whenever Emma was home the whole house was upside down, doors slamming, raised voices, the record player blaring out and all the time Kim was trying to get on with her quiet, gentle life (she was a student at the time) and I was trying to earn our living, run the house, be chauffeur and also get some private life in for myself.

Emma loathed on sight any men I brought into the house. Some of them were very nice, she admits that now, and some of them were pretty awful, but the thing that got

Emma was that most of them were married. She thought
they were all bums for deceiving their wives and if they had
children then that was the last straw — she kept identifying
with the children and how they'd feel if the marriage broke
up and so on. She really was very damaged by the divorce,
very bitter, and I think she still needs to get things a bit
straight about it.

But having the baby was, in its way, her solution to the
pain of it all. There was never really any question of
abortion or adoption and there was never any question of
marrying the father or even of keeping up with him. She
didn't want him, she wanted the baby. And, in fact, as soon
as she knew she was pregnant, she and the boy finished
with each other. There was terrible drama there too: he'd
hoped they were going to stay together but he had no job
and he couldn't look after himself at all, let alone a wife and
child. Emma had tried several times to end it, but he'd
threaten suicide and so she didn't.

When she was pregnant I think it made her stronger
about what she really wanted and so she broke with him
and he took an overdose and flung himself in the river from
which the police fished him out. Up to then, though, Emma
had been as caring about him as she is with everyone —
very tender about his feelings and letting him decide
everything. Nearly all that time, from the separation to the
time she got pregnant, which was about three years, she
was very switched-off; she always seemed to be not quite
there when she was with you, as if trying to work
something out in her mind the whole time. She looked
remote when she wasn't shouting or weeping, her weight
went up and down, she was on the Pill — or at least she'd
had it prescribed by the family doctor and she bought
supplies but I don't know whether she used them or not.
She also experimented with LSD at one time and we had
quite a tussle about that but I don't think she ever seriously
went in for drugs.

After about a year of living and working with her father
she was suddenly alone there in the flat, except for working
hours when her father came in. As soon as the divorce had
been finalised, you see, he married his girlfriend and
moved into her house.

Emma's terribly under-educated, of course. She just stopped learning when the family started to break up. She's marvellously creative and it's all unchannelled. She paints a picture here, makes a belt or a doll there, today she'll make a skirt, tomorrow she'll do an ingenious bit of sculpture out of rods and chicken wire. She plays the guitar and makes up her own words and music. It all tumbles out of her. She's got an IQ of 148 which, I know, doesn't really mean a thing in terms of intelligence, but it does say something about a lot of mental energy going spare inside her. And you can see sometimes she seems to get very frustrated by the limits of her abilities.

Now that she's got the baby she has started to think about making a living. We still mutter a bit about taking a course or something but I reckon it really isn't the time now, when the baby has to be minded — and nor does she really. She can still earn some money doing some work for her father and she probably will. Meanwhile she's on supplementary benefit to the tune of £11.80 a week, she gives me £5, and she's responsible for her own room and the baby's room, feeding the chickens and cats and dogs, looking after the boiler, chopping the wood, all the fencing and garden work, so she's no slouch.

She felt very guilty, at first, about lumbering me with a baby in the house — and, of course, it was the most hostile and selfish thing she could have done, since most of my work has to be done at home and she knows it's very demanding work. But having started the baby, what else could she do? And now that she's contributing so much to the home in terms of work and sharing the load I don't think she feels nearly so guilty. What I have to do is guard against finding her so helpful and so companionable that I couldn't manage on my own here. I don't want to hang on to her, consciously or unconsciously. She doesn't think much of marriage at the moment, which figures, but she might want to live with someone else or a number of other people later on, or she might want to have someone of her own living here. But it's all in the melting-pot. Who knows where any of us will be in a year? I never think too far ahead now.

Kim was very upset, no, she was downright angry, when

Emma came home pregnant. Well, we had got a very
smooth life going here after Emma left. It was always a
tremendous relief, after the upheaval of Emma's visits, to
sink back into our quiet ways with the occasional dinner
party. For a long while she wouldn't even admit, in Emma's
presence, that there was going to be a baby at all; she'd get
up and walk out of the room if it was mentioned. When
knitting and a pram and a cot and things started to appear
she'd act as if she hadn't seen them. But then, when the
baby was here, she was sweet with it — you could see how
badly she wanted to let go of all her disapproval of Emma
and just accept the whole thing, the way I had to. She never
did say anything, but she held the baby and she bought him
a fluffy animal and as soon as he was able to smile he always
smiled most readily at Kim and so now there's no tension
there. But what really settled their kind of feud, which was
making me dread the two of them in the house together,
was that Kim got engaged when the baby was about a
month old and she's going to be married in a couple of
months and she has a lovely cottage to go to so that's
made everything easier here at home. This is what I mean
about not knowing what's going to happen. A few months
ago I thought we were going to have real trouble and
friction in the house. It's terrible for mothers, I think, when
their children have conflicting needs — you get so torn,
wanting both to be happy.

I haven't found any bad feeling or anything about
Emma's baby. Everyone knows she's not married but
there's been absolutely no shock or condemnation or
anything. People have been marvellous, in fact. A woman
who serves in the greengrocer's kept asking me about
Emma all the time she was pregnant and she was avid for
news of its birth. Then when Emma took the new baby out
for the first time we took him to the greengrocer's first and
the woman ran out so excited and slipped fifty pence under
his hand. That really touched me.

I haven't told the people I work with; I haven't told
anyone who doesn't know me well enough to come to the
house anyway and see the baby. I've got no earthly reason
for hiding the fact of Michael's presence but I've got no
earthly reason for announcing it either. Emma has told all

her old friends and anyone who matters to her. We've had some portraits done of her and the baby and I shall go on having them done from time to time — I love family records like this.

I entirely think of him as one of the family. He has Emma's surname, our family surname, and he's one of us in every way. We don't talk about the father much, no need to but Emma sometimes chats about how to put to Michael that there isn't a father around. Sometimes I think it would be better to tell him he's dead — but that would be a lie so I think one's got to think of something that will reassure him and fill in the gaps. It's funny, the only times I've got a bit niggly at anybody's reaction to the news of the baby is when someone immediately says, 'Who's the father?' — I mean, before they know anything about Emma's well-being or the baby's welfare or how we're all managing or anything. I find myself saying, 'What's that got to do with it?' which is stupid, really, because it has got something to do with it, of course, the father. But it's hard to realise this when there's absolutely no contact and the boy was never around here anyway, he's completely unknown to every-body Emma knows now or knew beforehand, and when someone asks a question like that I tend to think it's just bloody nosey. What good is it going to do them anyway if I say, 'Joe Bloggs is the father'? They're no better off. I wonder sometimes if they're not hoping for a marvellous bit of scandal, like if I say, 'Don't tell anyone, swear not to, but actually it's Jim Callaghan's boy'.

As for how I feel about the baby — well, I love him. I suppose this sounds a bit sentimental but the truth is that I couldn't fail to warm to anyone who could change Emma from the lost, unhappy, depressed person she was to the easy, loving person she is now. I've always, in a way, felt like that about the girls' boyfriends. I've loved the ones who made them happy, you know how a girl's face changes when she feels loved and happy, it sort of opens out and their whole manner is lighter and they look so gorgeous and I nearly burst with pride and love. And I've always loathed the ones who make them jumpy and anxious and kind of put-down.

I know there are going to be quite a few problems ahead

for Emma with Michael, and not just money ones. And I don't know how I'm going to feel when I'm getting on and there's a great big lumpy adolescent boy in the house with football boots and things all over the place — that's if Emma hasn't moved on. But for the present, he's brought new life to the house that died a little when my husband went. I love holding him and have to be restrained from doing so at the wrong times; I don't seem to mind his crying. I've got used to being a granny but still like to be told I don't look it. One friend said, 'Anyway it sounds much younger to be an illegitimate grandmother than the legal kind.'

'I only saw my Mum twice before I went home for good when I was nearly fifteen. I went once for tea and once for a holiday. I didn't like it, I didn't get on with her. My brother and one of my sisters had been brought up there. I pitied them.'

20   Tracy on the run

Tracy grew up in a children's home from the age of two. When she was fourteen and a half her mother claimed her back and she returned unwillingly to the family. This consisted of her mother, her father, who's a postman, two younger sisters and a younger brother. One sister had also been brought up in a children's home.
A year later Tracy ran away and since then she has been living in a series of remand homes and girls' hostels.
The warden of the hostel, where Tracy's living under the terms of a probation order, said she was a girl who was easily led. She travels light. She has just her few clothes — a sweater or two, and jeans which, when we talked she was wearing in current teenage fashion, rolled up to mid-calf with striped socks. She also carried everywhere with her an expensive photograph album, wrapped protectively in a polythene bag. Inside the album are carefully mounted coloured snapshots, two to a sheet and on the facing page, a corresponding caption, wittily composed and carefully printed in white crayon.
These are the pictures (reminders of happy childhood holidays) they gave her when she left the children's home to go back to her parents. None of the snaps gives a clue to the fact that Tracy grew up in an institution. Ther are no pictures of kids all dressed the same, or of her in clothes which look as though they're second-hand. The dark-haired middle-aged woman who appears in most of the photographs could easily be Mum, especially as the children with her, neatly turned out in sunsuits and sandals, might be sisters. In all the pictures of the group together, the youngest child who is fair and pretty, is closest to the

woman – holding her hand or laughing up at her. This is Tracy,
throughout the early part of her childhood, with her house-
mother, Sister Marion. When Tracy was twelve, Sister Marion
suddenly left the children's home to get married. There are no
pictures of Tracy after that time. She has since grown into a
well-built girl with rather heavy features. Her hair has darkened
and she uses a grip each side to keep it off her face. She speaks in a
matter of fact tone, avoiding your eyes as she talks. In the same
expressionless way, she mentions an abortion and two suicide
attempts, not glancing up for a reaction. Only when she imitates
the way her natural mother spoke to her, does her voice betray
emotion and then it's full of scorn.

I didn't know I had a Mum until I was nine. They didn't tell
me, I thought they were dead. Then one day Sister Marion
told me about my Mum, she said she wanted me to go
home with her for a day. I didn't want to go. I was happy at
the Home. There were twenty-eight of us, all girls – the
boys lived down the road in another home. We were a small
group; I was the pet, see, the youngest. We had good food,
nice clothes, we had everything we wanted. I liked it there.
I didn't feel different from other kids – I was quite all right.
We had lovely holidays, a lovely time. Then Sister Marion
told me about my Mum and said I had to go home with her.
Well she's a big woman – she did smile at me that first day,
but there was something behind her eyes I didn't like. She
frightened me, she's always frightened me. Anyway all the
time I was at home with her I was thinking what the others
were doing at the Home because they were going on an
outing and I was missing it. I would much rather have been
with them.

    I only saw my Mum twice between the time when I was
nine and when I went home for good when I was nearly
fifteen. I went once for tea and once for a holiday. I didn't
like it, I didn't get on with her. My brother and one of my
sisters had been brought up there. I pitied them.

    When I was twelve Sister Marion left to get married. She
must have been oh, forty or forty-five. After she went I got
into a bit of trouble because I larked about a bit and they
sent me down the road. There was a housemaster there,
see. They mixed us up, after that, the boys and girls. I liked

it just as much. We were small groups, I had a great time, it was smashing.

Then when I was fourteen and a half my mother said she wanted me back for good. I know why it was; she wanted me for the work I could do, she wanted me for the money. I didn't want to go. But they said I had to, they made me go against my will. It was horrible, I hated it. My Dad said my mother was schizophrenic, she'd had an operation on her brain before I was born. He said she never used to be like the way she is. She couldn't bear any noise – even the sound of a spoon rattling in a cup would send her barmy. She frightened me. My Mum didn't like me. She wanted me to leave school, that was part of the trouble, and I didn't want to. I wanted to be a nurse. I've always wanted to be a nurse, I know I never will, I'm not clever enough, but I've always wanted to be a children's nurse.

I used to go to school and work in a hairdresser's on Saturday mornings, shampooing hair. My Mum was always after me to work. Cor, the work I did. She used to say, 'Do so-and-so *if you don't mind*.' It was the way she said *'if you don't mind'* that got me.

I ran off when I was fifteen and a half to go to live with a friend of mine who had three brothers: two of them had been in prison and one had been in Borstal. They had a bad name – drugs and that – but they were good to me. The oldest brother was married and separated from his wife but he had the house, to look after their kid. Well after four months we was down in the town, a whole group of us, and the police busted us.

They said I ought to leave the neighbourhood and they sent me to a centre ten miles away. It was a homely place, free and easy, I liked it but I run off. I was going out with a boy, then we got busted. After that I was sent to a remand home for reassessment. It was a strict place, I liked it – I didn't want to leave. There were thirty girls there – I couldn't go out when I wanted. I didn't mind. I'm used to it, see. I went to college and took an O-level in cookery and needlework, I like needlework.

Then my social worker sent me to another girls' hostel. We had freedom there, we could do as we liked. But I got into

trouble because I was going out with this American black
and I was staying at his place and when they found out they
said I should go back to my own county, I was taking up a
place in the hostel another girl could have, so my social
worker fixed me up here.

Well I only stayed three weeks that time because there
was this girl there and she said, 'Let's go down to the
seaside for the weekend' so we ran off. When we got back
we hadn't got anywhere to go so we slept in a bus shelter.
Cor, it was cold. The police picked us up and I went to
another girls' hostel. They got me a job as a machine
operator in a factory but I got thrown out.

By then my care order had finished, and I got a job as an
auxiliary nurse, living in; that was when we stole the record
player from another girl – actually my friend stole it but I
spent the money.

I was sent to Holloway on remand; I was there three
weeks, it was horrible. I wrote to my boyfriend for the first
time from Holloway. I didn't expect to hear from him but he
wrote back. He understands, his parents are divorced.

I thought I'd be sent to a remand home when I came up
for the record player. I'd already been to a last-chance
hostel, I expected them to send me to a remand home. But
they put me on two years' probation and said I had to pay
compensation of £42 and my probation officer sent me
here.

I'm waiting for my boyfriend to come home from
Germany, he writes to me four times a week. After we're
married in September, if all goes well, I'll go to Germany
with him in December.

We want to have children, we want to give them
everything we never had. I shall bring up my children
whatever happens, even if he dies, because he's going to
Northern Ireland. No one's going to take my kids from me.

At least I'm free. I'm not worried about my parents, I
haven't got any. If they died tomorrow, it sounds awful but
it wouldn't mean nothing to me. Other girls are fond of
their families, I haven't got one until I have my own. My
Dad, he says he's finished with me, since Holloway, he
says I'm a whore, I'm horrible, I'm a criminal.

I'm not very optimistic, I don't like to hope. I like reading,

I read about suicide, medical things and drugs and people who can't get off them. I always seem to be reading about things like that.

I had an abortion just before Christmas. I didn't know the father was married, he'd asked me to marry him. I've made two suicide attempts; once I took an overdose of Valium and once I slashed my wrist at my sister's. It wasn't very deep, it didn't leave a scar.

I don't know what it is that makes me run off. It's when something gets me, if something gets through to me – not just anything, but it can be a little thing.

I feel very strongly that it's all wrong for parents who have given up their children to be allowed to take them back again. Magistrates can say blood's thicker than water – they're not thinking what the children are thinking. They shouldn't be allowed to come along and take a child back who's very happy where she is and spoil their lives.

It's all right when the child's grown up and ready to leave the Home and going for a job, to tell them they've got a family. Let them find out who they are then if they want to. But not when they're growing up and happy. It's not fair. If the parents want the child back let them wait until they're grown up, or when they're getting married, to make a nice family group for the wedding picture.

PART FIVE

Getting back

'I'd imagined that she'd be longing to meet me. I dreamed of getting to know her very well, not sharing a home exactly, but I thought it would be nice to have half my holidays with her. I had it all worked out.'

21   Susan and the search for her mother

Susan is at a teacher training college in the Midlands. She has a lovely merry face, short curly hair and a Devonshire accent. Her home is with her adoptive parents in Plymouth. For as long as she can remember she has wanted to trace her natural mother. At seventeen she started the search and a year later she had completed it. This is Susan's story of that search and what she found.

I'm illegitimate. My real mother and father had been engaged for four years and then they parted but they met again and that's when it happened. They decided they'd get married after all but thought, 'Well, it's not a very good start for marriage, with a baby', as they both had careers. So my mother thought it would be better for me to be adopted. She had a good job teaching in Germany at the time and I don't think she wanted to give it up; she was twenty-five and had an interesting life going for her.

I was born in Manchester in 1958. My mother chose it because it was an anonymous town. She didn't know anybody there, she came from Wales. So she lived under another name in lodgings and went to a maternity hospital to have me, and then to a mother and baby home which was nearby and linked with it, I think. She was there for a month and then she didn't even go back home. She signed all the papers during the month and the adoption went through very quickly.

Apparently I had two weeks in a council home and then I came to my adoptive parents. My father's an engineer and mother's a teacher too. I've got one older brother who's also adopted; his natural mother kept him for about two years but she couldn't cope so he was adopted later which must have been worse for him really. My parents couldn't have children of their own.

I knew I was adopted very early on, I can't even remember not knowing. I think they told me when I first asked where babies come from. Also it was quite funny — we were one of three houses in a row and all the children in them were adopted. Just in our street, in these three houses in a row, there were about eight children, all adopted, so it was almost abnormal not to be . . . it was a bit funny if you had your own.

I first started thinking about my natural mother when I was about twelve. I had a very good friend at school then and she'd never known anybody who'd been adopted and that's how it started. She thought it was most peculiar — you know, 'Don't you want to *see* her?' and questions like that — and I suppose I started thinking about it. Anyway, it's the age, isn't it, for wondering about relationships. So I just kept asking my parents for more information but they didn't have very much.

They showed me all the forms and everything. They were willing to help, I could look at the papers any time — they were just kept openly in a drawer. They didn't seem at all put out by my wanting to know, which is unusual. But all that was there was simply my mother's name and the fact that she was a teacher, her age, and that she liked golf and embroidery, which I found out was a very bad picture of her indeed. I don't know where they got that from. I thought, 'Gosh, what a funny mixture!' It didn't say anything about my father at all. That was all. You get a lot more nowadays, I know this because I baby-sit for an adopted girl who's three; her papers have got every O-level her mother took and almost what mark she got in them, great foolscap sheets about her from the adoption society — just everything about her.

My parents said I'd have to wait until I was eighteen and then I could get my original birth certificate with an address on it, so I just kept that at the back of my mind. I thought, 'I might do something about it one day, but I'll leave it until I'm eighteen.'

But one day, when I was looking through the adoption forms, I decided to write to the Social Services Department in Manchester and ask them for some more information. I didn't actually want to trace her then — I wanted some more information. I waited about a month and then I got this letter from the social worker saying she hadn't been able to find my papers — they were all in the basement, it had been so long ago — so she couldn't give me much information; later, she told me she was holding it back. I sort of kept writing. We had a great correspondence for six months and she gave me a bit more in every letter. I think she wanted to find out how serious I was and what sort of person I was, that's why she didn't give it all to me in the first place.

I'd started this in the September. Then in the January I joined Jigsaw, which was a register that adopted children could join who wanted to trace their mothers, and mothers who wanted to find their adopted children could join too and the idea was that you might sometimes get both sides joining. At this stage I definitely wanted to trace my mother in person which worried my parents a bit. They were really more worried about my mother than about me in a way. They didn't want her life ruined by me turning up on the doorstep. So they said, 'If you join Jigsaw, that's all right because she has to get in touch with them too and you'll know then that you both want it.'

Jigsaw wrote back and said, 'Your mother hasn't joined but we'll keep you on the list.' In fact, when I did get in touch with her, she'd never heard of it.

So I waited and I kept writing to the social worker and in the end I think she realised I was serious and she suggested I went up to see her. That was in April this year, just after I was eighteen. So I went up and had about two hours with her and I don't think she knew what to do for the best. It was tricky for her. She didn't have my mother's address but she had the address of my grandparents and she thought about giving it to me and then about making enquiries there on my behalf but then she decided not to and said 'I'm not going to do anything.'

I don't think she expected me ever to find my mother really. She gave me a bit of a talking-to and said she didn't

190 Breakaway

think it was a very wise thing to do. She just said, 'Let me know how you get on.' She definitely wanted to fob me off. She told me these great horror stories of a boy she knew turning up and finding his mother was a prostitute and so on. She had letters there from my father and my mother and she wouldn't let me see anything, which I thought was a bit silly. I suppose they had addresses on and I would have memorised them and so she was a bit worried.

But then I did know that my mother was employed by an education agency because that was on the original information that my parents had so I wrote to the agency and I sort of made out that she was a friend. I certainly wasn't going to pour out the whole story, I don't think they would have helped me if I had. I just said I was looking for a friend who was employed by you in 1958 to 1959 and they sent me back her address immediately, no question of it at all.

That was, in fact, her parents' address in Wales. I was very lucky, it was miraculous, to have got this address. So I wrote to my mother at that address; I worded it very carefully — 'You know me as Margaret' (that was the name she'd given me) 'and I'd be glad if you got in touch with me. . . .' I was worried in case anybody opened it, you know, if they weren't living there anymore, the grandparents or any of the family. In the newsletter I had from Jigsaw it said to be careful and how to word it very carefully, so I did. I waited for about a fortnight and I didn't hear. I was quite depressed then. I thought she'd got the letter and wasn't going to answer it, which I thought was a bit mean.

But in fact she'd married and had children and now lives in Durham. So she wasn't at her parents' address where I'd sent the letter. It went to her father and he kept it for her because she was, in fact, going up there at Whitsun.

But, being me, I didn't wait very long. So after a fortnight I had the idea to ring up Directory Enquiries and get the phone number of her parents' home. And I thought, 'My word, is this the number for my mother or just the grandparents?' so I rang up first to establish which. I pretended I had the wrong number. It was quite funny because I asked for somebody, I can't remember who, and he said, 'No, I don't know about that, I'm a grandfather' —

and it was funny because he was *my* grandfather and it was tempting to say, 'Yes, I believe you're *mine*.' So I established that he was there and then, of course, I wondered if my mother was there. I wondered if she was single and living at home, I didn't really think she was because I felt she would have replied. So I rang up again and asked for her by name — Diana — and he said, 'Oh, you've written to her', and I said, 'Yes', and he said, 'I wondered about it because you put Miss and she's been married for fifteen years.' I must have seemed pretty odd so I made up a great story about being a friend from university (which I told my mother later so that she could carry it on) and then he gave me her phone number and address in Durham. This was all in one night.

So then, after ringing him, I rang her. Her husband answered and I asked to speak to her and she said, 'Hullo' and I said, 'Are you Diana?' and she said, 'Yes' and I said, 'It's your daughter.'

There was silence at first, it was terrible.. She was very shocked, I heard her gasp. She didn't know what to say and nor did I. It was an emotional moment, specially like that on the phone. In a way I would have preferred to write but I was in a state and I thought I'd rather ring up. And it's a good job I did because she might have opened my letter at the breakfast table or something, and if her husband didn't know. . . .

So then I said, 'Have you told your husband?' She said 'No'. Immediately I thought, 'Oh, there's going to be trouble here', so I said, 'Is it all right to talk?' and she said 'yes, he's just gone out', which was lucky because she really wanted to know what I was doing.

She was glad I was doing A-levels, she asked me which subjects. 'What do you want to do?' she said, 'and what interests do you have and have you got any more brothers and sisters?' She knew that I had a brother because they sent her a photo of the two of us when I was about six months and my brother was about four and a half. But she didn't mention my father at all, not then, she didn't mention him at all. I didn't like to press the point because I thought she'd probably like to forget about him, anyway we didn't stay very long on the phone. She said, 'Well,

what are we going to do about it?' I said, 'I'd like to write'
but she was very concerned that she would write first.
Because, I suppose she wanted to put her point of view
across before I got mine in. I asked her to send a photo and
she didn't want to, but I persuaded her to.

She wrote in about a fortnight's time, very briefly and
said she was thinking a lot about it and didn't know what to
do for the best but said she'd write again and that I wasn't to
write to her before I got her next letter.

I waited another ten days or so. In the meantime she rang
up my mother, which was rather a peculiar conversation.
She said she wanted to know a bit about me but she said she
didn't want to meet me and she didn't know how to put it.
So Mum said it's best to put it clearly in the next letter so
that you don't keep her waiting about, it's not very fair.

In the next letter she made it clear. She said, 'I don't want
to meet you'. It was a blow. It made me very unhappy for a
while. I would have liked to meet her. Perhaps it was
difficult because her husband didn't know, but that could
have been got over. I could have gone up and stayed in a
hotel or something and she could have met me in the day-
time but that would have been a bit furtive, I suppose. At
one point she said, 'I've got relations near you actually,
perhaps I could meet you there,' and then she said, 'better
not'. I don't think she wanted to start a relationship. She
told me that she'd lived under an assumed name when I
was on the way and it was like another person and that's
how she wanted it to stay. She went back to Germany and
within a fortnight she'd met the man she married. You
know, I think she just wanted to put it out of her mind.

She said in the letter, 'I can get the phone to myself on
Tuesday nights.' You see, she couldn't ring me up when
she felt like it. She had to make sure her husband and
children were out. So she said she'd ring me up on a
Tuesday night and she did – and we had a great long talk.

She told me all about my father. She called him 'the other
half'. 'I suppose you want to know about the other half',
she said. She said he'd married too and has children and
he's a farmer in Wales but she didn't tell me much about
what sort of a person he is. She did ask if I was placid and I
said, 'no, I don't think I am' and she said he was very

placid, extremely placid. 'Well', I said, 'I don't seem to have inherited that!' She asked me if I was any good at science and I said, 'no, terrible' and she said, 'so am I. I've got brothers with first-class honours degrees in science and I'm the black sheep of the family' and I said, 'We've got that in common then, because I'm no good at science.' It was little, ordinary things, you see, we talked about. She agreed to send me a photo. And later I sent her three. She was very pleased with them but I don't know how she'll keep them, she'll have to hide them away somewhere. She's got a secret to keep now. She said she didn't tell anyone about me except her parents.

But she didn't once say she wished I hadn't got in touch. She said, 'I'm glad you got in touch.' I think she was pleased. She said, 'I've often wondered how you turned out because at eighteen there are so many things you could be doing. You might be married. You might have a baby. You might be doing so many different jobs and different things. It's not like a five-year-old. You know what they're doing!' She said she was pleased to have news of me but 'I just don't want to carry it on.' So after that phone call I asked if I could write and ask her a lot of questions and she said I could.

So I wrote and asked her about hobbies and interests and things like that. I found we both play the piano – well, I've just started. She likes a lot of things that I do, reading, cooking, I was very pleased about that. I also asked her a lot of things about health. Any particular diseases in the family, for instance. I wish adopted children could have more of a medical report because I've had a couple of things and the hospital has asked, 'Is it inherited?' and, of course, you don't know.

She answered all my questions. I thought she might avoid some but she didn't. And I told her again that I'd like to meet her and that I'd like to write more but, if she didn't want to, then I wouldn't press the point. Even though, actually, I could have done because, although this sounds horrible, I do in a way have power over her. Her husband doesn't know and her children don't know and I could make quite a fuss if I wanted to. I think she was quite worried, you know, quite frightened that I might say, 'If

you don't meet me, I'll tell your husband.' Of course, some
people might, some rather nasty people. They'd have to be
rather unhappy and disturbed to do that and, luckily, I'm
not. My childhood and family life has been perfectly
normal.

So that was it. I had three letters. The last one was about
two weeks ago. And it has stopped completely now. She
said she'd like me to respect her wishes. She thought it best
not to write anymore because she didn't want to meet me
and it would have been stringing me along. I can see that
but. . . it's a big disappointment. I had been expecting
something very different. I didn't dream she'd be married.

When I was fourteen I used to think that twenty-five was
very old and I thought by the time she'd got over having me
she'd be about twenty-seven or twenty-eight and she'd
never marry then. I really thought she'd be on the shelf. I
thought she'd still be single so that was a shock when my
grandfather said she was married and it was another big
shock when she told me her eldest child was fifteen — I
thought, 'Oh gosh, that was quick off the mark' but I
suppose it's natural to want to replace a baby pretty
quickly.

I also imagined she'd be longing to meet me. I dreamed of
getting to know her very well, not sharing a home exactly,
but I thought of holidays. I had it all worked out. I thought
it would be nice to have half my holidays with her. I even
told my parents this. I think, had it come to that, they
wouldn't have been very pleased obviously, but they never
thought it would be like that. They were much more
realistic. They said, 'Well, gracious, she'll be married,' and I
said, 'Of course she won't, she's much too old. . . .' And
Mum said, 'Well, even if she's single, she's probably made
a good life for herself and perhaps she won't want to know
you.'

The Jigsaw Newsletter had said that most women want
to meet their children and I'm wondering if that's true,
because if you're married and you have another family it's a
bit unlikely. I think that's a bit off the mark.

I think what started me looking for her was partly that I
wanted to know more about myself, and partly wondering
how she was and what had happened to her, whether she

was happy. Sometimes I think well, really, she's not like me really and perhaps I wouldn't want to meet her. She's quite a career woman and I'm not really like her. She went back to teaching when her youngest child was three. And that's quite a funny thing, her being a teacher of infants because, before I even knew that, I'd decided to do infant teaching so she's doing exactly what I plan to do. And when I had the photo of her, that didn't fit in with what I'd imagined. She's just a sort of ordinary person and she doesn't look like me at all. She says I don't look like anyone in her family. Of course, I might resemble somebody in my father's family but she didn't know any of them very well. Perhaps I'm more like him although some people aren't like either of their parents at all.

Contact is all finished now. But I'm glad I've done it even though it didn't turn out as I would have liked. I've had a lot of information about her and about what she's doing and I'm really glad to have that. On the other hand I can see its such a difficult point because if I hadn't been very careful I could well have let it out to her husband and it could have wrecked the marriage. If you've been married for sixteen years and suddenly say, 'Oh, I've got an 18-year-old daughter. . . .'

It wouldn't have been enough for me if a third party had found out all these things, that's why I think tracing should be easier. I did need to speak to her. I'm glad now that the social worker didn't contact her first as she was going to do. If she had done, I think my mother would have written back and said, 'I don't want to contact her', and then I would have been left thinking 'why not?' and 'what's she like?' So I'm glad I did it because any other way might have given me the wrong sort of picture of her. On the phone she kept saying, 'I don't want you to think I'm a hard person or anything. I just think of you dispassionately.' You know, I think she forced herself to and she doesn't want to go back on that. She's not going to send me a birthday card or anything. I asked her when her birthday was. It was a bit peculiar when she said, 'I'm not going to tell you the date' but I think she was afraid I'd send her one. So she said, 'I'll just tell you that it's the end of November.'

But I understand this because I think if it was me and I

was married and had a family I might be the same. I don't
think I'd ever give up a baby for adoption though. But then
I wasn't in her position and I wasn't in 1958. Because it was
very different then really – a lot of muddles after the war. I
don't think it's easy today but people then gossiped more.
She came from a small town in Wales and my grandfather
was a teacher there, a well-respected family – and that's
why she went away: not because they pushed her out –
they were quite happy to have her there – but *she* thought it
would be better. And I admire her for that. She picked a big
city where she knew nobody. It could have been anywhere.
And she got lodgings and waited for me. I said to her 'Oh, it
must have been lonely' and she said, 'Yes, it was.'

My Mum and Dad have supported me all the time I was
searching for her. But they were worried about her. They
thought of her in the position she's actually in now,
married, with children. They were worried that she hadn't
told her husband and as it turned out, she hadn't. So they
wanted me to be discreet at all times. They didn't want me
to go around telling my story to everyone along the way.
They thought Jigsaw was a good idea and were sorry she
hadn't joined it. When I joined Jigsaw they thought that
was it, that I'd wait and if she joined it, fair enough, and if
not I'd be happy. They thought that would satisfy me. I
think they were a bit shocked when I said, 'I'm going up to
see the social worker.' And once she tried to fob me off they
thought, 'That's it now.' And then I started up again, with
the letter to the educational agency. I don't think they
believed I'd get an address and when it came they were
quite surprised. But they helped me to word the letter I sent
up to Wales. They made suggestions and said, 'Don't write
a great emotional letter saying, "I am your daughter" and
everything else, in case anybody else finds it', which was
very wise advice.

I think they would have been quite happy if my mother
had agreed to meet me. But not if I'd gone back to stay with
her regularly. You know, I think they would have been a bit
hurt. But I think maybe that was a bit mad, that idea of mine
about sharing the holidays out.

One thing that worried them a bit was that it all
happened in the middle of my A-levels. My natural mother

was worried about that too; when I told her I was doing A-levels she said, 'What? You shouldn't be doing this in the middle of exams.' It was just like a mother: she said 'Have you got an exam tomorrow?' and I said I had and she said, 'Oh, you mustn't keep on the phone then. You should be revising.' I thought, 'Oh, you just can't get away from it. . . .'

I think adopted girls will always want to try and trace their mothers – well, some of them, not all, of course. Apparently the Adoption Society told Mum and Dad that if there's any, as they put it, trouble, and they want to find out, you'll find it will be the girls more than the boys. My brother has no wish to trace his parents. Boys tend to be more, 'This is my home and that's that', whereas girls tend to be more emotional and curious, particularly about their mothers. Perhaps the longing might come back when I have a baby myself and I'm a mother but I don't think so. I think finding her has closed the door really. I won't do any more about it, certainly.

If another adopted girl wanted to find her mother I'd say, 'If you feel strongly about it, do it.' But I'd say, 'Be very careful, and always have stories ready', which sounds awful – but I had lies ready all the time, like being an old university friend and so on. Don't blurt out your story to everyone – that could be disastrous – and be prepared to find that she won't want anything to do with you. I mean, mine did write. She didn't just put down the phone on me, something she could have done. But all the same, she was frightened. I expect she wondered if I was in Durham and was going to pop in from round the corner. So I didn't rush it.

In a way, now it's all over, I feel more grown-up and more complete. It's been with me a long time, the search, and I can't really believe it's over. But I think I feel sort of finished now.

22 Conclusion

All the stories in this book except Susan's are, in their different ways, about rejection – a girl's rejection of her parents' values, of their control over her life, of their attitudes to sex and relationships; or the parents' rejection of the girl's bids for independence, her sexuality, her role in the family, her self-discovery.

Susan's story, on the other hand, is not about anyone rejecting anything. Her search for her natural mother was essentially a search for a missing link in her identity. Her breakaway took place without her knowledge when her unmarried mother had her adopted more than eighteen years ago. So her bid to fill in the gaps about her background was a way of breaking in, back to her beginnings, the final constructive step in her teenage endeavour to sort out who she is. At the end of her story she says, 'In a way, now it's all over, I feel more grown-up and more complete. . . I think I feel sort of finished now.'

But in this search for her identity Susan is no different from the other girls who gave me their stories, nor, I daresay from any other teenager of either sex. From Elizabeth, the meditator, to Alison, the anorexic, from Francesca, the tearaway, to Emma, the unmarried mother, there are undercurrents throughout their stories of efforts to answer the questions 'Who am I? Am I really like this, or is it just the way my parents see me? Will this action or that action make me more the real "me"?'

And just as Susan could not feel 'complete' without reference to her natural mother and her actual beginnings, so the other girls, far from rejecting the family itself, consistently showed that the quality of family life was the biggest influence on their sense of security or insecurity, that their relationship with their parents – or lack of it – coloured all their relationships, and that the family was a vital reference point for their self-image and the basic self-confidence with which they embarked on adult life.

Those who rejected or lost their families have made, or speak of making, another family of their own – not necessarily in its conventional form but a 'family' all the same. So it would be hard to go along with the current idea that today's teenage girls are overthrowing the whole family idea in favour of communal living, full-time, lifelong careers, babies without husbands, cohabitation without marriage or any of the other life-styles that are undertaken by a small minority but which so alarm some parents and all the self-appointed guardians of 'the family'.

It's unrealistic to expect marriage and family life to conform to centuries-old models. The diversity of human needs and natures and the ever-increasing choices in self-fulfilment and in personal relationships means that people are always trying out and often succeeding in new ways of living. It is only for them, who are living this way, to say whether it seems worse or better than the old ways. All we can say is that it is different.

But my point, from the evidence of the girls who spoke to me, is that basically today's girls are not all that different from their mothers, or their grandmothers. I must admit that, before my researches, I thought they were. I thought they were striving for success as measured by many men – earning-power, material goodies, job-status and a swinging sex-life. I was also under the impression that where the pressure of women's lib had not directed a girl to these goals they invariably influenced her all the same in another way – by making her feel guilty about preferring home life under her parents' roof or going straight into marriage from home.

But after all the meetings and talkings and listenings, my conclusions are quite different. When the concepts of getting on and making your mark were mentioned they came second to three others. The words that kept cropping up spontaneously, over and over again, were security,

confidence and relationships. Every single girl who talked
to me, regardless of her particular breakaway point, spoke
of wanting to be secure and safe, of wanting satisfying
personal relationships. Most of them were much concerned
with understanding themselves and others, and with
establishing cooperative rather than competitive links
with their fellow men and women.

A lot of the problems that arise in families when
daughters are adolescent would be more smoothly worked
through if parents and the girls themselves understood
this. They get crossed wires about the real needs of the
maturing girl. Perhaps this is common to the whole of
society's interactions, at all ages. We consistently react to
people as if what they are making most noise about is what
they actually want and we don't bother much to listen with
that inner ear which reveals the real anxieties, fears and
needs hiding behind the shouting and door-slamming and
compulsive acting-out. Anglo-Saxons have the additional
burden of being unable to express fully their warm, loving
feelings, especially between parents and their adolescent
children, lest – well, lest what? Lest they would be thought
sentimental and sloppy? Lest they be hurt? Lest the sky
fall?

But parents need now to be superhumanly flexible. They
need a keen ear as to what degree of 'holding' and 'letting
go' best suits an individual daughter. That takes a great
deal more knowledge of emotional growth and psychological development than most parents have, or think is
necessary. If I could make the world better in one move, I'd
opt for education for parenthood – starting in the teens.

All this is true, of course, for sons as well as daughters.
The competition between the sexes as to which has the
rawest deal out of life is a disservice to both. Men have a
tough row to hoe in the battle for survival and in the
acquisition of a basic self-confidence. Women have a tough
row to hoe in the struggle for personal integrity and
autonomy – and they have the added snag of actually
needing to depend on others when they are bearing and
rearing their young. Rather than competition, what's badly
wanted between people is compassion and at the family
level what's wanted more than controlling is understand-

ing. Many people, including parents, are still trying to impose 'what ought to be' instead of listening to 'what is'.

I'd go further and say that all that I've heard from girls while compiling this book, and all that I hear from men and women of all ages, week by week, through their letters to *Woman's Own*, makes me think that we're in for a very rough ride indeed unless all of us, both men and women, cultivate and cherish the so-called 'feminine' qualities in the spectrum – sympathy, caring, fellow-feeling, intuition, a tranquil, less 'on-the-defensive' view of life.

There will always be breakaways from the family — teenage girls driven from home, walking out or clashing with their parents' expectations. No family is without its tensions and emotional conflict, unless it's completely lifeless. But perhaps we can be better prepared to deal with these breakaways so that there's not so much bitterness and estrangement as a result, so that the breakaway girl has a fair chance of somewhere safe and pleasant to go to, and finally so that the break can be turned into a healthy growing-point for the girl herself.

They had just robbed the laundry van.

The only thing that the criminal duo managed to steal successfully was two pairs of tights from their girlfriends' underwear drawers to disguise their identity – excluding the four nicked sacks containing used towels from the staff toilet blocks, valued (pre-wash) as worthless.

The judge managed to stop laughing just long enough to pass a custodial sentence for attempted armed robbery, assault and criminal damage. And since the dumb duo were from Limerick, home of the eponymous ditty known as a limerick ...

Two criminals concocted a plan
To steal from a wages van
But when they raided the lorry
It didn't contain any lolly
So now they're doing time in the can

HOSTESS WITH MOSTESS

When it comes to sexy professions, we deem firemen, nurses and air hostesses worthy occupiers of the highest positions in personnel hotness. This unfairly ignores all the country's hot fruity accountants (certified and chartered), road sweepers and dinner ladies. Yet it remains a ludicrous stereotypical preference we appear content to promulgate as a national trait. For example, I once bought a DVD titled *Naughty Nurses Get Dirty on the Job* – disappointing, since it featured nurses arriving late for their shifts and not countering MRSA by using disinfectant hand gel when entering the wards – more tardy than tarty (OK, not really, but you see my point about the nurses-equate-to-sexy orthodoxy).

Air hostesses are, or more accurately were, in less enlightened decades, considered to be especially glamorous. Singled out for their desirability, stewardesses were often assumed to be young, slim, tall, pretty, single and, crucially for girlfriend potential, out of the country a lot! (One for the old-school, there.)

Stewardesses are certainly unique. For starters, 'stewardesses' is the longest word in the English language that you can type using only one hand. Someone who undoubtedly spent considerable time thinking about stewardesses whilst using one hand was a petty thief and all-round medallion-man/chauvinist git from the edge of Kent that bleeds into South London. He was the sort who thinks more of their car than their girlfriend. Taking full advantage of his air stewardess girlfriend being away for several days a week with continental stop-overs, he would instigate several inter-continental stop-overs of his own – usually at the flats of Scandinavian girls that he had met clubbing that evening.

He might have got away with being one of infidelity's frequent flyers, if it were not for the array of incriminating blonde hairs, empty condom packets and unfamiliar perfume odours regularly discovered on his clothes. It was this rudimentary inability to cover his tracks that ought to have signalled he was ill-suited to a criminal lifestyle.

Returning to his flat one morning to collect her possessions, the betrayed air hostess recalled a charming remark when he had once branded her 'only good for sewing'. So she proceeded to sew several rinds of camembert into the hems of the curtains, ensuring the relationship ended with not only a bad taste, but also a bad smell. This was the 1980s, so décor was used to being a bit cheesy – though not often literally.

A few months later, whilst presumably high on the cheese fumes, the jilted love rat entered a bookies with a shotgun and a note demanding the takings. Two details are worth recalling here: it was a viciously cold day, with the country gripped by ice. All racing had been abandoned. Hence there were no takings. However, the manager said he could not read the stick-up note and would have to go into the back to get his glasses. He didn't wear glasses, but instead phoned the police. He then opened the till and said, quite honestly, that he had put the day's takings in the raider's bag. It totalled £8.40, which was nowhere near enough to buy some new curtains.

'Right, listen and do what I say or I'll blow your head *******
off you ...' (not only is his language unsuitable for a family

book, it's not even suitable for a non-family book like this) '… phone me a taxi now. And it had better be here in two minutes or I'll blow your ugly [lots more swearing … and even more swearing] face off.' Nice man. But surely this was clearly a little late in the planning stage to be considering the getaway vehicle.

He ran outside panicking, saw some large lettering on the side of a car with a raised structure on the roof, and assumed it was a taxi. So he got in, shut the door, and told the driver to get his foot down. The driver obliged and they sped off to the nick – as he had just voluntarily got into an arriving police car which had scrambled to the scene after the 999 call. Basically, he had captured and arrested himself.

Doors to manual – as his ex-girlfriend may have said. No doubt the same instruction goes for the cell doors too. And he'd better hope that whatever prison job he got didn't render him amongst the perceived sexy professions.

GORDON BENNETT

Prior to banks becoming central to the nation's financial system, and black holes for public money, individuals would historically have hidden their money at home.

Organisations would instead have preferred holding their wealth reserves in object form, often as treasure. Indeed, the storybook depiction of pirates stealing treasure chests is not too far removed from a regularly encountered reality. Oxford and Cambridge colleges would have locked their considerable wealth in treasure chests stuffed full of sparking silver and effulgent gold. These would usually be secured in purpose-built towers.

Although heavily fortified, they consistently attracted robbery attempts. One of the largest-scale raids occurred at Worcester College, Oxford in 1769. Overnight, the entire college treasure collection had been expertly removed. Solid silver antique tankards, plates, candlesticks, punch bowls and bejewelled boxes were hot-fingered away without any visible signs of a break-in. Understandably, both the college and local authorities were mystified.

Mystified, that is, for exactly one week, until local girl Lucy Bennett walked into the silversmiths in Oxford's High Street and attempted to sell complete sets of the stolen silver from the well-publicised robbery, all branded with the distinctive Worcester College crest.

Lucy was the daughter of the college's butler, and had 'borrowed' her father's key whilst he slept. Claiming at the trial that she required the money for her wedding – she had married a man called Gordon a few days earlier – she was transported to the colonies for seven years.

To clarify, her punishment was an all-expenses-paid, return travel trip to the wonderfully warm climate offering all-year bathing opportunities of Australia. That'll teach her. And will have saved her a fortune on the honeymoon costs.

Until the nineteenth century, offenders were routinely transported to Australia. This practice must seem confusing to subsequent generations of Aussies who visit the Motherland of Britain (let's face it, to work in a bar). Having swapped unblemished blue sky and uninterrupted sunshine for the grey inside-a-Tupperware-box environment of an overcast cold UK, it must be difficult to fathom how being sent to Australia constituted a punishment.

READY STEADY CROOK

Many consider themselves 'self-employed' rather than criminal (several MPs amongst them), but those who have turned to crime as a way of escaping the dreamless drudgery of the 9 to 5 existence may be surprised to find that the criminal life does not offer an escape from damaging work-place hierarchies. Particularly in prison.

There are strict stratifications of offered respect in jail: incremental terraces of assigned status. These range from the lowest (a cell in solitary in the nonce wing/investment bankers) up to the career profession villains, e.g. the Grouty character in *Porridge*. Murder, extortion, armed robbery and running a dance school without the correct licence all guarantee top bunk status in the jailhouse.

Occupying the bottom bunk status of the criminal hierarchy was the pettiest of petty thieves from Middlesbrough. After smashing open a bubble-gum dispenser outside a newsagents with a hammer (we're not dealing with a classy Raffles-type villain here), the sweet-toothed delinquent had an abundance of confectionery – enough unhealthy sugary snacks to induce diabetes in a woolly mammoth – and plenty of small change. So when he boarded a bus as his choice of getaway vehicle, and the driver tapped the 'Correct fare only' sign, he was surprised to find that he was without the required coin denomination combination.

That's no problem if you are a petty criminal determined to end up in borstal. All you need to do to get home is steal a moped. Well, it was either that or just take two minutes to get some change and catch the next bus.

He selected a nearby moped, but struggled to start it as the owner had secured an immobiliser anti-theft device. The dismayed thief was shocked to encounter this level of security – it's like you can't trust anyone these days. Unperturbed, he picked up the moped and started to carry it across a car park, enabling him to work on hot-wiring the vehicle in more private surroundings. Unsurprisingly, carrying a locked moped across a public car park aroused sufficient suspicion for the car park attendant to leave his sentry box and challenge the erstwhile moped dragger, forcing him to abandon the newly nicked bike.

Not to worry. Completing a crime-wave hat-trick, he next decided to steal a car. Breaking into a vehicle, he had no trouble hot-wiring the motor, and set off home. Unfortunately, the soft rock on the car stereo was deemed so horrendous to his taste that he had to change it as an immediate priority. Hence he popped open the glove box and started flicking through alternative CD choices. This essential distraction from the road ahead ended with a loud 'Wham!' as the CD player churned out George Michael and risked serious irony overload.

When his eyes did eventually return to the road, the hot-headed hot-wirer could slowly make out, through the steam hissing upwards from a damaged radiator like a geyser, the back of a white van he had just hit. Closer inspection revealed the rear-ended vehicle to be a police transit van.

As the policeman later revealed in court, they were poised to open the back doors – so had he waited two seconds, the villain could have deposited himself inside the police van. It would have been the ultimate self-service arrest. Unexpected criminal in the packing area – as may also be said about beardy TV chefs.

PIMP MY BRAIN

Rated a full 10/10 on the scale of despicable humanity, a West End-based pimp tried to entice two passing gentlemen on the fringes of Soho with his 'new girl'. The 'new girl' was a smuggled Albanian prostitute, and the passing pair of gentlemen high-ranking CID officers. Handcuffs were quickly deployed in a bedroom environment once the policemen had followed the pair upstairs to their flat.

Hopefully the prison authorities will ensure that the pretty-faced Albanian pimp will be bending over backwards to offer some serious morale-raising favours to his fellow showering prisoners – in a programme of restorative (poetic) justice.

AD FAB

Newsagent windows have long since provided a communal message board for local jobs and services. Existing before the Internet age, the handwritten adverts continue to survive healthily despite the rush towards digital in most other modes of communication.

These ads are the ideal information hub to locate a missing cat, find a babysitter, or recruit a driver for a bank job. OK, admittedly that last one is reassuringly rare.

An aging career criminal, at a loose end during a brief period of his adult life when he was not in jail, placed an advert in a Walthamstow newsagent's window in the 1980s that read: 'Wanted: Experienced driver to carry money around at high speed. Must not like the Old Bill. No shooters.' Although applauding his anti-gun crime stance, the local police were informed and contacted the advertiser.

Proving that he was not the sharpest chisel in the burglar's toolbox, he'd even used his own name in the advert. No pseudonyms for him – after all, the police have enough to do and welcome any considerate attempts to ensure their job is made easier. He was soon back inside, out for just long enough to enable his cell to be decorated. The senior swindler continues to grow old in the clink, and is estimated to have sewn about 25% of the UK's mailbags by now.

BAD SANTA – FROM THE GHETTO TO THE GROTTO

An unemployed man in South London responded to a Job Centre advert to work as Father Christmas.

Unlike a lot of men of a certain age who dress up as Santa Claus each Christmas – the snow-white Santa whiskers look is readily available for most men of a certain age by merely not shaving for a fortnight and staying off the Grecian 2000 – he was a professional Santa, paid for working in the grotto.

When he arrived late for his first morning, with a worryingly pronounced smell of super-strength lager, his elves took the decidedly modern step of reporting Santa to HR. However, it soon transpired that HR was already watching him closely – on CCTV.

Regrettably, this particular Father Christmas fundamentally misunderstood the rudimentary concept of being Santa Claus, and instead of distributing presents chose to nab a sack full of spoils for himself. Store security intervened when the Father Christmas fraudster attempted to leave the grotto one evening with a coffee maker and other assorted grown-up goodies stashed in his Santa sack. Perhaps he was taking his work home with him and planned to wrap them in the workshop? Instead, his reverse Santa activities ensured Saint Nick was nicked.

GOVERNMENT BONDS

Visitors to UK Job Centres were surprised to see that the latest vacancies offered by the Government's Department for Work and Pensions in 2012 included an advert for a hitman.

Of course, MI5 and MI6 would not use such utilitarian language, hence the role that genuinely appeared on the Government's website sought to recruit a 'Target Elimination Specialist'. In case this left room for opaque ambiguity, the recruitment ad stated that the successful applicant would be expected to 'remove people' and would receive training in firing a sniper rifle. A proven ability to 'cross borders by unconventional means, assume new identities, fly jet-packs and pilot miniature submarines' were also listed as desirable skills. Basically, they were looking to fill a James Bond role.

A visitor to the Job Centre in Worcester Street, Oxford, observed: 'I'm looking for some part-time warehouse packing work, but I might apply – even though my miniature submarine piloting skills are a bit rusty nowadays.'

The job vacancy posted on the Government's official website clarified the role further: 'From time to time the UK Government has a need to remove people whose continued existence poses a risk to the effective conduct of public order.'

Unsurprisingly, a spokeswoman for DWP confirmed that the job should not have been posted. No sh*t, Sherlock. Though there was probably an advert for someone to take out the person responsible for uploading the original advert.

NOT SUITED FOR CRIME

Here is an original approach to burglary. Significantly, this strategy has only been attempted once. That may be because it is an immeasurably stupid way to steal antiques and A Very Bad Idea.

A swindler had visited a palatial country house in Perthshire on several occasions in 1933, and coveted the precious antiques contained within, which he correctly assumed were valuable. Engineering a fabricated reason for revisiting the homeowner's stately pad some weeks later, the amateur conman orchestrated his crime. See if you can spot how this plan may have compromised the likelihood of a speedy getaway.

Excusing himself after he had weaselled an invitation to stay for afternoon tea, he announced his departure, saying he would walk to the nearest railway station. In fact, he merely pretended to leave. Audibly shutting the front door from within, he remained in the hallway, where he hid inside a displayed suit of armour.

At nightfall, the armoured thief came to life like a magically awakened statue, and proceeded to go around the house stuffing small valuable antiquities into his stealing sack. There were, of course, a couple of disqualifiers for this being awarded Perfect Crime status.

Firstly, the metallic clanking of a rattling suit of armour crashing through the house like RoboCop ensured the entire household was awake, in dressing gowns and loading their muskets.

The inevitable confrontation with the clunking crook in their midst directly exposed the second fault of going out burgling wearing a suit of armour: namely the available speed for running away. Although the police required thirty minutes to reach the remote house, the ungallantly behaved knight in armour had barely reached the front gate.

The clattering crook would have lost a 100m race to someone wearing diving boots and a ball and chain. A chance was soon

presented for him to experience the running speed of someone wearing a ball and chain, as one was fitted in jail after he tried to abscond whilst on remand.

SUPERGRAN

When two motorcycling tearaways, both in their twenties, decided to burgle the isolated Hampshire house of a lone elderly lady, the words 'unguarded candy' and 'sleeping baby' possibly sprang to mind.

Targeting the property, they discovered no one was in. After parking their motorbike in the driveway with the engine still running to ensure a quick getaway, they commenced their pernicious plundering of the old lady's house. Just as they were noisily forcing open cupboards and filling pillowcases with the frail grandmother's jewellery – and probably Werther's Original toffees – she returned home from a shopping trip to nearby Alton.

About to unlock the back door, she noticed that a window had been smashed and realised she was being burgled. Although there was no time to change into a cape, the crime-fighting grandmother sprang into superhero action mode.

She returned to the front drive and crunched through the gravel until reaching the robbers' motorbike – then pushed it over, thereby disabling the running engine by causing it to flood with petrol.

Next she entered the house, wrenched an antique gun from a wall mount, charged up the stairs and screamed at the devious duo. Fleeing downstairs, they attempted to barge her out of the way, and earned a sound biffing with a gun barrel in the process. Unable to start their tampered bike, the helmeted thieves were wrestled until they ran off into the woods, with the grandmother still in focused pursuit. She flagged down a passing motorist and used his mobile to dial 999. The summoned police arrived and headed for the woods, where they quickly rounded-up the burglars. Outfoxed by a grey fox. The judge in Winchester Crown Court applauded the plucky pensioner for her display of bravery.

Outside court she informed awaiting media: 'I'm glad it is all over, but I feel sorry those two have taken this ridiculous course in life.' Banged to rights by Supergran.

SANTA SLEIGHS THIEVES

When a pair of Christmas criminals attempted to rob a publican, they had clearly forgotten about the spirit of Christmas. Two masked men in ski masks jumped on the landlord whilst he was depositing his takings at a bank in Prestwich, Greater Manchester. 'Where is it?' they ordered, prior to frisking him until they found the tell-tale bulge of a concealed cash pouch.

However, they had failed to take into account the existence of Santa Claus. A man convincingly dressed as Santa was standing outside the bank, promoting a nearby business, when he leapt into action and barged the thieves. He chased them away, and delightfully had time to shout after the retreating villains: 'I'm going to put you on my naughty list for this Christmas!'

The rattled rogues fled empty-handed, and jumped into their getaway vehicle: a BMW (which appears to be the first three letters of the gangster-wannabe alphabet in Manchester).

Santa had foiled the seasonal swindlers and chased off the Ho-Ho-Hoodlums. Try telling them that Father Christmas doesn't exist!

POLICE NOTICE: DUMB CRIMINALS OPERATE IN THIS AREA

Two thieves decided to pull into a Nottinghamshire lay-by when they spotted a small lorry parked unattended. Prising open the vehicle's back doors, they hastily transferred the contents into their own van, and screeched away at speed – tripping a police speed camera into flashing action as they made their getaway. This proved a helpful detail in securing their inevitable subsequent conviction.

Back at their hideout (OK ... flat), the dishonest duo excitedly opened the van's back doors to appraise their haul. Was it gold coins, unmarked non-sequential banknotes, or the world's largest diamond? No. Instead their entire haul consisted of just two boxes – all that had been left in the truck. These cartons contained two items: tampons and budget razors. When combined, perhaps the thieves could have peddled them as the ideal his'n'hers gift set!

As soon as the thieves attempted to move the razors, they got nicked. (I said 'they got nicked' – you know, as in a shaving cut ... no? Is this thing on?)

DOUBLE OR NOTHING

Sometimes criminals like to keep their business affairs within the family. When an eighteen-year-old girl, 'camouflaged' in a commodious bright red jacket on a hot day, was arrested in a London shopping centre for greedily stuffing tagged sweaters into an enormous sack like an inverted Santa, store detectives began monitoring her on CCTV. After all, what could possibly be suspicious about someone wearing an oversized coat in summer whilst dragging a capacious bag along the floor stuffed with numerous cashmere sweaters? Security apprehended the sweating sweater swiper.

But prison was apparently not to her liking. She had been there before, and had definitely not enjoyed the experience. Normally, this is how the concept of a deterrent works. But not in this case, as reaching that conclusion would require a modicum of cranial processing skills.

The shoplifter decided to plead 'not guilty', even though she could not have been caught more red-handed if she had been busted stealing tins of leaking crimson paint. Pre-trial, the shoplifter with a diminutive IQ informed her Dublin family that she might be going back to prison again. Given that this was her third separate arrest for shoplifting in just one week, after earlier receiving a suspended sentence from a lenient judge, this was a fairly obvious prediction. Ladies and gentleman, there is a new prophet in town.

At this point in her criminal career, she hatched a cunning plan that would almost certainly have been rejected instantly by *Blackadder's* Baldrick. But not by her sister.

She persuaded her sibling to attend court on her behalf, and claim she was the person charged with the shoplifting offences. The transparent ruse was immediately discovered, given the accused's existing familiarity with both police and court staff, and the judge despatched both siblings to the cells. 'We don't think her sister is very bright either,' commented an incredulous court official.

READING THE TEA LEAVES

A self-declared clairvoyant was described in court by a judge as a 'con man and charlatan' (is there any other type of clairvoyant?).

Claiming supernatural powers, the court heard about his history of befriending elderly and vulnerable individuals, with a penchant for the recently widowed. Whilst visiting one such recently bereaved confidante for afternoon tea, he looked up from straining the Earl Grey and announced he was receiving a visitation from the spirit world.

Pretending to be a mere passive receptor for transmissions from the other side, he relayed a message from the elderly woman's recently departed husband, revealing that there was a new will hidden inside the grandfather clock.

To be stringently fair about his clairvoyance skills, this revelation was undeniably accurate – though mainly because he had just placed the will in the clock case whilst the old lady was in the kitchen slicing some Battenberg.

The 'will' revealed that exactly half of the bequeathed fortunes should be left to the clairvoyant. But his deception was rumbled when the will's signature was exposed as bearing no relation to the deceased's handwriting. Bet he didn't see that coming.

And no, the judge – traditionally the only person in court who is allowed to attempt humour – could not resist cracking the obvious gag in his summation, informing the parasitical pilferer after he had been convicted of forgery, theft and deception at Wolverhampton Crown Court that: 'I am sure you have foreseen that you are going to prison.' A good gag? You be the judge.

SPIDER MAN

As a general rule of pilfering, the Top 5 items that thieves prefer to steal have remained fairly consistent for decades: money, booze, cars, fags and electrical items. Hence it represents an imaginative departure from swiping the usual clichéd swag when a thief decides to focus on stealing less predictable items. Especially when they are probably the first villain in the long and ignoble history of thieving to ever steal that item.

A twenty-three-year-old male had departed from the traditional thief's opening line of 'Give me the money, now!' Instead, he commenced his robbery with 'Give me the Bolivian spider monkey, now!' Presumably he specifically named the species in order to avoid the following scenario:

Thief: 'This is a stick-up. Give me a monkey.'
Cashier: 'Here you are.'
Thief: 'No, not £500. I want an actual monkey.'

Breaking into Chessington World of Adventures, and crucially leaving incriminating DNA in the process, the thief bagged his fellow primate and scarpered from the scene. There were no sightings of the stolen Bolivian spider monkey named Sponge Bob, until he was observed two days later playing frisbee with children on Clapham Common.

This would have made an intriguing sight for the man on the Clapham omnibus. How a zoo escapee came to be playing frisbee in Clapham remains mysterious. A detective constable informed the BBC: 'I have no idea how Sponge Bob travelled the 12 miles from the zoo to Clapham. It is difficult to see how he got there by his own steam. We are almost convinced he was taken by somebody, due to the way the fences at the zoo were cut.' Top detecting, and all deduced without contacting 221b Baker Street.

But you have to feel for Sponge Bob – one moment he's playing frisbee in the park, the next the cops pounce and take him back to the pen – and, after his breakout attempt, he's got to be looking at a stretch in solitary.

Of course, Sponge Bob's experience of being returned to his barred enclosure with his recent liberty removed was wholly replicated by the fellow ape who stole him.

NO CON TEST

Jake the Fake has spent a greater percentage of his life in the can than most baked beans.

Firstly, you will not be surprised to know, his name is not Jake. That's because he is a master of disguises – or, more accurately, a novice of distinguishes. His attempts to con 5-star hotel receptionists into giving him a suite on credit have been consistently undermined by his thick Mancunian accent and prominent facial tattoos – obvious barriers to assuming new con man identities. Anyone sitting in a hotel lobby in Manchester early one evening in 2012 would have overheard the following conversation:

'Alright? You lot has got a room for me, yeah?'

'What name is the reservation under, Sir?'

'Smith.'

'What initial, Sir?'

'A.'

'We don't appear to have an 'A. Smith', Sir.'

'B?'

'No.'

'C?'

'We don't seem to …'

'D?'

'You realise, Sir, I pressed the button under the counter at A?'

JUST IN THE NICK OF TIME

A knife-wielding thug entered a takeaway food shop in Halifax and proceeded to demand money with menace. Cool staff pointed out that they were not open yet, and were still preparing sandwich fillings. Told that they would be open in ten minutes, the robber decided to sit down and wait.

Although the thief was almost certainly the only person to be shocked by the events that subsequently transpired, a member of staff had earlier phoned the police with unavoidable predictability to report the incident. Two policemen arrived, and bungled the premature pilferer into the police car.

He did not have to wait for the cell door to be opened for him.

OUT ON THE TOWN BIKE

An oversexed twenty-one-year-old male from Boscombe, Dorset stopped when he spotted a sex worker plying her kerbside trade underneath a traffic light – the locality being a known red light area (although sometimes green and amber too).

Pulling over to negotiate a price for her favours, he agreed to hand the twenty-two-year-old escort £30 for engaging in some illicit coupling. He immediately mounted the (… wait for the joke …) kerb, as he had visited the red light zone on a bike. The prostitute led him to her self-styled make-out den, a romantic setting charmingly emblazoned with ambient, mood-setting, er, rubbish and barbed wire fencing behind an industrial estate.

Choosing to focus on the agreed sex rather than the insalubrious surroundings, and determined to obtain his £30 worth, the two-wheeled kerb crawler proceeded to mount (… be patient …) his bike again and rode it the brief distance towards a steel railing where he could secure it with his trusty bike lock. Well, there are lots of criminals about.

Then the fireworks really started to erupt. He may have only paid £30 to a jaded prostitute with one eye on her watch and another on her next client, but the earth genuinely moved for the couple, with sparks literally starting to fly. Mainly because he had pushed his bike straight through a gap in the railings and secured it to a detached insulation guard on an electricity sub-station.

This acted as a convenient distress flare, enabling the police (who were already in the vicinity as part of a crackdown on street prostitution) to easily discover the couple in a compromising position, and the pair were duly arrested. The electrical explosion had given away their position for all to see (doggy, since you ask).

Whereas the unfortunate banged (to-rights) hooker received a three-month jail term, her bicycling client merely received a caution for outraging public decency, even though the two-wheeled john surely realised it takes two to ride tandem.

But this charging and sentencing discrepancy was the reluctant conclusion reached by the police after consulting the 1985 Sexual Offences Act. The law states that an offender, in order to be prosecuted for kerb crawling, must either be on foot or in possession of a motor vehicle. However, the punter did not get away with just a discharge (er … that was the joke … no, I suppose it wasn't worth the wait), as he received a caution. Though his girlfriend reportedly ensured he received a discharge soon afterwards – from their relationship.

ZIMMER SHAME

The aforementioned cycling duo were discovered during a crackdown on prostitution in Bournemouth and Boscombe in

2006, codenamed Operation Planet. This targeted law enforcement initiative netted a ninety-five-year-old punter, who was
reprimanded for kerb crawling. The aged paramour, arrested after
picking up a prostitute in Bournemouth, was caught driving a
blue car – no doubt matching the colour of his favourite pills.

He was released with a caution. Although, if the geriatric
john had succeeded in getting the prostitute into his bedroom,
he would probably have just thought, 'now, what did I come
upstairs for?'

A LETTER OF THE LAW

An East London thief became Britain's worst cat burglar; not
by stealing a cat, but by abseiling from the roof of a three-storey
building, where he attempted to break into an office.

Clumsily, he fell too quickly and dislodged a large capital letter
'A' from a company's displayed name sign, which subsequently
hit him on the head, resulting in hospitalisation. Police arrested
him when he was discharged from hospital. Surely a (upper) case
for both the Crown Prosecution Service, and advocates for the
return of capital punishment.

THE FINAL CHAPTER

An overweight Scotsman from Perthshire knew he had to pri-
oritise weight loss and commence an exercise regime. Presumably
he then started to eat a more healthy Scottish diet, and moved to
consuming deep-fried salads and deep-fried fruit.

Unfortunately, the additional exercise came from increasing his
housebreaking activities, which led to a tragic death sentence. No,
not capital punishment, but an ill-advised library raid.

Stumbling through the window of a large country house,
the thief discovered a huge haul of antiquarian books.
Enthusiastically loading them into his van, the sweaty swindler
made numerous trips from library to vehicle, straining under
the ponderous load of the ancient tomes. But he was greedy.
Wheezing and sweating under the physical work, the burgling
bibliophile collapsed from exhaustion and suffered a heart attack.

MUGSHOT

When parked outside a friend's house in Surrey, a woman's car was broken into and an iPhone – imprudently left in full unobscured view on the passenger seat – was, somewhat inevitably, stolen.

Less inevitable was what occurred next. After initially being informed by local police that the case was unlikely to be resolved, at 3 p.m. the next afternoon she received the notifying 'ping' of an incoming e-mail. It was from the thief.

No, the thief wasn't anxious to improve the quality of his service 'because you the victim are important to us', asking her to fill in a short questionnaire evaluating the service of her robbery. Instead, the crook had taken a picture of himself on his new phone, and accidentally engaged the app that the rightful owner had set to automatically upload photos to her Facebook page.

She called the policeman back. He recognised the freshly uploaded self-portrait shot of the photogenic felon as a notorious and pernicious local burglar, and drove to the robber's house to arrest him. Not for the first time.

ELECTRIC LET'S BE AVENUE

Norfolk police were depressingly familiar with one criminal, who seemed unable to grasp the concept that shops require payment. One thieving raid resulted in him being arrested for stealing a packet of cornflakes (relax, there's no cereal offender joke coming up).

But the Norfolk constabulary made perhaps their easiest arrest when another serial offender broke into a Norwich flat in 2013 and snaffled a student's laptop. Tracing the thirty-three year old hardly required investigation – the burglar was electronically tagged at the time, and thus his movements to and from the crime scene were all digitally recorded as hard (drive) evidence. He got five years.

APP-REHENDED

Walking through York city centre one evening, a local was continually bothered by a Polish national asking him if he could use his phone. Suspecting that the requester had been drinking, and was planning serious mischief, he repeatedly declined the invasive requests. Until, that is, the pursuer produced a knife and held it to his throat. Running off with the phone, the thief was heard to gloat.

The victim knew that discovering the identity of the thief may merely constitute a waiting game. Given that he had set up a linking app with his wife's phone to automatically upload pictures, it was not long until the face appeared on the victim's other phone. The mugger was well-recognised at the nick, and his face has probably appeared on as many Wanted posters as members of boy band The Wanted. Yes, really.

He was picked up by the police, and yet another shot was taken of his over-photographed face as his arrest mugshot. They then automatically sent his face to prison.

SCOUTING FOR TOYS

Scouts and Girl Guides enjoy an affectionate status in the UK, and thus light-fingered criminals who rob from these organisations can rightfully expect harsh sentences. A receiver of one such severe sentence from an unyielding judge was a thirty-five-year-old woman who worked in an accountancy capacity for one of the youth groups. She forged the signatures on cheques and blew the illicit gains on diamond jewellery, holidays and expensive toys.

The game was very much of the up variety when the Inland Revenue questioned the repeated large cheque deposits in her bank account, whilst she claimed to be earning an insufficient amount to qualify for paying income tax.

However, presumably she is eligible to receive her Major Criminal Fraud badge. The woman was ordered by a judge to return every penny of the snaffled loot. One option for the embezzler to raise the required funds could be to spend every day of the next three years in prison doing permanent bob-a-job week. Surely that heavily tattooed butch inmate could think of something she'd like her new pretty cellmate to do?

DON'T PUSH IT

When a robber attempted to hold up an Abingdon shop, staff recognised him as a regular customer – even before he accidentally removed his mask in front of the shop's CCTV camera.

Grabbing some till takings whilst flaunting a toy gun, the bungling thief's getaway consisted of multiple attempts to push the pull door. Eventually, the floundering felon concluded that the door simply needed to be pushed harder. Much harder. Taking a run up like a fast bowler, he launched himself at the door, only to bounce back with such a momentous force of proven Newtonian physics that he crashed into a confectionery display. Struggling to get back on his feet, he repeatedly slipped on the spilled confectionery – flailing around like a camel on an icy lake.

Concussed, he was picked up by police, who remarked to the *Oxford Times*: 'His actions show he's not cut out for a life of crime.' Duly arraigned, he received three years.

CRIMINAL NAME CALLING

You and I don't rob banks. There are many reasons for that, but the over-riding one is this: we're not stupid. Unfortunately, a sizable proportion of our fellow humanity are demonstrably less keen to distance themselves from such a description.

Continually cheating Darwinism, their genes are expanding – as are our prisons. The point here being that robbing banks or shops is surprisingly difficult. Most criminals don't undergo training courses or purchase books titled: *Career Guide: How to Rob a Post Office*. Thus they tend to pick up the basics from TV: stocking on head, recruited getaway driver, etc.

Most villains also choose to have a note, as this evades providing a voice recognition clue. Robbers in Kent once bungled a betting shop raid in the 1970s with the following dialogue:

'Give us the bag, Mike.'
'Don't call me Mike.'
'Why not, Mike?'
'Shut your friggin' mouth, George, or I'll fill it.'

George and Mike were known to the police. Soon afterwards they changed their names to prisoner Nos 18836 and 18837 respectively.

STILETTO IN THE GHETTO

Two acquaintances of mine went abroad on a stag weekend and paid a hefty admission price to see the Warsaw Ballet. Turned out to be the worst Pole dancing ever.

OK, so that's merely a bit of comedic invention – a joke to lighten the mood ahead of recounting exactly what happened to the idiotic mugger below. This story really does involve pole dancing. And a great deal of discomfort.

A drunken repugnant City worker, well known as a beery, leery troublemaker at various West End lap- and pole-dancing establishments, was ensuring that the dancers were wearing padded bras – he being mainly responsible for padding those bras via a liberal insertion of banknotes into the dancers' underwear. However, he had ideas of inserting other things in mind. This led to some of the performers encouraging him to continue offering them an ever-faster supply of increasingly high-value banknotes. When it became obvious that house rules were not about to be broken, and private dancing was all he could (un)reasonably expect, his evening ended in non-fulfillment. The only udders being squeezed that night were metaphorical ones, as the dancers milked this particular cash cow until it was emptied.

Next, a combination of frustration, drunkenness and generally being a bit of a git led to him hatching a stupid criminal plan. He would wait in the alley at the back of the club for the women to leave by the stage door, and then snatch their purses in order to reclaim his evening's vast expenditure. A faultless plan.

Eventually, a dancer departed through the door. Jumping out from behind a wheelie bin, he attempted to grab her bag. Not in any mood to let go of her bag, and supported by two of her colleagues, the trio proceeded to whack the drunken mugger. Indeed, they whacked him with such force that, after repeatedly landing high heeled kicks to his unspeakables, the club's bouncers came running out to intervene – not to assist the girls in nullifying the mugger's threat, but to drag the girls off him, shouting, 'He's had enough, girls.'

The demure dancers chose to respond to this comment by declaring, 'We'll decide when he's had enough!' prior to one of them taking a run-up like a free kick specialist and landing another well-aimed stiletto between the sticks.

Not that this would be the horny punter's most painful encounter of the evening: that would surely arrive later when he explained the bruises to his wife, whom he had reportedly told he would be spending the night at choir practice. Given the hefty Jimmy Choo he received to the groin, he may now be the first chorister in history whose voice has transformed from treble to baritone, through tenor to bass, and then back again to treble.

Charges were dropped when the punter chose not to press ahead with a complaint for assault, matched by the dancers' decision to withdraw a formal report of attempted mugging. The punter, though, is banned – a decision presumably made for his own safety. Although he can probably now sing a lovely rendition of Mendelssohn's famous high-noted passage 'O for the Wings of a Dove' or 'Great Balls of Fire'. Silver linings.

COUPLE WORK OUT HARD EVIDENCE

On a dark evening, when a drug-dependent burglar noticed a house without lights, he decided to lob a brick through the back-door window and indulge in a spot of opportunist thieving. But the pickings turned out to be slim – as did the owners of the house, since their residence contained a fully functional private gym, but little else apart from necessities and a huge stock of health food and low-calorie energy drinks.

Unperturbed, the unfit burglar attempted to place dumb-bells into his bag. Only when attempting to pick up the bag, did this particular thieving dumb-bell acknowledge that he was incapable of lifting it. Eventually deciding to leave the gym equipment *in situ* due to its hernia-inducing heaviness, he bagged some fitness DVDs and a few protein vegetable shakes. If he had hoped for a night tossing gold bullion into his swag bag, then this was an incontrovertibly poor harvest.

However, going through his illegal haul the next day, the scoundrel believed he had stumbled across a plan to trade up his paltry pickings. Some of the snatched DVD cases turned out to be decoys, housing privately made DVDs of the abode's healthy young couple engaged in some seriously acrobatic upstairs physical workouts – but not necessarily on their gym equipment. They were shown pumping more than just iron.

For reasons that only a drug-addled idiot thief could reason, this constituted A Very Good Idea: he decided this was a great blackmail opportunity. The next stage on the inevitable route towards prison was characteristically simple. He wrote a note, saying that he had the private homemade porn in his possession, and in order for it to be safely returned to its owner and leading lady, he would require £1,000, or else the action would be uploaded to the Internet. Helpfully, he had included a phone number. A home landline number, as well as his mobile.

The couple merely passed this note to the police. His address was traced, and he was arrested within two hours of posting the ransom note.

After the conviction, the distinctly non-camera-shy couple received their DVDs back – though presumably not until the police had invested considerable time in studying the hard evidence, from every conceivable angle, in case they had missed something. Eventually their homemade filth was returned by the, er, filth.

VIDIOT

There's stupidity. Then there's platinum-tipped, weapons grade stupidity. Crossing over from the former to the latter category is a thief from Rochester. After breaking into the house of a

candidate standing for local political election, the crook swiped a
few profitable goodies. Undeniably the best item of his thieving
picks was a state-of-the-art digital video camera, augmented by
related extras.

Keen to show off his spoils when he returned home, he
proceeded to film his own house, noting off-camera that his
girlfriend needed to do the washing-up (bit sexist!). He then
attempted to film his girlfriend, who batted the camera away,
prior to providing the viewer with a guided tour of all the other
rooms in his home.

Finally, the film concluded with the thief turning the camera on
himself, and confirming his full name (rather aptly like a rehearsal
for an anticipated court appearance). He then taunted the authorities with the line: 'This is my house. Yes, and a stolen camera that
I stole. But it's OK, the stupid cops won't ever figure it out.'

The short film is mainly shaky footage – next time he ought to
steal a tripod too.

Shortly afterwards, local police raided the house of a notorious
local fence and retrieved a considerable haul of stolen goods,
which they set about reacquainting with their owners. As soon as
the camera's recently reunited owner settled down to watch some
video he had recently shot, he was surprised to see his footage
prefixed by eighty seconds of a criminal's face, pledging with
vanishing confidence, that he stole the camera and would not get
caught by the dumb police.

Handing the camera back to the police, the incriminating
footage was uploaded onto YouTube. Several keen identifiers
came forward, including a man who had CCTV footage of the
same villain breaking into his car. The local force charged the
non-camera-shy robber. Not that they had trouble knowing
where to find him – he was already in prison awaiting sentencing
for separate offences.

WHEN A SAINT GOES MARCHING IN

A raid on a Southend supermarket did not turn out to be that
profitable for a mathematically challenged thief. Approaching

the cashier with just one item in his basket, an onion, the villain handed her a £20 note to ensure she opened the till. This accomplished, he grabbed the contents of the cash register and scarpered towards the door, leaving behind him pandemonium, ringing alarms and an abandoned onion.

Totting up the missing proceeds from the till, the store discovered that the raider had successfully stolen £14.35, whilst the cashier had significantly kept hold of the £20 note he had handed over to make sure she activated the till opening. Thus he lost exactly £5.65 on the raid.

Local shopkeepers displayed a 'Wanted' poster of the thief afterwards, though presumably in the hope of attracting him into their shops.

DISORGANISED CRIME SQUAD

A sixty-one-year-old resident of St Peter Port, Guernsey, provided a novel defence after being arrested for indecent exposure. He claimed to have merely been holding a jumbo hot dog in his hand. It transpired under cross-examination that he was most definitely NOT holding a hot dog. Nor was it jumbo.

When two girls strolled past the entrance to his flat one evening, they spotted him engaging in an activity historically associated with causing deteriorating eyesight. Hence it was somewhat ironic when he claimed in court that their eyesight was probably poor. Giving evidence, the girls recounted how he beckoned them over to observe his meat products, though they sensibly declined this hideous offer, preferring instead to notify the Channel Island authorities.

The phantom sausage holder even arrived at court with a saveloy specimen, which he claimed was a replica of the one purchased at the fish and chip shop next door on the evening of the offence. The outlandishly bright red colour of the saveloy might have been a cause for medical, rather than judicial, attention.

However, it transpired that there had been previous incidents where he had been convicted for holding various pink-coloured elongated meat products in public. An arriving policeman had also spotted the defendant displaying his pork sword without accompanying chips on the night in question.

The judge decided the defendant was not being frank(furter) with the court and a guilty verdict was quickly reached.

WATCHING THE SOAPS

There are hardly any TV repairmen these days. This must have a huge knock-on effect for those who rely upon the profession continuing, particularly the plot writers of porn films.

In 2006, a student at a North Wales university decided that since his TV was broken, he would merely watch films on his computer. If only there was pre-existing pornography somewhere on the Internet that could be searched for. He decided that since there were no opportunities to see naked girls on the Internet, he would have to record his own films. In the university. And starring several of his fellow undergraduates. And (… see if you can spot the controversial bit …) naked without asking their permission.

Firstly, he placed a camera in the plug hole of a sink in the female bathrooms. Unsurprisingly, this produced several watery shots of women brushing their teeth, and was not the sort of scorchingly erotic Babestation featurettes he was presumably imagining. Tired girls in pyjamas flossing represents a highly specialist market of deviant erotica.

Unperturbed by this initial and screamingly obvious setback of stupidity, he continued in his ludicrous plans to make his own secret movies. Next, he spent hours designing and building a hidden remote digital camera inside a shampoo bottle. Well, it was either that or get a degree.

A specially adapted gel bottle – which was suspiciously enormous – got placed on the ledge in the female communal bathroom. Surely now he could capture erotic images of beautiful frolicking women lathering soap over their gorgeous pendulous breasts. Finally, his gel-o-rama masterpiece was ready and secured in the ladies' bathroom with the record switch pressed down.

The new approach resulted in capturing footage featuring lots of steamy scenes. But not the sort he envisaged. Turns out that your modern girl favours taking a shower over having a bath, and showers create constant hot steam. Steam was all the camera recorded.

Back to the drawing board. Now seriously behind with course-work, and any flailing grip on social reality, the perpetrator focused on devising a plan to overcome this latest setback. The resultant plan was so cunningly terrible, it would guarantee him a place in the finals of the World's Biggest Idiot Championships.

In case the over-sized gel bottle, with the cumbersome camera concealed within, alerted insufficient suspicion, he put up an accompanying sign proclaiming that 'all the showers are broken, and girls must take baths instead'. This would surely not incur any raised eyebrows, and the girls would just nod compliantly. Perhaps next week he could add a 'girls must wash each other's breasts very slowly' sign too.

Needless to say, an appearance in Caernarfon Crown Court followed – as did a permanent expulsion from university. He was

charged with six offences governed by the Sexual Offences Act – though surprisingly not the lesser charge of 'Imitating a scene from daft 1980s high school movie *Porky's*'. He left Bangor University soon afterwards, with a degree of shame.

SANTA CLAUS IS COMING TO JAIL

There are undoubtedly times when turning to a life of crime is a barely coded cry for help. This, it transpires, can also involve an actual cry for help. Such as an occasion in Wigan when a delivery van driver for the town's Tesco store heard a disturbing cry of 'Help! Help!' coming from the top of the store's chimney.

Nightshift workers had earlier reported hearing the sound of someone sneezing in the chimney – maybe the trapped villain was suffering from a bad case of the flue! (You're welcome.)

As it was approaching Christmas time, maybe a premature Santa was in the chimney? But all through the house a creature was stirring – and it definitely was not a mouse. In fact, Santa was an unemployed, and evidently overweight, twenty-year-old burglar. He informed police that he was hiding from drug dealers who were owed money, but this story was soon dismantled, as it was a clear case of an attempted break-in.

Should the store ever require a Santa to work in the shop at Christmas, then his CV at least now contains relevant experience of sliding down chimneys. He even brought a sack with him. Though he may be unsuitable for future work as Santa, given he clearly suffers from Claus-trophobia (OK, I'll save it for a cracker).

How he planned to get back up through the narrow chimney after filling his sack with bulging plunder is not known. Then again, he had not succeeded in working out that the chimney was insufficiently wide. At least a diet of bread and water for the next few months should help the burly burglar shed a few pounds.

MINDLESS CRIMINAL

When it comes to excuses for crimes, what better than the old classic 'I can't remember'. James Murdoch famously employed this technique at various Select Committee appearances, though he presumably cannot recollect appearing before any Select Committees.

However, the ultimate attempt at absent-minded finesse was used by former Austrian President Kurt Waldheim, who 'forgot' that he had been in the notorious Nazi SS. Well, let's be honest. Who amongst us hasn't committed an offence and then forgotten about it? Most of us have left the photocopier jammed at work and forgotten to return, or left the printer out of paper, or the toilet roll finished and unchanged. Or rounded up an entire community and burnt down their village.

This approach matched the actions of a serial burglar from Manchester. Having been caught red-handed, and with matching prints and accumulated evidence directly linking him to at least forty other break-ins in the North West area, he was remaining tight-lipped in custody. Until a deal was brokered. Since he was more guilty than a puppy sitting next to a steaming poo pile on a brand new carpet, he decided to change his plea in court – realising that 'I don't remember' was unlikely to win over a jury in response to repeated invites from the prosecution to explain why his fingerprints, clothing strands, DNA and CCTV images were associated with so many crime scenes.

Asked in court why he had steadfastly denied the charges earlier, he replied, 'I forgot committing the burglaries, but now about 100 have just all come back to me. Yeah, thinking about it, I did do all those break-ins.' The judge remembered to send him to prison for a long time.

PLASTERED ON THE JOB

A pair of plasterers must have taken a major plastering job after getting plastered. The troublesome twosome had finished plastering a Liverpool property when word reached them that their boss was going to instigate a surprise visit to inspect their work. Since their work was competent, and they had completed it within the expected timeframe, this ought not to have caused excessive concern. Except for one salient detail: the competent plastering they had completed was on another property, where they had been moonlighting all week.

Having plastered their extra-curriculum property, they panicked, and decided the best way to hide the fact that they had not done any work on the house where they were supposed to have been all week was to burn it down. Petrol was sprayed over a bed, and then a toilet-paper wick was lit from the letterbox.

Returning to the property to see how successful their arson attempt had been, the bungling duo narrowly avoided crashing into the approaching fire engine. Unfortunately, the dim pair had plastered their whereabouts too. Witnesses reported seeing their distinctive van, advertising their company and phone number, driving away from the smouldering property. Large cracks soon appeared in their alibis – and plastering.

RAIDERS OF THE LOST ARK

Crooks in Brighton decided to target a Barclays bank cash machine located in an external wall. Arriving with a top-of-the-range digger, stolen from a quarry in Lewes the day before the theft, they wisely supplemented their stealing vehicle with a speedier getaway pick-up van. Or so they thought.

Crashing into the wall, the digger scooped out the machine and effortlessly deposited the heavy item into the back of the pick-up. The JCB driver skipped out of the cab and hopped into the pick-up, ready to speed away. 'Go, go, go!' he screamed over the sound of the reluctantly starting ignition. Perseverance resulted in a spluttering ignition noise as the car rattled on the spot but stubbornly refused to go. With alarm bells ringing – both the figurative and literal varieties – the foiled felons decided to abandon their two vehicles and plundered cash machine. They were then spotted by witnesses running away into the dark streets of a pre-dawn Brighton.

Since cash machines are refilled in the morning, as a deliberate policy to ensure they contain limited cash overnight when they experience less use, there would have been a relatively small sum involved even if the haul had been successful. It is also worth pointing out that the digger – which was rejected and left at the scene – would have been worth around £100,000. D'oh.

IPHONE IDIOTS

Some people cannot wait. The day before the new iPhone 5 was due to go on sale, bandits decided to ram-raid the Apple store and grab as many as they could before the flatfoots arrived. Unfortunately, Apple scrumping is nowadays a more high-profile crime than in the past, requiring refined technology to steal advanced technology.

The thieves had a BMW 4x4 which they drove through the store window. They then industriously filled loot bags with iPhones and Apple Macs. Calculating that they had to leave within three minutes or dramatically increase their chances of being apprehended, the gang's leader gave the signal to depart. Alas, reversing is always difficult, particularly under pressure, and he took multiple attempts to steer the car out of the shop, after it looked likely the vehicle was going to be permanently stuck there.

Arriving police immediately discovered that the vehicle's licence plates had been knocked off in the ram-raiding, radioed the control centre to obtain the address where the vehicle was registered, and then popped round and duly arrested the owner. Plus the store had not received any of the new iPhones anyway. What a stupid iDea.

PRIME TIME CRIME

When a woman decided to steal an iPhone from a fellow reveller at a Brighton nightclub, she probably thought she had stealthily secured the gadget without any comeback. After all, her venal activities were cloaked by the club's near darkness, pumping backbeats and coruscating lights. Her thieving was surely safely hidden from any prying security cameras. Safe, that is, from all cameras apart from her own.

Attempting to unlock the stolen phone in the backseat of her getaway car, the brunette triggered an app that had been set up on the device to take a photo. Instantly, the mugger's mugshot was sent to the real owner's email account, where it was immediately forwarded to the police, where it was in turn forwarded to the BBC, where it subsequently appeared on both prime time BBC1 and ITV. Other than that, and her picture being featured in nearly every national newspaper the next day, no one saw her do anything.

Perhaps stealing the phone was a snap decision.

SNOW MORE PUNS

Metal thieves in Dudley, West Midlands stole piping and gas meters from domestic properties immediately after heavy snowfall in 2013. Police were called to investigate one break-in, where they promptly followed the clear trail of footsteps and paw prints (the raiders had brought canine accompaniment) that started at the crime scene.

Tracing the distinct trail, officers trekked 1.3 miles to the main culprit's hideout, where they found the thief, the metal and the canine accomplice. Police expect the arrested man to follow a clear trail through the criminal justice system.

THE CRIME UNRAVELLER'S WIFE

An Oxfordshire groom-to-be was becoming increasingly reticent about exchanging vows with his fiancée and thereby joining a family he was already on record as describing as 'scary'. In fact, his feet could not have been getting any colder if he slept with them stuck outside the door of an undersized arctic tent.

Thus a criminal mastermind plan needed to be hatched. The fact that it is about to be listed in this book prompts you to expect that it was not a particularly clever plan. And you'd be correct in making that assumption.

For he decided the best way to avoid getting married was to wait until the dreaded wedding day itself, and then stage a break-in at his own flat. Causing criminal damage, and announcing himself with a cheery 'hello' to his basement-dwelling landlord upon arrival, he proceeded to make considerable noise. Windows, mirrors and crockery were smashed, settees and tables were upturned. When the landlord trotted upstairs to investigate the disturbing sounds from above, he found the runaway groom in confessional mode: 'I've done a burglary and will have to be arrested.' The police were called and soon established his motive. He was actively choosing prison over marriage.

Unfortunately the police refused to imprison him, but he was fined for wasting police time and causing criminal damage. However, the boys in blue did unhelpfully point out that stealing your own possessions does not, as a point of law, constitute theft. Who knew?

Upon hearing of the groom's preference to be sent down for life, rather than enter into an until-death-us-do-part bond with his beloved, his intended understandably called the whole thing off. So, that was a happy ending then. Of sorts.

THE LONG LEG OF THE LAW

Like a brow-beaten, punch-drunk boxer opting to retire too late, several villains delude themselves that they can carry on their criminal careers far too long — only to reap predictable and unpleasant rewards. Britain's grey prisoner population has increased three fold over the last few years, with the *Daily Telegraph* reporting that the UK's oldest lag is a ninety-two year old. He has probably forgotten what it was that he came inside for.

Agility is hardly optional in the fast world of smash and grabbing. When a disabled pensioner from Glasgow decided to help himself to a travel case in a department store, he left something behind at the scene. Whilst attempting to flee at (relative) speed with the stolen item, he tripped and left behind a prosthetic leg.

Attempting to leg it from the scene without a leg did prove predictably difficult. When it came to his defence in court, he simply didn't have a leg to stand on.

HUNG BY THE NECK

Showing a fittingly ironic disregard for prison slang, a twenty-three-year-old woman from Nottingham stole numerous chokers from several of the city's fashion stores. So frequent were her relentless shoplifting sprees that she was given a custodial sentence when she refused to name the third party who was purchasing the stolen chokers and other accessories.

A choker, for those not *au fait* with the transient trends of fashion, is a type of necklace, traditionally worn high on the neck and often manufactured out of fabric, especially lace.

Unbeknown to the pathological choker raider, the similar word 'chokey' is Victorian slang for her inevitable destination: prison! As in many a villain's pledge: 'I ain't going to chokey no more, I'm going straight.' In her case, she was going straight to chokey.

If *Countdown*'s Dictionary Corner specialist Susie Dent was here now, then … well, three things actually. (1) She would almost certainly be able to reveal that the etymology is the Hindi term *cauki*, meaning a lock-up; (2) I'd demand that she altered the spelling of the word 'team' in the Oxford English Dictionary, ensuring from now on it is spelt 'teiam', just to shut-up all those annoying workplace motivating managers dispensing their clichéd aphorisms; (3) I'd ask her to consider recording an audiobook, reading just the rude words from the Oxford English Dictionary.

Inevitably, the choker thief is currently choking in chokey. Police raided her house and found numerous boxes of stolen chokers, hairbands, earrings and necklaces. Perhaps they'll charge her with being an accessory. I said 'an accessory'… oh, never mind.

UNAWARE OF THE COMPETITION

A couple burst into a department store intent on robbing it. Greed being a potent motivator, the Bonnie of this particular modern-day Bonnie & Clyde operation was temporarily distracted from the pressing robbery by a poster strewn with palm trees draping their leaves lazily into an idyllic atlas-blue ocean. Targeted advertising had its desired effect and she began fixating on the poster's competition to win a 5-star resort Caribbean trip.

Sensing that the art of a good robbery is to get in and out as quickly as possible, Clyde continued with the plan. Unfortunately Clyde, the chimp from the Clint Eastwood movies, would have

brought more cranial processing capacity to proceedings. After swiping goods, including ... and do enjoy this next detail ... items from the SALE table (presumably they put back the full-price items they had initially stolen after spotting that they could steal the exact same items with 20% off elsewhere) they swept past pursuing security guards.

Falling, rather than running, down the escalators, they fled into the twilight and reached their getaway motorbike. This left the shop and police with little to go on, other than multiple eyewitness testimonies, security guards' accounts, multiple-angle CCTV surveillance camera shots, and ... oh, just one more thing Columbo ... the Caribbean holiday entry form shown being completed by Bonnie on CCTV and dropped into the store's special competition posting box. Other than her full name, date of birth, address, email, home phone, age, work phone and mobile number, the police had absolutely nothing to go on.

BRITISH SUMMER CRIME

Three members of the British army were despatched to monitor a security checkpoint during an overseas peacekeeping initiative. One bearded local quickly established himself as a regular checkpoint user, noticeably for the fact that he was permanently pushing (significantly never riding) a shiny bike whilst carrying a large bag packed with a suspicious cargo. Whenever the three soldiers (let's call them Private Matters, Major Incident and General Coincidence) looked inside the capacious bag, they discovered fragments of ripped plastic sheeting and torn cardboard. Odd. But nothing that looked remotely illegal.

Crossing the security point one afternoon, the suspicious local bumped into an acquaintance and proceeded to inform him that, 'These stupid Britishers don't know that I'm stealing two bikes a day from the factory where I work, and then selling them on the other side. They can't even work out that I'm stashing the packaging in my bag.' His friend expressed concern that he had surely just implicated himself in their presence. 'Never,' he counselled with an unwarranted hubristic confidence, 'They'll never know 'cos they can't be bothered to learn our language.'

One of the three British soldiers was fluent in the local dialect, as were the local policemen whose custody the bike snatcher was placed in. He had stolen his last bike.

WOOF JUSTICE

A thief already serving concurrent suspended sentences should surely have considered retiring from the thieving business. After all, his predilection for being caught was a sure indicator that thieving was not his true career forte.

However, under issued threat of a suspended sentence or not, he parked up his 4x4 Planet RuinerTM in a Gloucestershire car park, and went about trying to remove a bronze statue valued at £3,000 from a public park in Cheltenham. Two passers-by alerted police to his noisy activities, and a police dog named Zak responded to the crime with his handler.

First on the scene, he chased the statue stealer. Sniffing his scent, Zak traced the miscreant metal meddler to a courtyard, where he proceeded to sink his teeth into his work – snapping his powerful jaws shut on the villain's left buttock. The resultant scream could probably be heard in the neighbouring city of

Gloucester, as could the noise caused by him toppling over a huge metal statue – which had initially alerted other park users to his unlawful activities.

On hearing of his toothy canine encounter, the rather unsympathetic judge stated in open court, 'Good, I hope it hurt!' Somewhat predictably, the *Daily Telegraph* reader comments approved of that judicial response.

SOMETHING SMELLS FISHY

A Cheshire shoplifter decided he was going to raise his standards. Hence he decided to stop robbing the Pound Shop and cease accumulating convictions for robbing discount stores. It was time to move on up, and acknowledge that thieving from charity shops was not an accomplishment that would induce swelling pride in his grandchildren. Basically, he needed to raise his game and reach for higher returns from life. Indubitably it was time to seize the day before dusk fell – rather than seizing the chocolate invitingly kept near the door at Aldi.

He decided to shoplift from Waitrose instead. How jolly upmarket of him.

After downing several drinks in a nearby pub, he entered his local Waitrose superstore. Seeing their extensive range of bourgeoisie-pleasing products (tip: if you have a posh friend visit, drive them past the nearest Waitrose en route to your scummy estate – it will help calm them), the Cheshire scally filled a basket with unfamiliar-looking products. Without doubt, the most bizarre of these was an octopus, bagged from a temporarily distracted fishmonger.

The upwardly mobile shoplifter was apprehended attempting to exit through the entrance door holding a basket containing goods of the decidedly unpaid variety – including a raw octopus and a hot chicken. Or, more accurately, a hot octopus and a hot hot chicken.

The long arm of the law (all eight of them) felt his collar. Maybe he thought the octopus charge wouldn't stick – if so, he failed to take into account the many tentacles of the law and the suckers it has to deal with. Pleasingly, when passing sentence, the judge branded him a prolific criminal and gave him eight weeks.

Incidentally, an octopus is capable of foresight, planning and tool use, and is thus considered to be the smartest animal without a backbone (you may add your own Nick Clegg joke here).

NOSEY BURGLARS

Five burglars forced their way into a pensioner's home in South Yorkshire. Being a pensioner's house, they found limited plundering opportunities; not the lavish jewellery and antiquities they were optimistically expecting, but probably lots of Werther's Original toffees, cat ornaments and those slippers that zip up at the side. However, their attention was suddenly drawn to an urn sitting above the mantelpiece. The fact that it was an urn ought to have provided an opening clue as to the origin of its powdery contents.

Mistaking the contents for cocaine – mainly because they're idiots – the raiding quintet decided to snort the white powder. After a while they concluded that they weren't getting high and decided – going that extra mile in the name of proven stupidity – that this was because they simply had not consumed enough. So they snorted deeper, harder and longer.

The returning victim saw the lights on at her property, heard a suspicious commotion and called the police. Whilst the crooks were being arrested, she informed them that they had snorted the ashes of two Great Danes and her late husband.

CRIME FIGURES ADD UP

People who work in cake shops should justly campaign for the same rights enjoyed by bar workers. Whenever fuller-figured customers waddle up to the serving counter and demand more cake, staff should be permitted to refuse service on the grounds that, 'No, you've had enough already, fatso!'

When a Croydon cake shop proprietor was removing items from the oven, he was surprised to see a customer waiting at the counter to hand him a note. He was even more surprised to see the note proclaiming that the overweight customer was armed and required money. The baker refused to hand over cash, at which point the customer decided that the armed robbery was to be downgraded to a smash and grab raid.

Snatching what he thought was a cash register, the corpulent cake fan grabbed an adding machine from the counter top and fled the scene. Mistaking the adding machine, which contained no drawers or cash, for a cash register meant that the thief had managed to steal a cumbersome calculator, with the added bonus of a (nearly finished) paper roll.

Police later traced the villain by his car, which appeared on CCTV – there being something about this case that just didn't add up.

NEWPORT GAG NELL

A caller giving her name as 'Nell' from Newport, Wales, reported a local resident for impersonating a police officer.

'Did the individual have a helmet?' asked the policeman on the front desk.

'Yes.'

'Did he have a uniform?'

'Yes.'

'So,' clarified the duty sergeant, 'may I enquire as to what reason you have for suspecting the individual was indeed a fake bobby?'

'Because,' she explained, 'we never see a policeman walking around Newport.'

FALLING FROM THE STRAIGHT AND NARROW

Presumably planning to see in the dark by the glow of his own luminescent brilliance – a sturdy surrogate for actual torchlight – a myopic burglar from Manchester decided to rob a remote house at midnight without the aid of any attention-attracting lights.

Holidaying in Cornwall, because he believed that rich people frequented the county, he decided he would randomly select a house to rob. 'Cleverly', he turned his car headlights off before reaching his destination. ('Cleverly' really did require inverted commas in that last sentence.) This resulted in him hitting a tree. Unperturbed, and with only superficial bumper and bonnet damage, he persevered with the plan, making his way along the perilously steep track near the Cornish coastal path – mixing darkness, altitude, unfamiliarity and rugged terrain, just like in the laborious five-minute set-up scene that starts each episode of *Casualty*.

The dimly lit dim-wit tripped, fell and bruised himself. He then fell again in the rugged terrain, twisted his ankle and got lost in the dark. So he dialled 999. A set of specialist housebreaking tools, and a mobile phone that allegedly included, amongst its scrolled contacts, 'Phil the Fence', made the CPS's workload a lot lighter. The local constabulary were used to traversing the paths and operating without streetlights. Now the captured crook regularly experiences lights out at 10 p.m.

CRIMINAL SPORTING BRUISES

Most professions are nowadays gender integrated. There are female dentists and rugby players, alongside male nursery teachers. All professions are equal (well, they will be the day I finally see a male make-up artist in a TV studio). And stupid criminals are likewise a wholly integrated lot when it comes to advance cross-gender nincompoopery. Furthermore, cross-dressing is *de rigueur* in some criminal quarters, especially if you want to fool the authorities into looking for a woman – specifically a 6ft 3in woman with two-day facial stubble and a fly-half's gait.

A deluded pervert decided all that was required to witness some sporty girls undressing was to obtain a South London gym membership. Then, simply by putting on his mother's dress and lipstick, he could arrive at the gym and head for the women's changing room. Once there, he would settle down on the provided wooden benches in the locker room to observe a free floorshow of stripping augmented by the glistening post-showered bodies of nubile ladies. It would be just like the Internet, but in 3D and without buffering delays. What a superb and entirely foolproof plan!

Apparently he had been in the changing room for two seconds before a muscular female weight trainer told him he was in the wrong locker room. Needless to say, his insistence that he was indeed a lady played out like a *Little Britain* sketch. He now appears on the sexual offenders' register. The swelling may finally be receding, as it was ladies' martial arts night when he chose to visit.

HAND IT TO THE BANDIT

It's an ageless dilemma highlighting the inconsistency of gender politics. A man who has multiple sexual partners is revered by society as a 'stud', whilst a woman who behaves similarly is branded as 'your mum'. Or at least that's what I hear a lot from the schoolkids on the bus in the mornings, whenever they sensitively discuss such issues.

But one self-described male stud (or slut, if we prefer assigning judgemental non-gender-neutral descriptions) sought an opportunity to bed numerous women and then steal their stuff. Screwing people twice over, it could be said. Or three times, as he also worked in a bank.

Stalking the nightclubs of Manchester, this 1970s throwback gigolo dressed and behaved like a time tourist from another decade. It was an age of wide lapels and narrow minds. You can imagine his chat-up lines: 'I have a mat of chest hair: it says 'welcome'.'

He would target women of a certain age, ply them with intoxicating compliments and drink, reassure them of their intense ageless beauty, then invite himself round to theirs for a nightcap followed by a Dutch cap. After concluding any messy animalistic activities, he would wait until his one-night beau was snoring contentedly into her Laura Ashley pillow whilst dreaming of introducing him to her mum, and then tip-toe out with his reclaimed trousers and the homeowner's DVD player, jewellery, purse and anything else that could be easily sold without the requirement of paperwork.

This plan worked relatively well until one Sunday morning when a former victim recognised him. Furthermore, he was holding two pillowcases, presumably just filled with another victim's valuables. But he scarpered before the summoned police arrived.

However, she spotted the criminal Casanova again a few weeks later, alongside most of her stuff. He was manning a car boot stall when she next phoned the police, who arrived and duly arrested him. 'What really annoyed me,' she informed the court later, 'was not just that he valued me so low, but that he thought my designer label clutch bag should be priced at 75p.'

WITLESS FOR THE PROSECUTION

The un-ignorable plight of the mentally ill in this country has often been ... ahem ... ignored. Or so it would seem. Those unfortunate enough to suffer malfunctioning mental faculties have often discovered that the establishment's response is basically one of semantics. Nowadays it is care in the community, with particular emphasis on the buildings used to house patients. Formerly called lunatic asylums, they were re-named mental hospitals; nowadays they're generally called 'luxury apartments' – given they've been sold off for high-end housing.

So it takes a peculiar sort of lowlife to steal from a charity shop nobly raising money to aid those with enduring mental deficiencies. One teenage hoodlum entered a mental health charity shop in North London and picked up a coat, asking the staff if he could try it on – in both senses of the phrase, given he then implemented stage one of his morally vacuous plan: Operation Nick Winter Clothing.

Wearing only a seasonal T-shirt, consistent with the prickly, inescapable July heat, the aged volunteer shop assistant, sweltering in the thermometer's mercury-boiling conditions, momentarily paused from fanning herself to point to the shop's fitting room.

When he drew the curtains to emerge from the fitting room many long minutes later, the customer rejected the coat by placing it on the counter, and muttered that it was too small. The reason for it being suddenly small was probably related to the fact that he was now wearing two buttoned shirts and two matching sweaters, with a short leather jacket topping off the outfit. Not that this looked suspicious in cactus-wilting conditions. The old lady challenged him, prompting the teenager to accuse her of being deranged since he claimed to have entered the shop dressed like a member of Robert Falcon Scott's search party.

Another shopper dialled 999 and a passing policeman quickly arrived at the premises and gave the teenager a severe dressing-down. No doubt followed by a prolonged spell in the cooler.

CHARITY BEGINS AT WORK

A charity shop worker frequently dipped her (regularly fingerprinted) mitts into the till. Quite how frequently was made exquisitely clear at her resultant trial. In order to make the job of law enforcement appreciably easier for the police and Crown Prosecution Service, she had enthusiastically maintained a detailed written log of her criminal pursuits. Her Warrington charity store was targeted from the inside on numerous occasions, with all the evidence carefully compiled in the diligent culprit's diary.

One entry read: 'Good day in shop £124 – £80 for me, oh yes!'

Another said: '5th June: Bloody good day at shop £213. Man brought bag of coins in – £75 for shop £35 for me, well I had to count it.'

On 13 April her crime diary recorded: '£37 for shop £15 for me, hee hee.'

And in another entry she bragged: '14th July: A good day as far as I'm concerned. £50. But not so for shop.'

Other penned diary entries included:

'2 March: I was in charge at Charity Shop and it was a good day for me: £91. Oh yes.'

'18 May: Shop quiet £87 only got £30 for me.'

'3 Nov: Good day at shop for me. £60. So got money in bank for tomorrow & £35 to spend. Oh yes.'

There are no more entries after December, as presumably January to December of the following year were immensely repetitive: 'Bad day for me: slopped out. Exercise yard. Lights out.' Or, 'Good day for butch woman in the top bunk.'

Particularly noteworthy is the entry for 13 April, ending with the villainous, dastardly laugh 'hee hee'. How she must have bemoaned not possessing a long moustache that could be curled for villainous effect. Regrettably, other entries are not populated with a Mutley-like theatrical laugh, but sprinkled generously with the term 'oh yes', like a freshly amoral Churchill dog.

CRIMINALS LOOS THEIR FREEDOM

A major tool in Peterborough attempted to steal some major tools. Passing a building site, he saw a bag of expensive-looking tools left invitingly in a large open bag. The bag had handles, which he interpreted as a sign telling him to abscond with it. Perhaps not the best demonstration of fine judgement, but his judgement had already been given the afternoon off after he took the lunchtime decision to partake of neat vodka.

Picking up the clunking bag of metallic spanners was predictably a noise-generating experience. Rattling like a timpanist in an echo chamber, he unsurprisingly gained the attention of some of the building site workers. Spotted, he decided to hang on to the tools and hide in a nearby portaloo.

Unfortunately, he became disoriented by a combination of the dark, the badly balanced tools, and the 70% proof Polish vodka. The portable toilet toppled over. When the authorities arrived he realised he really was in the sh*t, and had to be saved from drowning in poo. The police arrived and knew instantly that something just didn't smell right about this case.

MAN STEALS OWN CAR

'We would like to charge him with possessing an idiotic brain,' said the policeman, in an unguarded moment, to a shivering bystander who had put on a thin dressing gown and stepped into the street at 3 a.m. to see what was responsible for the commotion.

A stolen car had been driven through a front garden, splintering the wooden trellis fence and giving the roses a grade one pruning of military shortness. The car had come to rest so close to the front door that the police were forced to use the back entrance.

The culprit, who had stolen the car and caused damage to the Wiltshire property by crashing into it at speed, was stubbornly failing to see the funny side of events. This choice of reaction rather separated him from the rest of the street, who were sniggering behind twitching curtains. Because the car he had broken into (by smashing the driver's window with a rock), hot-wired and driven into a front garden, had both belonged to … that's right, the driver and homeowner.

After consuming heroic quantities of alcohol, he had decided that driving home was definitely an excellent idea. Congratulating himself on making such a good decision, his brain – sabotaged by numerous pints of bitter – was unable to inform him that he had parked his vehicle in the pub car park a few hours earlier. Normally, given the circumstances, this would have been a good thing, as it would render him unable to drive home with a blood alcohol reading off the scale: at that point, even Amy Winehouse would tell you to stop and go home.

Instead, he staggered along the side streets until he eventually ended up at the pub car park, where he smashed his way into a

car, and then drove the short distance home before deciding to
park in his hallway.

A substantial fine and driving ban followed. Plus his licence
now has more points on it than a pin-covered tetrahedron.

DIAL M FOR MUPPET

Several people have successfully saddled redundancy and
ridden it towards a rewarding new career. There are numerous
examples of the jolting shock from redundancy prompting
recipients to undergo career changes that involve retraining,
starting a business, or generally steering themselves towards a
more fulfilling career.

A Polish builder reacted to being made redundant from the
construction industry by changing his career to burglary.

Fortunately for him, whilst equally unfortunate for his
numerous victims, he discovered initial success in his newly
adopted profession. Until the day he decided to break into an
unoccupied house whilst the owners were away for a weekend
break in the West Country.

Having stuffed electrical items and jewellery into the traditional
boodle bag (why don't burglars syphon out printer ink? – there
is surely nothing more valuable per gram than that commodity!)
he decided to help himself to something from the fridge, then
the snack cupboard, and finally the drinks cabinet. Bored with
flicking through the TV channels, he spotted the house phone
and decided he would speak to some of his relatives. Dialling
numerous Warsaw, Krakow and Gdańsk numbers, he spoke to his
mother for over an hour, his wife back home, and then rang three
professional work colleagues (i.e. three housebreakers he had met
during a brief spell of incarceration).

Such was the Polish housebreaker's professionalism that police
were initially unable to trace any leads. Until, that is, a few days
later, when the homeowner discovered an unaccountably high
phone bill. The itemised statement listed the numbers of nearly all
of his immediate family and some other sought-after villains who
are now helping police with their enquiries.

CELL PHONE

Police responded quickly after receiving a call from an agitated woman informing them that there was a drunk and disorderly man on her premises. When the response car arrived, officers were surprised to see that the address was a domestic property, and that 'the individual in a drunken and disorderly state' turned out to be the woman's husband. Furthermore, he was sleeping peacefully on the lounge carpet.

The two constables patiently explained that there was nothing in current law that enabled them to charge a man for being drunk in his own house. The woman contested this verdict, stating that she had seen the police pick up drunks from the pavement and take them into custody. Once again, the two officers explained, with eroding patience, that this was different to being inside one's own private property, and not blocking a public highway.

Suddenly the woman became newly compliant, accepting the officers' explanation and thanking them for explaining their justification for being unable to intervene.

She then opened the front door, picked up the prostrate and motionless husband, and dragged him onto the pavement outside.

'There,' she declared. 'You'll be able to arrest him now and throw the useless scumbag into the cells.'

IT'S A RICHMOND'S WORLD

Someone who buys a Porsche has not demonstrated a sensible allocation of resources. Yes, you can pay £150,000 for a car, but £15,000 will enable you to own a car that does just about all the same things, on exactly the same roads, as the one ten-times the price.

Hence, being impressed by a Porsche owner is akin to being impressed by someone who has just spent £15,000 on a kettle. Nevertheless, shrewd and guileful marketing ensures that Porsches are much coveted – and many feel compelled to correct you if you negligently abandon the pronunciation of the final 'e' in Porsche. You're supposed to pronounce an 'er' sound at the end. Especially when you're speaking to a Porsche fanatic and describing him as a 'toss'. Well, you know what they say about men who drive big expensive cars: they probably have a … (pausing to build comedic tension) … better-paid job than you.

But there is another way of obtaining a £150,000 Porsche, with or without the 'e'. Namely steal one. And in the case of a stolen Porsche in Richmond, it was very much with an 'e'. Indeed, several – as a twenty-two-year-old car thief had popped a handful of ecstasy tablets, troughing them down like M&Ms to such an extent that he must have been rattling along the pavement in his chemically enhanced state of euphoria. When he spotted a parked luxury car, his E-dosed brain slowly whirled into action ('if I steal car, car can be sold for money which can be used to obtain more drugs, booze, fags and Elizabeth Gaskell novels'). OK, one of those wasn't true – he didn't smoke.

Unthinking, he picked up a stone, smashed the window and activated an alarm. Two uniformed beat officers were walking two metres behind him along the street, and immediately slapped the cuffs on his villainous wrists and read him his rights. It may be a contender for the quickest-ever police clear-up rate; the amount of time between the crime being committed and the villain being safely apprehended in custody was approximately 1.2 seconds.

However, there is a potential American challenger to the record: a thief in Snellville, Atlanta, patiently joined a petrol station queue and then requested: 'Give me all the money in the register' (with swears redacted). Struggling to suppress laughter, the manager complied with his request, fully aware that the man behind the robber in the queue was a uniformed police officer with handcuffs ready primed!

A BRIEF HISTORY OF CRIME

It may be tempting to believe that crime rates in rural Cornwall are so low that the only thing the local constabulary deal with is the occasional encounter with a drunken sailor. Unfortunately, this does not appear to be the case. Following a Freedom of Information request, Devon and Cornwall police published a lengthy list in 2012 of thirty-three robberies that had all taken place at the same location: a police station.

On one occasion, a tea leaf had managed to steal some, er, tea leaves (one packet of tea) and a second-hand mattress. Quite why, or how, someone could, and indeed would, steal a dirty second-hand mattress from the drunk-tank holding cell is beyond most people's comprehension.

Elsewhere in Cornwall, a local petty thief with the obvious ambition of becoming a pretty thief, stole eyeliner. 'Sporty chick' eyeshadow, foundation, lip-gloss and lipstick were stolen from the handbag of a local woman – who happened to be an on-duty uniformed police officer.

Make-up thefts are surprisingly common, as one glamour aspirant demonstrated under oath at her trial for shoplifting. This young lady had her designer-label collar felt by police in Derbyshire. When asked in the interview room why she had stolen so many L'Oréal products, she genuinely justified her actions to the police by proclaiming, 'Because I'm worth it.'

NO SMOKE WITHOUT BEING FIRED

When police, acting on a tip-off, arrived early one morning at the property of a thirty-year-old male, they made a discovery consistent with their informant's prediction. Inside the garage were numerous black bin bags, all stuffed with generous quantities of cannabis.

Desperate to avoid a debut spell in the slammer, the druggie produced an excuse. The sort of excuse that could only really be imagined by someone on, er, drugs. Starting his excuse with the classic line, 'I know this looks bad, officer, but …', he went on to ensure his excuse sounded, as well as looked, bad. Here it is. He informed the arresting police officers that none of the marijuana was intended for smoking, but instead he was merely collecting it for recycling. That's right. It was for the purposes of composting, not consumption.

Also, the Cardiff resident had been sacked from his last job for smoking, and had decided to give up – hence he would never smoke now, just compost, he pleaded to the police. Unfortunately for the green-minded dope head, he did not encounter a similarly green outlook amongst the policemen's levels of naivety, and he was duly banged to rights after initially receiving a £14,000 bail bond. On his way to the police car, the arresting officers observed a sign saying 'Keep off the grass'. If they managed to refrain from offering that as good advice to the suspect, they were stronger-willed than most.

RAIDERS OF THE LOST LARK

Apparently nothing ever happens in Scorton, a small village plonked down seemingly without too much forethought in the rustic North Yorkshire countryside a few miles from Richmond. Locals recalled that it had only been in the paper once, and that was when they closed the village school. And even this was only the local press.

But the village made the national news with a bang one day in late 2012, as did two thieves when they decided to deliberately drive their pick-up truck straight through the wall of the village shop.

The ram-raiders splintered the shop's door and then detached a cash machine from an internal wall. Piling it in the back of the vehicle, they sped away in the early hours of the morning towards Richmond, the munificent thieves even leaving some banknotes at the scene. Unfortunately for them, they caused another crashing bang when the inexpertly loaded cash machine tumbled off the back of their pick-up vehicle.

A local, disturbed by the commotion outside his window, discovered the cash machine, with money flickering in the wind like the clear-up operation after a ticker-tape parade. Presumably when he informed police that 'it fell off the back of a lorry', they believed him.

Sadly, the only part of the thieves' activity that does not appear to have been witnessed was the moment the returning villains parked the getaway vehicle at the hideout, strolled around to the back of the pick-up, and discovered that the cash machine had vanished. Perhaps they thought it had been stolen. (Typical! The problem with this place: too many villains.)

It is worth noting that had the criminals not lost the booty at the start of their getaway, they would have experienced an equally disappointing feeling upon examining the contents of their crime. The machine would have contained virtually no money, as one of the shop's proprietors informed the *Northern Echo*: 'There would have been a minimal amount of cash in there as we fill it up ourselves from the business and it usually runs out by the end of the day.'

AROUND THE HORN

A part-time shoplifter, yet full-time idiot, made several visits to a Brighton museum, where he aroused suspicion amongst gallery workers, who regularly saw him circling a rhinoceros horn exhibit like a hungry vulture.

One afternoon, these harboured suspicions were spectacularly justified when the sound of crashing glass rang throughout the museum. Sure enough, the horny thief had absconded with the rhino horn. The thief was suffering from the deluded belief that eating rhino horn filings would greatly enhance his sexual potency.

It certainly ensured that he ended up in bed straightaway – as the rhino horn had been treated with a highly toxic cocktail of chemical preservatives, and the thief spent several hours of restless agony in a Sussex hospital.

And he didn't escape the rhino charges. Charges! See what I did there? Oh, please yourselves.

COAT D'AZURE

With the autumnal nights drawing in, signalling the inevitable slide towards winter, a Bournemouth man decided it was time to get a new winter coat. Normally, following the rules of social convention, this would involve a selection process followed by payment, but this man only intended to do the former.

Entering a seafront hotel, he immediately located the cloakroom. Conveniently, there was even a sign advertising the location – a helpful courtesy, which may as well have read 'free booty'. Here he flicked through racks offering a wide selection of mainly gentlemen's overcoats, all belonging to big-framed individuals. Having deliberated sufficiently, he chose a warm, expensive-looking blue azure coat and then went outside to catch a bus to the town's Park & Ride facility.

During the next few minutes he was joined by several other waiting passengers at the bus stop, though only one of them was without a coat to offer protection against the invasive sea breeze. Unfortunately for the thief, the lone coatless individual recognised the garment as his own. He, and the other passengers in the queue, were policemen attending a conference in the hotel on policing and surveillance techniques. The only positive lining for the thief was that he did not have to get the bus after all, but had a chauffeur-driven lift. To the nick.

TREE-MENDOUS CHEEK

Like the overwhelming majority of the UK population, I have no idea what bankers do. But I still hate them. Obviously. Mark Twain said a banker is someone who will lend you an umbrella when it's sunny, but ask for it back when it's raining. He said that 125 years ago. There's a clue about the venality of bankers within the title of their trade newspaper: 'The FT' spells 'Theft'.

Remember all that spent rage and splenetic anger, now surely reappraised as misplaced, we used up on banks purely because of their insufficiently short pen chains? Bookmakers and Argos would benevolently allow their customers free tiny pens, but not the super-rich bankers. Their pens were spot-welded to an infuriatingly inadequate length of chain, like a badly behaved dog.

Nowadays we're actively nostalgic about those old-fashioned banks that just sent the occasional acidic letter enquiring about your overdraft, posing the not unreasonable question 'Dear Mr Smith. We've noticed the size of your overdraft, and just sought clarification as to whether you're still banking with us, or we are now banking with you.' How we affectionately recall the anachronistic bank manager – whose welfare we used to reference in casual conversation ('that'll cheer up my bank manager') – whom I imagined was slightly avuncular and always wore pin stripe accessorised with a bowler – even in summer – and sensibly carried an umbrella.

Remember when professions such as banking and journalism were respected as noble ones? (OK, you need to be quite old.) Those old school banks are now a Wetherspoons or luxury hotel.

One such former bank that has now become a luxury hotel in Oxford's High Street is rather given away by its imaginative choice of name: The Old Bank Hotel. Two students from a nearby High Street college drunkenly stole an ornamental bush from outside the hotel, and took it back to their college.

Hoping to nip a recent crime spree in the bud with the giant secateurs of modern police surveillance technology, Oxford's constabulary was sent to investigate a spate of crime from outside the hotel.

Within five minutes, the police had discovered that the trail led to a nearby college. Literally – as the teenage thieves had left a tell-tale breadcrumb trail of soil from a leaky plant pot, which officers were able to follow along the street, through the fifteenth-century oak doors of the college, across the quadrangle, up a staircase, and right up to where it terminated at the room of the culprits. Morse and Lewis were not required to solve this one.

Mystified as to how their perfect crime had been detected, these master criminals were rusticated the next day. If only the tree they had stolen had belonged to the taxpayers and been worth £735 billion – then they'd have got away with it. And got to keep the tree.

TOP MODELLING JOB

It was the best of crimes, it was the worst of crimes.

One critical cause of the credit crisis rarely receives exposure, and hence it rarely receives its deserved share of the blame: mathematical modelling techniques. Computer advances enabled banks to process modelling projections, which led to huge rises in speculative funding. The three most common models are

complex and prone to irrational performance; they are (in alpha-
betical order): Black Scholes Model, Markov Chain Model and
Naomi Campbell.

Like technology itself, criminal stupidity is constantly evolving
to fit the latest criminal opportunism. Hence a financier at a
leading bank decided that he would tamper with a mathematical
modelling computer programme, allowing a supposedly invisible
sum of money to be syphoned off from legitimate transactions
into his own off-shore bank account.

Arrogantly believing that such mathematical computer models
would be beyond the processing capacity of any but the most
enlightened derivatives-literate actuary, this masterful Moriarty
made a number of mistakes that would make a five year old
laugh over the rudimentary gaucheness involved. For starters, his
illegal gains were deposited in an account he named ... there's
a spectacular example of ineptitude coming up, so do prepare
yourself ... 'The Slush Fund Account'. Obviously that was the
best possible name to camouflage it from any potential prying
auditors, a bit like painting 'Stolen' on your car, or 'Illegal Drugs'
on your holdall before approaching customs.

Otherwise, by the standards of City traders, his scam was
almost legal.

IT'S HAMMER TIME

Why be a judge, when it involves training as a lawyer then practising as a barrister for decades? You could just apply to be an
auctioneer and immediately get a free hammer with the job.

An unemployed labourer was passing an Essex building
site when he spotted an opportunity to obtain free hammers.
He clocked a bag of tools left with its zip invitingly half-open,
like a woman with a teasing display of cleavage. The concept of
deferred gratification being evidently alien to the thief, he immediately dipped his hands into the bag, snatched three expensive
hammers, and then legged it along the road at full tilt.

It was probably during these early stages of his getaway
procedure that he contemplated the necessity of planning.

Since the building site was on the outskirts of town, at the end of a long access road, the thief's initial surprise tactics soon risked being thwarted by the builders' access to motorised transport. Sure enough, the four burly builders decided to hop into their van, to compete in Britain's most one-sided race. One unfit, overweight bloke carrying three heavy hammers and a bag of other cumbersome tools attempts to outrace a white van along a 1-mile stretch of private road.

Rather than apply any hammer-based justice of their own, the builders called the police and this particular DIY crime spree was at an end.

For random criminal stupidity – just like MC Hammer would say if he worked at a museum gallery – 'You can't touch this!'

CRIME FILES

In the highly stressful and pressured crime scene, tension filling the room like a gas, a tinderbox environment where even the tiniest mistake can lead to a conviction, the margin for error is becoming ever more compressed by perpetually evolving police technology. A criminal's freedom is highly flammable – the slightest spark of error and the whole caper is blown.

The difference between leaving a bank with unimaginable riches, or spending the next decade sewing mailbags at Her Majesty's pleasure, can be down to minuscule details. Or leaving behind your full name, date of birth, full address (both home and work), next of kin contact details, National Insurance number, and several pages of folded A4 detailing the entire crime including full name and contact (for 'contact', I do of course mean 'arrest') details of the entire hapless gang and their criminal job descriptions.

Yes, that's what a Liverpudlian bank robber succeeded in doing. And he pleaded not guilty. The jury took eight minutes.

HOT-FOOTING IT WITH HOT GOODS

TV and movies are responsible for building a false image of the villain, often applying a faux cladding of intellect and cunning to disguise the reality of cognitive malfunction. Criminals, we are encouraged to think, ranging from Moriarty to Columbo's confident opponents, are only caught when their hubris causes an error in the otherwise intellectual chess match between the twin combatants of law enforcers and law breakers. Thanks to popular culture, our imagined default robbery villain is often sophisticated, perhaps sharing characteristics with The Professor in *The Ladykillers*, rather than some toe-rag non-entity nicking fags. The criminal reality is, of course, markedly different. And much thicker.

For example, bus getaways are surprisingly common in the world of stupid criminals. Decidedly rarer is the walking getaway, when you have a limp and need a cane. A would-be shop robber in Edinburgh decided to make a getaway on foot – which is ironic, as he only had one good one.

With alarms activated, the grey-haired villain hobbled out of the shop, and the chase began. (You may want to imagine the pavement pursuit sequence that opens the movie *Trainspotting*, where Ewan McGregor's shop-robbing character is pursued in a frantic chase along Edinburgh's streets to the accompanying beat of Iggy Pop's 'Lust for Life'.)

Two shop staff leap over the counter and out of the door, clock the fleeing villain on the pavement to their right, and commence full athletic pursuit. Meanwhile, our crippled cane-carrying criminal staggers, ambling slowly past approaching shoppers. (OK, you may need to hum 'Lust For Life' at 33rpm rather than 45rpm.) The fleeing bandit taps his stick in frustration as he gives up attempting to overtake a granny with some particularly heavy shopping. Whereas Ewan McGregor leapfrogs over the bonnet of a car, this grey transgressor stops for a recuperative lean on a parked car's bonnet and a nice rest after fully twenty seconds of 'pursuit'. His two pursuers are already on the scene, even though they've already stopped to phone the police on their mobiles and never had to select a higher gear than 'brisk walk'. It takes fully twenty-five seconds to catch him, but five minutes for him to negotiate the steps into the police van.

A MAN WALKS INTO A BAR

Good manners are important. When a forty-two-year-old entered a well-known High Street bank in Winchester, Hampshire, his request started out meticulously polite, prior to becoming most rude indeed: 'Good morning, I'm here to rob you today. Give me £5,000 and I will f*** off. Do not keep me waiting or I will shoot.'

Staff decided it was worth giving him £1,600 in order for him to f*** off as pledged. Indeed, he turned out to be a very fast f***er off-er, departing at such speed that he left £350 on the bank carpet. Unusually, his getaway was not a vehicle, but a building – as he fled to a pub next door. Here he presented the money to bar staff, and informed everyone that he had robbed a bank and the drinks were on him.

Unfortunately, he was not a hands-on representative from the Inland Revenue ensuring that banks pay appropriate taxes, but a disturbed individual acting alone. The police quickly arrived to perform their Sheriff of Nottingham role against this modern-day Robin Hood.

A DENTURE HOLIDAY

A forty-three-year-old criminal from Leeds committed a somewhat toothless crime.

A man with no teeth attempted a stick up but had to repeat his rehearsed line 'This is a hold-up. Put all the money into this bag!' more than five times, as he was incomprehensible to staff. When the incident was reported to police, the authorities instantly recognised the culprit from earlier bungled robberies, where he had displayed similarly poor crime scene diction, and promptly arrested him.

AHEAD OF HIS CRIME

A thief was prosecuted at Lincoln Crown Court in the early 1980s for illegal possession of a fence – probably a first in British legal history. The man had stolen the fence and then attempted to hawk it at various locations around the city (thus rendering him vulnerable to the charge of fencing a fence).

Thus the fence fencer had landed himself in court. The jury were instructed not to sit on the fence – which was ironic, given that a witness testified that the arresting policeman had sat on the fence stealer when capturing him after a lengthy chase.

Presumably the fence filcher also asked for several other (of) fences to be taken into account. (What? That was hardly an of-fence-ive pun.)

BURY THE EVIDENCE

When uniformed offers in Bury, Greater Manchester discovered a suspect acting suspiciously in a known drugs areas, they intervened and discovered bags of cannabis with intent to supply, alongside other narcotics paraphernalia and a mobile phone.

Back at the station, the suspect denied that the items belonged to him, stating that the drugs equipment, scales, cannabis and phone had all been left behind by the previous occupant of the house. Moreover, he had been meaning to take them into the police station but had never got around to it until now. Yeah, sounds credible.

He then requested to go home, and thanked the police for finally ensuring that he had handed them in. This defiantly maintained defence was in no way undermined by the mobile phone ringing during the police interview, and the caller confirming the name of the suspect prior to asking to purchase some more drugs – 'the same quantity of crack as yesterday please'.

The police incarcerated him, after first explaining that his cell had belonged to a previous owner – another drug dealer.

BIRD BRAIN

It was the night before Christmas, and all was not still. A thief broke into the pigeon shed belonging to fancier Philip Pearce, who had bred pigeons for fifty years, and swiped three of his precious prize birds. Then on Christmas Day presents arrived, descending from the sky and landing on the roof to bring forth gifts – no, not Santa Claus, but the three pigeons returning to their loft. Because that's what they do: they are homing pigeons. They are specifically pigeons who return home. Clue in the name.

The thief had demonstrated beyond reasonable doubt that he was not the brightest bulb on the Christmas tree lights.

Mr Pearce informed the *Peterborough Evening Telegraph*: 'They were back by Christmas Day … The thieves made a mistake when they released them as whoever took them obviously didn't know much about homing pigeons.' The Birdman of Peterborough Prison doesn't quite command the same authority as Alcatraz, but both birds and their takers are safely back behind bars.

MUMBLING BUNGLING

It's an unremarkable Tuesday in a mundane provincial town branch of a northern building society. The branch has been announced for closure, and the unmistakable shadowed shape of the gallows is hanging over it and the employees' jobs. But they carry on professionally, and dutifully open the shop only a minute late.

At 9.01 a.m. a cashier unlocks the door, whilst another sits behind the desk. Waiting for her computer to finish logging-in, she sips her morning take-away latte, leaving a ghostly lipstick-trace on the rim whilst gaining a white-foamed moustache.

It's 9.02 a.m. and a lone raider bursts through the newly unlocked door and approaches the seated cashier. He barks an order at her: 'Poouuttt th…th…th…th… muuunnnneeee immm bbborgg.'

'What?' asks the cashier reasonably, casually continuing to sip her coffee with her right hand, whilst her left invisibly fumbles for the alarm beneath the desk.

'I saaaaaad …' continues the criminal.

'You're sad?' enquires the teller, the alarm button now located and pressed.

'Naaaaaaawwww. Oh, this is hopeless,' he says with sudden comprehensibility, like a tuned television that abruptly departs from fuzz to reveal pin-sharp picture clarity when eventually picking up a micro-tuned channel. Because he has just removed the restraining uncomfortableness caused by his pinching balaclava.

Pin-sharp clarity is also an accurate description of the branch's multiple CCTV images of the raider's unsheathed face. Combing his hair back into position with his fingers (well, if your photo-fit image is going to be circulated on that day's news broadcasts, you want to look your best), he tries again. 'Right. What I was trying to say was, can you put the money … oh, you've gone,' he says, as the cashier disappears behind the descending metal shutters.

Standing in the middle of the carpet, he rotates on his heels – scanning the room like a lighthouse, searching for any possible escape route or hiding place. There aren't any. He politely asks the other cashier, a middle-aged lady still standing near the door, if she has any money he can have.

'Sorry, love; my bag's behind the screen now,' she replies, before asking, 'Have you got a gun or anything?'

'No, couldn't get one,' he replies forlornly.

'Do you want to wait for the police?' she asks.

'Er … yeah alright,' he complies.

CRIMINAL'S COLLAR FELT

According to professional security guards, a common excuse given by trespassers when asked to justify their presence on a guarded site is: 'I'm walking the dog.' One criminal, attempting to break into a freight yard in Greater Manchester, had even brought a prop to support his phoney alibi: a dog lead and collar.

Rather dismantling his excuse's credibility was the distinctive absence of a dog. Walking around the premises with merely a dog collar ensured suspicions were rightly activated, and summoned police found a hole cut in the perimeter fence. Henceforth a police dog was released to fetch the thief – a real canine with actual, not pretend, teeth.

I'm surprised he didn't claim that someone had stolen the dog – after all, there's a lot of crime in the area.

CAMERA SHY

A car dealership wisely decided to invest in some professional CCTV monitoring equipment when opening a franchised forecourt in a potentially insalubrious area of the West Midlands. Quite how insalubrious was proved on the first evening after the sophisticated monitoring system was installed.

A man left his house opposite the new car showroom. Slowly scaling each individual pole that supported a camera, he struggled for a considerable time to nullify each lens. Initially unsuccessful, he returned home, and then reappeared with additional tools for another attempt at dismantling the cameras one by one. Again he climbed and scaled each pole, then sat in front of the camera whilst he fiddled, tampered, selected the appropriate tool or located a spanner that fitted.

We know this minutiae as his face appeared directly in front of every single camera for several minutes, whilst he was photographed more times than Kate Moss has probably managed in a lifetime.

Arresting him the next day, police confirmed that he was a familiar drug dealer and didn't welcome the threat of cameras monitoring his trading area. Presumably his frequent visits back to the house were to adjust his hair and make-up prior to being filmed.

FREEDOM DELETED

A burglar indented a perfect footprint in soft ground whilst forcing open a window to burgle a property in suburban Essex. His shoe size would almost certainly be an equivalent number to his IQ. For, once inside the property, after ramming as many discovered valuables as possible inside a holdall, he decided to take a few relaxing moments of me-time, whilst still at the crime scene, to check his Facebook account.

When the homeowners returned several hours later, they were understandably dejected to discover that their home had been burgled. But despondency turned to surprise, as they discovered their computer was displaying the logged-in page of a stranger's Facebook account. It didn't take long for the authorities to update the burglar's status to 'nicked'.

CAMBRIDGE GENIUS

A man broke into a Cambridge residential property, rummaged through some upstairs drawers, and stuffed a pillowcase with relatively low-cost items. Perturbed by the small value of his haul, he went downstairs and discovered the drinks cabinet. Deciding that putting bottles into pillowcases was hard work, and that he deserved a refreshment break, he sat down and helped himself to a glass of something restorative from the spirits section of the cabinet. And then another. And another.

Eventually he fell asleep on the sofa in a self-induced drunken stupor. When the homeowners returned, their turning key failed to rouse him – as did a summoned policeman, who testified in court to taking several minutes to revive him.

SCARBOROUGH FAIR COP

Shop staff suffered a terrifying ordeal when an armed robber wearing a motorcycle helmet burst into their Scarborough shop and menacingly demanded money. However, the police were able to intercept the crook as he pulled up outside his house after returning from the raid. But how, Sherlock? Because the bandit's own name was painted on his crash helmet in particularly large lettering.

THE DAY OF THE JACKASS

Two tourists from (old) South Wales visiting Australia on a working holiday became particularly high-spirited one evening – mainly because they had consumed 1.5 litres of spirits at a beach party as a precursor to breaking into Sea World on Queensland's Gold Coast.

Narrowly avoiding swimming in the shark pool by random chance rather than forethought, the pair evaded becoming fish food by opting instead, at the last minute, to swim in a pool with dolphins. They then broke into the penguin enclosure and stole a penguin. Jackasses were the breed of penguin.

Back at their holiday apartment, one jackass (the penguin) was discovered by another jackass (the penguin stealer) in the shower. The Welshmen, aged twenty and twenty-one, a bricklayer and a former soldier, had filmed and uploaded their escapades – thereby permitting a viewing acquaintance back home in Wales to notify the authorities. Branded as 'stupid' by the judge, the pair were fined £1,000 each. The shark pool, like justice for a Bond villain, remains an option if bail terms are breached.

Dirk, who was named in open court, was the smallest of the three jackasses (Dirk being the name of the penguin). Probably best to ignore advertisers' advice in future, and not p…p…p… pick up a penguin.

ROBBER BARON

Bank robberies can appear effortlessly easy in film and TV dramas. You walk in and scream, 'This is hold-up. Hit the deck!' – perhaps with the optional dramatic flourish of cocking a gun. It's an opportunity for shotguns and adrenaline to both be pumped. And to really raise the level of performance coolness, and give the *Crimewatch* re-enactment actors some meat in their roles, you could always fire off a shot into the ceiling as a scene-intensifier.

An East End robber attempted to hold up a bank in the 1970s after watching a similar raid on *The Sweeney*. Unwisely, he fired two shots into the ceiling for dramatic effect, only to be ignored by staff when he requested money, given that they rightly observed he was in possession of a double barrelled, two-shot gun. And was now demonstrably out of ammo.

In his head, the plan would go like this: berate the cashier, who compliantly hands over the money, and hop into a waiting expert getaway motor whose driver flashes you through empty city streets to an awaiting hideout where toppling piles of untraceable banknotes are distributed equally amongst trustworthy colleagues.

And here's how the sequence of events really happened: shattering the tranquillity of a quiet suburban Monday afternoon, a masked armed robber barged into a small Essex branch of a High Street bank. He opted to fire a shotgun cartridge into the ceiling. This caused an enormous amount of dusty debris to cascade downwards, enabling staff to ring alarms, secure shutters and seal exits. He was arrested within minutes.

Newly released but unreformed, the same villain wandered into a similar bank a few years later. This time he shouted an order for staff and customers to 'get down – this is a raid'. Pointing a gun barrel into the face of a terrified cashier, she calmly filled his provided carrier bags. (Nice green touch that: he'd brought his own reusable bags, as he has a bag – and sentence – for life.) After the bags had been stuffed with fake notes that are kept for just such scenarios, the robber then stormed out of the bank to where he had parked the waiting getaway vehicle. Only the car was not there, as someone had nicked it. Bloody criminals.

He then stole a bicycle – this being the 1970s, presumably his push bike getaway of choice was a Chopper and his bell-bottomed flares got caught in the chain. He certainly got caught by the fuzz.

Making a determined effort to top the day's criminal activities with one final charge of 'attempting to bribe a police officer', he was arrested whilst offering two policemen a carrier bag of fake money to turn a blind eye.

PHONE AHEAD

A forty-year-old debutant armed robber decided that preparation was the key to success. Hence he rang up a shop in Windsor before raiding it, to sensibly enquire how much money they currently held in the till. After all, it was hardly worth a bus fare into town if the shop had meagre takings in their cash register.

Without replacing the receiver, the shop manager dialled 1471 to obtain the caller's number, and instantly relayed the information to the police. The woefully ambitious robber then naively rang two more shops and requested the same information. Bizarrely, after receiving confirmation that their tills were healthily full, he requested that they had the money bagged and ready for him to rob, carefully informing them of the time he expected to be there.

Presumably he then phoned up the nick to see if they had a spare cell available for him.

NEIGHBOURHOOD BOTCH

Police in Manchester reacted to a tip-off from a vigilant member of the public. He had reported seeing a suspicious vehicle repeatedly stopping at mail boxes in several locations within the same area of the city. When police investigated, they immediately established that the vehicle was a mail van. And the man was … await the big shocking revelation … a postman.

To be fair to the informant, the van was not red – unlike the mailbox, where the police 'apprehended' the postman, which was emblazoned with a 'wet paint' sign. Otherwise, the culprit could have been caught red-handed. (Like I could resist that one.) The postman had been forced to use a relief van, due to mechanical problems. Perhaps the over-enthusiastic neighbourhood watch member next dialled 999 to report a suspicious man driving Britain's slowest getaway vehicle after he had been repeatedly spotted nicking empty milk bottles from doorsteps.

PUSHING THE ENVELOPE

Surely by now prospective bank robbers have been exposed to enough movies to realise that planning is an integral part of any bank raid. Simply devising a plan on the back of an envelope just won't cut it any more in the modern evolving profession of bank robbery.

Though this is plainly not true in Newcastle. Here, one modern-day Moriarty wandered into a branch of a well-known building society and slipped a note under the counter. It was a stick-up note, boasting of possessing a gun and demanding money. His note was written on the back of an envelope.

Flipping the ransom note over, the cashier – and subsequently the authorities – discovered the name and address of the armed robber. A same-day special delivery to the cells followed.

DANGEROUS ALLIGATOR SNAPS

A fifty-two-year-old ex-soldier was sentenced at Manchester Crown Court for illicitly pocketing £17,365 in Incapacity Benefit (amongst other false claims) after declaring he was barely able to walk. Investigators discovered photos of the false claimant wrestling an alligator in Orlando, walking a gangplank in the Canary Islands, riding a camel in full Lawrence of Arabia costume in Tunisia and training for a martial arts belt in sun-kissed Manchester, showing that he was perfectly capable of enjoying active pastimes in nice places (plus Manchester) and partaking of exotic foreign adventure holidays.

The prosecutor informed the court: 'He had filled out claims forms that essentially suggested he was virtually unable to walk. A large amount of documentation was discovered, including a series of certificates showing this defendant's progress from a white belt to a black belt in the sport of ju jitsu.' Now he's really in the sh★t-su.

After the trial, a fraud investigator informed the *Daily Mirror* on the steps of the court building: 'We all knew the game was up for him, especially when we found the alligator picture. We are all calling him Crocodile Dumb-dee now.'

The criminal also hot-footed it when his market stall was raided and the authorities discovered and confiscated 1,237 counterfeit DVDs and CDs. One of the illicit CDs was a compilation album by The Clash, which contained the track 'I Fought The Law And The Law Won'.

PUTTING HIS FOOT IN IT

In 2011, a Coventry burglar broke into a house on the same street where he lived and stole music gear and a high end mountain bike. Evidently considering this an easy bit of pilfering, he decided – there being no passing babies with candy – to return to the recently pilfered house and help himself to some serious seconds. His villainous dessert course was a motorcycle he discovered in the garage, which he wheeled the short distance down the road to his abode.

Unfortunately for the freewheeling felon, he kicked over a large tin of white emulsion paint on departing from the garage, leaving a subsequent trail of clear and distinctive white size-10 boot prints all the way from the crime scene to his house, connecting the victim's garage to the burglar's hallway. Police duly appeared a few hours later to connect the dots and arrest him.

The services of a highly trained tracker were not required – no Indian scout Tonto-type was brought in by Warwickshire constabulary to raise their wet finger and announce, 'Giant idiot passed this way one hour ago.'

GENTLEMEN THIEF

Police flushed out a criminal who had entered a pub and stole (… OK, you're probably not going to believe this next bit. But this happened. Really) … a used urinal. (I said you wouldn't believe me.)

A forty-two year old entered the Royal Oak public house in Southampton, consumed some lager, went to the gents to … er … recycle the same lager, and then decided to spend the next forty minutes dismantling the used and somewhat smelly urinal from the pub wall. Other drinkers must have assumed he was just taking the p*ss.

Then the police became involved, rolling up the sleeves on their long arms of the law to clean-up this latest criminal mischief. With the assistance of the *Southern Daily Echo*, the police ran CCTV stills of the toilet thief.

The public response to the local paper's campaign prompted the porcelain pilferer to enter a police station in his hometown of

Salisbury with the stolen urinal and admit his crime. The culprit did not stay out of bleach for long (come on, everyone loves a pun, right?). Eventually he proceeded to come clean – which probably involved much disinfectant. The urinal was subsequently returned to the pub and the pan pilferer was cautioned by police. Frankly, he must have been round the U-bend.

At least the usual, well-worn excuse for justifying mindless vandalism was not trotted out – that it was because youngsters just didn't have anywhere to go.

MAYDAY FORCE FIVE BE WITH YOU

So, you've just arrived at the quayside to catch a ferry but instead see it chugging away from the harbour as it heads towards Dublin. What do you do now? (a) get the next ferry (b) steal a moored modern fishing trawler and attempt to sail the mighty vessel miles across the pitch-black Irish Sea at night time, despite possessing no nautical or navigational experience whatsoever. You went for (b) too, right?

Because that was the choice made by two Irishmen, aged nineteen and twenty, after they had miscalculated how long it would take to consume another round of drinks – which is surprising, as they'd spent a large proportion of the day researching exactly how long it took to order and consume a round of drinks. As a consequence, they missed the ferry back to Dublin from Holyhead.

Boatjacking (yeah – I'm claiming that as a word) the trawler landed them in some very hot water. This is particularly ironic as they would almost certainly have been in some very cold water too had the coastguard not rescued them after several hours at sea, picking up a distress Mayday message from the stricken trawler *Le Bon Mawr*. Without any radio ability, a Mayday signal was picked up by fluke after it had been broadcast on the wrong wavelength by the calamitous captains of catastrophe. An RAF Sea King helicopter was scrambled alongside the Holyhead lifeboat to discover their position.

This enabled the coastguard to contact the stolen vessel, with the stowaway sailors amazed to discover that they were speaking minutes later – without any honey. It transpired in court that the robber was illiterate and a former cellmate had scribbled the note on his behalf. Although the note misspelled 'money', the judge had no difficulty spelling out 'prison'.

THIEF'S PERSONAL TRAINERS

Staff at an Ipswich sports shop were discussing whether they had served anyone famous. A midfielder on the cusp of Ipswich Town's first team who once came in to buy trainers was established as the biggest name their collective discussions could identify. Certainly it was clear that no one off the telly had ever been clocked visiting their particular little shop in unfashionable Suffolk.

Until later that day, when a stripy-shirted man with a French accent sauntered into the boutique and announced that he was interested in the window-advertised vacancy for a retail assistant. He soon exchanged his striped shirt for one with a predominant arrow design, after eagle-eyed shop staff dialled neuf neuf neuf and shopped the Frenchie.

They had just been watching the store's CCTV from the previous day when their discussions had failed to reveal any recognisably famous customers. It had proved to be revealing footage, showing a thief stealing trainers. It was the very same man who was now applying for a job, and unknowingly aiding police with their enquiries by completing an application form with all his personal details.

'Have you done any previous jobs recently?' asked the store manager.

'No, nothing for a while.'

'Really?' replied the manager, somewhat incredulously.

ROBBERS GOT CLEAN AWAY

A thief from Limerick had undertaken meticulous planning on how to conduct an armed robbery on a security van; he had watched a single episode of a TV cop show featuring a raid on a wages delivery. That constituted the research effort he was prepared to put into his unlawful endeavours. You can probably guess where he resides now.

ot his Dublin counterpart, after
t avoiding shipping, lighthouses
brewing. They had merely been
cles, and were discovered off the
miles further from Dublin than

Holyhead lifeboat informed the
of the sea whatever; they didn't
cabin light on.' Another lifeboat
BC Radio Five Live: 'They were
t know any nautical terminology
nesty they were quite frightened.'
olyhead and promptly arrested on

nakers, off-licences, newsagents,
For some reason robbers tend to
m of retail robbing environments.
ton decided he would definitely
lains' books, he instead attempted
hermore, it was a bookstore that
and had just opened for business

cept for a tiny float in the till as he
day, the villain risked his freedom
to augment his poor pickings, he
to his loot bag, including a huge
ould look up words such as 'heavy',
'incarceration'.

e of which were priced at more
e assistant immediately telephoned
tted the bookish burglar struggling
, resembling a short man pulling a
slower. The authorities threw the

SUPER GRASS

When officers received a radio communiqué informing them that a man had been reported by several members of the public openly selling drugs in Central London, two nearby foot patrols decided to respond.

They discovered a youth offering passing punters 'weed for sale'. Approaching the police, he proudly confirmed that he was merely ripping off punters, as he was selling fake cannabis. In fact, he was discovered to be openly selling actual weeds. He was arrested for a public order offence.

PARKING CYANIDE

The getaway driver is a key recruitment in any armed robbery gang. His skills can mean the difference between speedy exit or crash, slick getaway or years sewing mailbags for snout whilst turning grey at Her Majesty's pleasure.

One getaway driver was brought on board for a blag in North London. He dropped off his colleagues to commit the raid, and then faced the persistent town centre problem of finding a parking spot.

Forced to park several places away from the agreed spot, he made a crude sign on A4 paper which he displayed in the window, marked 'GETAWAY car'. This drew the attention of a local shopkeeper, who phoned the police. Needless to say, the police immediately recognised the driver as a longstanding professional acquaintance of dubious character and intellect. Backup was immediately summoned, and the robbers ran out into a waiting car which had the words 'POLICE vehicle' displayed above the front windscreen. Their shop raid had netted a paltry £30. But at least they hadn't got a parking ticket.

HEADLINING ACT

Two drug dealers were captured in an orchestrated police raid in Finsbury Park. Both were sent to prison for three years, after being found guilty of intent to supply Class A drugs. Earlier, the local council had distributed postcards requesting the public

to recruit an accomplice who con-
sional villain, his name synonymous
imes. Possessing a crime CV listing
d by an identical number of corre-
d basking in the reputation of being

riminal career, he planned one final
curtain on his lawless vocation. And
as not about to put in the required
ensate by undertaking painstaking
mination to ensure that the opera-
nined by lack of due diligence.
ilding merchants, and established an
ld monitor weekly arrival times of
h to record the seconds taken at each
duced a pre-computer-age manual
asuring and processing his assembled
operation would run like clockwork,
t while and result in a big wind-up.
ed robbery, at precisely 1100 hours,
he car park. The callous pair intent
ir vehicle into life, stamped on the
ly rammed into the side of the van.
le, they pushed a shotgun with ter-
es of the van's driver and passenger,
the back door. Unsurprisingly, they
e.
acks from the back of the transit van
— a sports car deliberately selected for
al, and purchased under a false name
he villains were soon out of the gates,
t laden with bags, and surely on their
t luxury.
eir venal accomplishment, they failed
ing into the car park — the van which
for the honest toiling staff.

to 'place an X marking the spot' if they knew the operational whereabouts of any local drug dealers.

Reacting to information provided from a returned card, police barged into a Hackney property brandishing warrants and truncheons. They arrested two men for possession and recovered large quantities of heroin and crack.

The dealers' improvised hiding place was not the most pleasant. Or illuminated. But the subsequent newspaper headline in the *Hackney Gazette* was much more illuminating. They chose to banner headline their front-page report with: 'Man Found With Crack In Bum.'

I FOUGHT THE DOOR AND THE DOOR WON

A would-be building society thief in the West Midlands fell for the old wasp in a jam jar trap. Tempted into the bank by the beckoning smell of sweet money, he then failed to find an exit out of the building. This is primarily because the counter shutters came rumbling down like crashing thunder the moment he produced a fake gun. With the induced alarm and panic hampering his already limited cognitive skills, the clumsy villain dropped the empty bag that he had optimistically brought for anticipated free lolly, and bolted towards the door.

Flinging himself at the door like a long-jumper springing off the board, he discovered it was a pull not push door. Ouch. Turns out that taking a sprinter's run up to a pull door results in a bloody nose, mild concussion, swathes of DNA evidence left at the scene from the aforementioned bloody nose, and four years in prison.

His hapless thievery continued when he made a further attempt to push the pull door, by which time the door had been automatically locked from inside the building. Not that the rubbish robber realised, since he continued to repeatedly push the pull door like a laboratory rat ignoring the button that rewards a peanut to instead perpetually press the one that provides an electric shock. Every time.

With the bank now entirely in lock-down mode, the door was only going to be opened again for the arriving boys in blue to

cuff the thick thief and lob him into the back of a police transit
van. Fittingly, he was allegedly reminded several times at the nick
that the cell door opens inwards, not outwards.

SLEEPER CELL

A known local lag was witnessed breaking into a Hartlepool
house in broad daylight. Police arrived quickly and searched the
property but found no one there. Nothing was reported missing.

Later that night, after the homeowner had retired to bed, he
hinged forward in awoken shock when hearing someone crawl
out from under his bed. The bungling burglar, who had been
known professionally by the local constabulary for over thirty
years, had decided to supplement his anti-psychosis medication
with a potent cocktail of heroin and cocaine, and had then fallen
asleep under the bed. The homeowner wrestled the rogue to the
ground and the police duly came back and this time found him
– pinned to the landing floor by the startled sleeper's housemate.
He was sentenced to a further three and a half years.

LETTUCE BE HAVING YOU

When a terrifying masked raider stormed into the village shop and demanded money, the armed robbery was defied by a pensioner armed with his trusty lettuce.

The shotgun-brandishing raider was taken out by diminutive eighty-two-year-old pensioner George Smith. Cool as a cucumber, this vinaigrette vigilante swung his shopping bag, containing several lettuces and a bottle of salad cream, landing repeated blows on the head of the gun-wielding hardened criminal.

Realising that the pensioner's bag attack was relentless, the would-be robber decided to scarper. After the career criminal fled from the village store in Speldhurst near Tunbridge Wells in Kent, police linked him to two similar robberies on village shops in the area. His curtailed crime turned out to be just the tip of the iceberg.

The tussling pensioner gave the thief a good (salad) dressing down. Later, the octogenarian salad swinger informed the BBC: 'The best method of defence is attack – so I did. I whacked him in the face and then clobbered him again. He ran off with the gun pointing my way. I took a couple of paces towards him and told him to clear off. And he did.'

Cos it was the right thing to do and the thief got a rocket, a policeman, with the shop on his beat route (beetroot! Oh, please yourselves), commended the pensioner's bravery. Police also recovered a set of burglary tools from the suspect, who was only 5ft tall (maybe he had a little gemmy? OK, I'll stop now).

RING OF DECEPTION

When choosing an engagement ring, there is a traditional convention that the band should cost at least one month's wages. Likewise, in the parallel criminal world, stealing an engagement ring worth anything less than a two-year sentence if caught is probably considered bad form. A criminal's fiancée could then gush, 'Oh darling, you shouldn't have – it must be worth at least four to six years? Certainly a minimum of three years with good behaviour. Oh I'm such a lucky girl/moll.'

Unfortunately a man named Simon (the prefix 'Simple' was added liberally in subsequent newspaper reports) proved he did not have the stomach for committing robbery and concealing evidence, as the twenty-eight year old from Dorchester was caught swallowing a £1,750 engagement ring in a jeweller's in Dorset.

Asking the shop proprietor to fetch two rings from the window display for viewing, the thief used this deliberate distraction to gulp down the platinum Princess Cut ring. After failing to retrieve the item with a strip search, police ran a metal detector over his body, which led to a positive result. A confirming X-ray revealed the exact shape of the ring floating in his stomach, which led the accused to choke on the evidence now confronting him.

Once arrested, police maintained a seventy-two-hour vigil until the ring re-emerged into daylight. Police had to twice re-apply for extensions to hold the suspect in custody, given his straining determination to withhold the evidence. The jewel-gobbler maintained that the X-ray, a sharply focused convincing photo revealing the ring's outline in fine detail, was actually just a piece of random foil – a foil that the police didn't swallow any more than Simon had.

Eventually nature, and justice, both took their course, proving categorically that he was now thoroughly in the sh★t, as was the reclaimed ring. The jagged edge of the platinum ring would certainly have proved to be painful for the swallowing swindler's legitimately owned ring.

Magistrates awarded him a twelve-week jail term, and the victimised jeweller informed the *Bournemouth Daily Echo* afterwards that another customer had had her heart set on the diamond ring but changed her mind when told what had happened to it. 'I don't want to sell the ring in my shop now I know where it has been,' the jeweller said.

WINDSOR HASSLE

A thief called Windsor chose a cop's house to burgle. Not the most intellectually auspicious start to planning a criminal caper.

Nevertheless, the burglar duly arrived at the targeted property whilst the Harrogate policeman was at home, patrolling his own lounge in his slippers. The policeman clocked the drug-dependent (who had imprudently been released on licence from prison hours before his latest ill-timed misdemeanour) ransacking his shed.

An inevitable chase ensued, which concluded when Windsor propelled himself over a 15ft garden fence by springing off a child's trampoline. However, in landing, the flying felon injured his leg and dropped his swag bag, which enabled the policeman to spring a surprise of his own. He phoned a colleague and provided the identity of the criminal hobbling away bagless from the scene.

The carelessly dropped bag contained more ID than is necessary to open a bank account, apply for a visa, join MI5 and work at GCHQ. The crook had also dropped his own wallet at the scene, containing money – which meant the burglar was technically down £90 on his own afternoon's crime spree, as well as losing his credit cards and driver's licence (not to mention his liberty).

On the bright side, at least he'll be getting free bread and water for the next few years. The North Yorkshire policeman later informed the press about his encounter with the injudiciously injured criminal: 'If I hadn't been wearing slippers, he'd never have got to the trampoline.'

LIFE'S A RIOT FOR THE PRIVILEGED

'London 2012: The Olympics' was watched by an estimated global TV audience of 3.2 billion, and its precursor, 'London 2011: The Riots', was watched by an estimated equivalent worldwide viewership.

Numerous intellectually challenged crooks were paraded through the courts afterwards, including the man from Hackney arrested after uploading photos of himself and his gang posing next to multiple stolen items tagged by comments such as: 'A TV that I stole from Comet last night on the High Street. Well wicked. Cops can't catch us.' Not really a case for leaving your calling card with Mrs Hudson to see Holmes and Watson; in fact, Inspector Lestrade would have comfortably solved that one.

However, rioters were attracted from all backgrounds. Including the privileged offspring of a multi-millionaire, who left the long drive of her parent's palatial mansion at the end of a secluded private road in order to, in her own words so eloquently spoken, 'go out on the rob'.

Nicking TVs, booze and fags, the straight-A student was so posh and pampered that her rioting crime spree actually involved being chauffeured from crime scene to crime scene by her family's employed driver. I'm surprised her butler wasn't involved too: 'I've just jemmied the shop shutters open, m'lady. Should one maintain an eye out for the filth, whilst I decant madam and madam's associates a cheekily dry sherry?' 'Yes, be a dear Jeeves and punch that copper for me. There's a good chap!'

The former Exeter university student and school prefect was caught smiling into a CCTV camera at a Sydenham petrol station whilst inside a car loaded with so many looted TVs, microwaves, booze bottles and fags that the back bumper was practically sparking along the tarmac. Sparks and petrol stations don't generally go together to ensure happy endings, and nor do criminals and CCTV.

Some of her accomplices bolted from the scene but were identified by forecourt CCTV cameras. Some of them, it transpired, were released on licence from prison at the time of the posh crime spree.

THE WENDY HOUSE OF CORRECTION

When a hard-working Witney primary schoolteacher awoke to see her car disappearing out of her Oxfordshire driveway at 3.45 a.m. one morning (well, let's face it, it's not morning yet is it, but a strange no-man's land between late night and early morning – hence her entitlement to be in a bad mood), she feared that she had become another crime statistic. But there was one unusual detail that both she, and her neighbour who had also been woken by the thief, had the tricky job of explaining to the police officers taking their statements. They concurred that the car had not had a driver when it pulled away and sped off at speed.

This detail was sufficiently unusual to start powering-up the swirling brain of a crossword-loving Oxford detective (no, not that one) – but the case would have been intriguing enough to prompt Morse into putting down his crossword, turning down the Wagner and sending down the culprits.

For a non-fictional Oxford detective was aware of only two readily known suspects, with more form than Frankel, capable of stealing a car whilst giving witnesses the appearance of the car being driverless. Have you cracked the case yet?

You've been promoted to inspector if you have, as both villains were ten-year-old boys, barely able to see above the dashboard, giving observers the impression of a driverless, juddering, unlawful Herbie or KITT. The diminutive dimwits then abandoned the stolen car, pausing only to spray-paint their names and signature tags on the vehicle!

The police were then able to take the kindergarten criminals for a long stretch in the (Wendy) House of Correction.

LUCKY GYM

After incurring a relatively minor thumb cut from a piece of apparatus at his local gym, a fitness enthusiast saw an opportunity – no doubt accompanied by the sound effect 'ker-ching'! After all, gym memberships are expensive, yet often rarely used. Especially since they sucker you in during those guilt-induced post-Christmas binge weeks of remorseful vulnerability, like a drug dealer cruising slowly past a school – only less moral.

He saw the opportunity to re-frame a slight annoyance into a debt-busting windfall. All he had to do was sue the gym for injury liability. Aware that the size of the claim would be directly proportional to the extent of the injury, the gym member decided to submit photos of his thumb that were a bit Tarantino. He downloaded some horror images from websites of appalling injuries and submitted these as his claim to the insurance company.

Surely he just had to wait and discover whether the size of the cheque fitted both his expectations and letterbox. It didn't. Although the size of the handcuffs certainly fitted his wrists.

Thumbing (sorry) through the claims, an insurance official had immediately noticed the discrepancy between the photos and the injury described. A custodial sentence followed for insurance fraud. Fellow prisoners reputedly nicknamed him Tom. The moral here is, as a rule of thumb, don't do insurance fraud.

CAKING A BUN FOR IT

Many people are currently serving sentences inside UK prisons for something they didn't do: they didn't run away quickly enough.

An example of this prisoner category includes a nineteen year old from Staffordshire. Passing a trendy farmer's market stall displaying home-baked creamy cakes, his monkey brain whirled slowly into action. It concluded with its limited processing skills: 'I see cake. Cake taste good. So eat cake. Now. Mmmm.' His basic error here (and this might be a hampering disadvantage to further criminal endeavours) was to enjoy the creamy hazelnut and chocolate confectionery, with defined banana back notes, so much that he forgot the rudimentary second part of thieving in broad daylight: running away.

A burly butcher from the meat stall opposite intervened by, as he later informed the local press with effortless erudition, 'head-locking the jumped-up little toe-rag until the Old Bill arrived'. You really can't have your cake and eat it.

WRONG MANIAC

Desperate captives will use any excuse, even if it's nuttier than a squirrel's droppings.

Take a Hull man in 2005 (as the police had to after they discovered him shoplifting), who was arrested in a supermarket and claimed that he was acting out of compulsion due to suffering a psychological affliction.

The five-finger-discount merchant, sensing that his incompetence would lead to imminent capture, had taken the precaution of writing down his ailment on a piece of card – a condition he presumably found on the problem pages of *Bella* magazine. Humberside police, not unreasonably for professional interrogators, decided to question him further on this psychological ailment that the thief assumed would be a literal get-out-of-jail-free card.

After fumbling through numerous pockets, the villain announced with theatrical disclosure: 'I am a nymphomaniac.'

This might have actually worked, given that it rendered several arresting policemen involuntarily debilitated with irrepressible sniggers, allowing a brief window for the literary-challenged larcenist to leg it. Instead, the thief stood his ground and attempted to correct his noun selection: 'No, that's not the one. Er. I mean …' he continued, through building laughter, before turning the piece of card over to reveal 'kleptomaniac'.

'Kleptomaniac?' enquired a WPC, before hopefully adding, 'Are you taking anything for that?' (Love a bit of music hall, me.)

MUMMY'S BUOY

A fisherman in the Norfolk area had complained to the local police that thieves were frequently stealing the buoyancy floats from the side of his boat whenever it was moored on the beach overnight. Given that the plundered items were large, cumbersome and, crucially, bright orange, they ought to be noticeable amongst a small community.

Eventually a suspect was caught, orange-handed, in a police net. The bait was an advert placed in a newsagent's window for buoyancy floats, which hooked the greedy landlubber. And yes, the evidence did float in court – whilst the thief went down.

MOTORCYCLE MAMA

Presumably keen to appear on the latest series of TV's *Cops With Cameras*, a motorcyclist from Skipton, Yorkshire refused to stop when ordered by police. This may well have been because he was travelling at a speed in excess of 100mph, so on flashed the rozzers' blue light and a high-speed chase commenced.

The motorcyclist was showing no signs of slowing down, yet the police kept their quarry in sight throughout the terrifying high-speed pursuit. Until, that is, the police car turned a corner and spotted a stationary motorcyclist standing next to his bike, submissively awaiting his capture.

Asked why he had had a sudden, if belated, compulsion to do the right thing, he informed the detaining officers that his mother was driving the car in front of him, and he would not have felt comfortable overtaking her at 100mph.

POLICEMAN CHASES HIMSELF AND AVOIDS CAPTURE

Tabloids have evolved their own language. Only in this context can you expect to hear officials referred to as 'bungling', academics as 'boffins', Swedes as 'sexy' and voicemail messages as 'public comment' (phew, satire). The damning finger of the tabloids was out in force in 2012, pointing at 'bungling' bosses who misinterpreted a CCTV image.

For nearly half an hour, an undercover policeman chased himself around a Sussex town. The CCTV police operator, presumably a transfer from the Keystone division, was in radio contact with a PC on the ground, after they were charged with the responsibility of monitoring an area which had seen a 'spate' of burglaries (why do you only get a spate of negative things like burglaries, never a spate of something nice like ice creams?).

The CCTV operator excitedly informed the officer that he'd just clocked a man acting suspiciously in the area, and gave him directions to the location of the suspect.

Off the PC set, his step and heartbeat increasing dramatically when informed, 'You are getting much closer to him.' Following radioed orders, the PC was hot on his heels, in hot pursuit, getting hotter under the collar, when the control-room monitor shouted in his earpiece, 'You're getting warmer, really warm now.' He was – it was a hot night – but still no sign of the target, even though he radioed back to confirm, 'I'm in the same street!'

With the excited operator screaming, 'You must be able to smell his aftershave now!' the pursuing peeler felt something else – the unmistakable musk of a rat.

Finally, a higher-ranked officer – presumably a member of the team not on temporary transfer from the Keystone constabulary – identified the PC giving forlorn chase and informed the officer that he had been chasing himself around the streets of Sussex.

ROADSIDE HANGING

A forty-year-old Richmond man stole a car, and promptly drove it into a dyke. The vehicle came to a halt upside down, but the villain was remarkably unhurt – mainly because he had been wearing a seatbelt.

Hanging upside down, he then elected to unclick his seatbelt. Ouch.

Scrambling out of the passenger window, he decided to flag down a passing motorist for help. The vehicle he decided to stop was a marked police car. The officers immediately recognised the vehicle from a description that had been circulated within the hour in the Richmond area, and arrested him. They also found substances in the crashed car, and arrested the man for being in possession of an illicit drug, a stolen vehicle and an acutely idiotic (sore) head.

WRITING'S ON THE WALL

Vandalism is nearly always preceded by the word 'senseless'. This implies that there must be a whole range of other vandalism, some of which is logical, considered or sensible:

'Well, me and my crew, right, we woz like smashing stuff at the bus stop as a conceptual homage to, like, Duchamp, you get me bro?'

'Really?'

'No – we woz bored and we're morons.'

Adding extra sprinkles of idiocy on an already large serving of moronic activity, two teenagers broke into a children's camping site near Stockport, Cheshire. Once inside, they proceeded to vandalise the hut by smashing crockery and activating fire extinguishers. One of the culprits wrote 'Peter Adisson was here' on the wall and 'British birds R gay' next to a picture of a blue tit on a *Daily Mail* poster featuring common British garden birds.

His ornithological recognition skills were too poor to avoid any potential tit jokes. This is a shame, so here are some of those missed tit jokes that he could have scrawled on the wall, appropriate for the different levels of the British press: 'Nice pair of tits' would have worked for a *Sun* audience. Or he could have gone highbrow with: 'George Osborne – the tit right in the middle of quantitative easing' (Radio 4 or *Guardian* audience).

The police entered his name into a computer and traced him immediately. Inspector Gareth Woods of the Cheshire police force informed the BBC: 'This crime is up there with the dumbest of all in the criminal league table. There are some pretty stupid criminals around, but to leave your own name at the scene of the crime takes the biscuit. The daftness of this lad certainly made our job a lot easier.'

COURT SHORT

'I would not normally be the sort of man who would go with a prostitute,' the prostitute-loving defendant announced in court, 'but that night I felt especially lonely.' He had succumbed to the non-deflectable affections of an aging well-known working woman ('girl' would clearly be pushing it) at a notorious red light area in Bradford. He was also in possession of multiple previous cautions and convictions for kerb-crawling, a point not lost on the prosecution.

'I accused her of half-inching my wallet,' he said. To which the woman replied: 'The only thing that can be described as half an inch was …' (you can guess how that ends).

Speaking of how sentences end: she was convicted of stealing a wallet and soliciting, and he was convicted of kerb-crawling. The police even sent a letter to his wife. So he'll be keeping his half inch to himself for a while.

RETURN TO BENDER

A thick villain in Northamptonshire, mysteriously low on money after blowing his cash on blow and booze, ordered a substantial amount of goods from mail order companies, and then claimed he had not received them.

Seeking compensation, or a duplicate despatch of the items that he could sell online for more cocaine and alcohol, he persevered with the scam. Furthermore, he also posted some items of jewellery by various special delivery means to an accomplice dwelling in nearby Kettering (though he later soon moved to Parkhurst!), insuring the items to an eye-wateringly high value.

The accomplice was persuaded to inform the insurance company that none of the goods had arrived. They had. Moreover, the jewellery that had been delivered was stolen property.

The suspicion bell was well and truly clanged and ringing at a deafening volume to attract the authorities' attention. Not only did the courier companies have clear tracking procedures, they also had legible signatures from the recipient as well as the exact times the deliveries took place. An insurance fraud investigator was despatched, and upon interviewing the Kettering-based buffoon, casually noticed one of the jiffy bags carelessly left on a hall table.

These criminal geniuses were presumably signed for upon delivery by the duty sergeant at the station cells.

SANG LIKE A CANARY

Newly released from Norwich Prison and clearly experiencing home-sickness for prison's free bed and en suite facilities, fine communal dining experiences, and exemption from utility bills, a robber made a detour on his way home after being released from prison – in order to commit an armed robbery!

This could be a bona fide Guinness World Record attempt at the fastest ever re-offending. Incidentally, in 1993 a Lincolnshire man surely made another world record – for the shortest time between gaining a legal right to drive and being caught drink-driving; after passing his driving test, he instantly celebrated by downing a bottle of bubbly that had been concealed in the boot throughout his test – and was soon stopped by the police.

But back to our Norfolk record holder. He tasted freedom, didn't like it, and quickly spat it out. Only a few minutes after being released from Norwich nick, he was back in custody.

Evidence that he wanted to get caught was plentiful, although denied at the trial by a subsequent plea. The twenty-eight-year-old man had sauntered into a Norfolk newsagent and instigated a hold-up. Unfortunately, his hold-up note was stamped with the prison name, and even his unique prisoner number. He also left behind a prison laundry bag at the scene, which contained all of the personalised documentation relating to his prison release. Another four and a half years doing bird promptly followed.

Still, Norwich Prison are thinking of getting Delia to take over the catering, to provide prisoners with scrumptious top-of-range Egon Ronay-starred food (not really – I think I might have read that one in the *Daily Mail*).

UNMAGNIFICENT SEVEN

Seven North Wales youngsters set up a Facebook page, blog and website dedicated to their crimes, complete with copious crime reports (let's rebrand them 'statements').

Their website was replete with photos of the gang reclining with their abundant ill-gotten gains, and even contained video links enabling surfers to see broadcast-quality footage of the rapscallions lifting the gear. Intent on improving their burglary experience for victims, there was even a comments section. Then the police arrived. Control, delete, freedom.

The Crown Prosecution Service was enormously grateful for all the file preparation and evidence already compiled for them by the gang. They just had to press print to generate the prosecution's paperwork.

VENDING FOR THEMSELVES

Two mendacious teenagers were reported to be targeting vending machines. These dispensers, which routinely charge the public £1 for a KitKat or a small sugary drink, might be perceived as approaching daylight robbery, but these two youths avoided the need to clarify any legal grey areas of what constitutes theft by smashing several machines with a coal hammer.

Police eventually caught one of the gang hammer-handed in Portsmouth. His suspected accomplice was picked up shortly afterwards, but there was only evidence to ensure a conviction for one of the duo ... until bail was given to the charged offender, which prompted the required sum to be posted by his accomplice – predominantly in coins! Coins that turned out to be traceable to an early vending-machine raid where owners had invested in additional security measures.

With the other gang member now eligible to be charged, it still took a long time for the penny to drop.

GRASS SNAKE

When a group of students moved into their new accommodation, it represented a big moment in their lives: the first time they had moved away from the reassuring familiarity of home.

Unfortunately, one of the group nicked another student's cannabis spliff from the kitchen table. And the crime was repeated later the same day – the second time in a day he had robbed the joint (so to speak).

This rendered the cannabis owner rightly angry – well, as angry as a dopehead can get. He challenged his flatmates, but the light-fingered marijuana thief remained at large. Although you would have thought the culprit might have been easy to identity in a police line-up ('wow like this row is, like, oh wow, so amazing man').

Instead, with the crime unresolved and the student fearful that his flatmates would continue pinching his drugs, he rang the police to report the crime. He was clearly two joints and a pipe short of a stash. The rozzers took his rizzlers.

WASHED UP THIEF

A bungled cash delivery robbery, which ended more *Carry On Thieving* than *Ocean's Eleven*, concluded with two thieves snatching a briefcase containing 'a very small amount of money as it was a wet weekday in winter', which immediately sprayed them with security dye.

Then two security guards comfortably overpowered the thieving duo, one of whom was heard to express concern about whether the dye would come out of his hoodie (there's an advertising demographic widely ignored and as yet untapped by the washing powder ad execs: 'hoodie, trainers and burglar's jemmy stained by difficult-to-remove security dye? Why not try new …').

Another criminal so inept that he failed to acknowledge security dye on banknotes, rendering them identifiable as stolen property, was a Birmingham-based armed robber who disguised

himself as Ali G. After being chased out of a shop for attempting to pass the clearly nicked notes, this criminal genius decided to put the banknotes in his washing machine.

Hopefully he was also charged with attempted money laundering.

READ HIS WRITES

Police in Oakham, Leicestershire, who were engaged in fighting a local crime spree, were pleased to have identified a witness whom they believed would be able to assist with their enquiries. Officers were despatched to take down the witness's statement, a seemingly routine procedure that immediately strayed a considerable distance from routine and wandered off into the comically surreal.

Having informed the officers that he was entirely illiterate, the policemen reassured him that this could be countered by one of them adopting the role of scribe, whilst the other would read back his colleague's handwriting afterwards so the witness could confirm that those were his spoken words.

Procedurally bound, the police also informed the witness that his statement would be preceded by the phrase 'I, the witness, being unable to read or write, hereby spoke the following declaration'.

Once all parties clarified that they understood the procedure, the statement was taken down orally. Here's the first line: 'I discovered that the deceased had been murdered when I read about it in the *Rutland Times*.' Nothing suspicious about that.

THEY HOOT HORSES DON'T THEY?

The thinking behind this was decidedly woolly. Woollier than Sarah Lund riding a woolly mammoth. Woollier than a horse's winter coat.

One grey Welsh afternoon in the winter of 2011, an Irishman arrived at the station in the centre of Wrexham during rush hour and purchased two tickets from the automated machine. Nothing unusual about that routine station activity, you may think. One ticket for him, and another for his travelling companion: a white horse. Yeah, I thought that last bit was unusual too.

He then led the horse across the bridge and onto the far platform, where he awaited the arrival of the train to Holyhead. 'Neigh,' said the onrushing station staff (and horse, obviously), pointing out that horses were forbidden from travelling on passenger trains as it was not a safe mechanism for equine transport. Turns out it's acceptable to pack humans into rush-hour trains with our faces stuck to the windows like rear windscreen Garfield toys, but not horses.

A train coming into the station sounded the horn to warn the strikingly pure white horse away from the dangerous platform edge. The man had earlier gone into a central Wrexham pub with his white horse. No, that is a reported fact, not the opening line of a joke. And no, the barman did not say to the white horse 'We sell a whisky named after you' (in the unlikely event you haven't heard it, the horse replied: 'What, Eric?').

In spite of breaking the law, and triggering the involvement of the local constabulary, transport police and RSPCA, the illicit

horse transporter allegedly accused station staff of not knowing the law. In fact, it is illegal to transport a horse on a passenger train – that's why on commuter trains you only see abandoned *Metro* newspapers, and rarely *Racing Post* or *Horse & Hound*. The man was also later spotted taking the horse to a nearby hospital.

The white horse was also reportedly seen tied up outside a well-known local massage parlour – presumably the horse wasn't the only one getting his oats.

TO CATCH APERITIF

Sozzled burglar Nigel of Kidderminster awoke from a lengthy sleep, then opened his cupboard doors one afternoon to encounter the horrifying discovery that he was completely out of booze.

Where could the booze have gone? Had he been capable of remembering any of the last thirty-six hours, then, as the only witness to the disappearance of numerous bottles of beer, wines and spirits, he could have pieced together a convincing testimony leading to the watertight conviction of the only culprit: himself.

Yet Nigel had neither time nor inclination to discover where his booze had gone. Clinking numerous empties into the recycling bin still failed to provide him with any clues or insight, but he was aware that he must get to the local off-licence.

Grabbing some cooking sherry and a particularly lively 'blended wine, product of Moldova' supplemented by some less well-known brands of vodka, he approached the till. Opening his wallet, he discovered innumerable receipts for booze from this same shop, but nothing else in the wallet that would enable him to add to his receipt collection. For he had no cash, and only a credit card that had been declined more times than Carol Vorderman has had forty-nine-year-old birthdays.

Nigel knew he had to think quickly. He was beginning to experience a brand new feeling, and he didn't like it: sobriety. Furthermore, he was aware that the longer he continued without replenished drink, the more his condition would deteriorate.

Then fate intervened. He passed a pub. His brain operated in slow motion. Pub = drink. Drink = good. Pub + money = drink. Not good. So he sneaked into the pub. It was early and staff were just opening for the evening at 6 p.m. Filling up on free peanuts – why waste money on food that could be better spent on booze? – he decided to slip several trays of free peanuts into his pocket. Admittedly this crime was literally peanuts, and, since they were free, it was not technically a crime. His next action was less criminally ambiguous.

Deciding to have a drink after his dinner, his nutty crime spree ended with him jumping behind the bar, yanking off several bottles of spirits, dipping his hands into the cash till, and then legging it towards the door.

The landlord chased him, and two customers entering the pub complied with the request to block the door. The barman then instigated siege negotiation skills: he offered the alcoholic assailant a free pint and said that he could stay and drink, as long as he returned the cash and bottles of spirits. The thirsty thief complied. The police duly arrived.

Nigel received a significantly reduced sentence since he had agreed to await the police's arrival without a struggle in return for a pint. However, the discovery of numerous bottles on his person (which he had nicked from the off-licence a few minutes earlier) didn't help his case.

DROPPING IN FOR A CHAT

A violent youth was out clubbing (i.e. at a night club) one Saturday evening in Hammersmith when he initiated a pernicious altercation with another youth, culminating in a prolonged clubbing (i.e. with baseball bats). The club's security personnel succeeded in breaking up the fight before it spilled out onto the main dance floor, and restrained the perpetrator to await the arrival of the police.

However, the youth had other plans, as he bolted through a fire exit and then escaped onto the building's roof. Two doormen pursued him, and a precarious rooftop chase ensued, ending

when the violent assailant, his self-preservation instinct neutral-
ised by drugs and drink, decided to evade his pursuers by jumping
through a skylight.

The skylight belonged to the local police station, where the
suspect was immediately arrested. He was subsequently charged
with criminal damage to the nick's ceiling window too – now
rebranded as a drop-in centre for offenders.

POLICE GET A LEAD

Arresting a menacingly short-haired individual straining to keep a
pit bull terrier connected to a lead, two police officers reminded
the suspected drug dealer of his rights. They then proceeded to
ask the Manchester-based prisoner whether he had third party
insurance as a dangerous dog owner.

'No,' retorted the prisoner.

'And why not?' enquired the police with some concern, given
that failure to obtain third party insurance would render him
guilty of a further criminal offence – after all, compliance with
the law is hardly voluntary.

'Because,' explained the about-to-be jailbird, 'he doesn't drive.'

The man, along with his unmuzzled snapping canine delinquent, were taken into cells and kennels – after belts and collars
were removed by the custody sergeant. Though the dog was
surely not considered worthy of suicide watch.

THE ROAD TO WIGAN PRISON

Twenty-year-old Stephen was due to appear in Wigan Magistrates'
Court. Unfortunately he had a bag of cannabis with him. Insight
gradually dawned that this might not look good in court – his
plea of not guilty for possession might be slightly weakened by
skinning up a joint in the dock.

So he conceived a plan. As plans go, it was down there with that
guy's decision to quit The Beatles in 1961 because they weren't
going anywhere.

He presented the weed to a court official and asked him to
mind his stash until he had finished in court. This entailed making

two bold assumptions: (1) he was going to be found 'not guilty'; (2) the court official was a massively corrupt idiot.

Handing the dope to the authorities, the dope (cannabis) ensured that the dope (the prisoner) was re-arrested after he had received his original sentence. His appearance in court that day ended with him being found guilty – though you knew that.

DOING BIRD

Cycling along a country lane late at night, I once heard the distinctive hoot of an owl. Soon thereafter I heard the owl hooting again for a second and third time. Eventually I decided to pull over and let him drive past, as I stood silhouetted in his headlights. Bloody owls with flash cars.

OK, so you rightly suspect that story couldn't happen. For starters, owls would have excellent night vision so wouldn't need headlights. And yet, a drunk from Glasgow was caught drink-driving by the Scottish constabulary. And it involved a bird of prey behind the wheel.

He had driven his car off the road and swerved into a tree. Fortunately it was a sapling tree, and in his semi-sober state he deemed both the human and mechanical damage superficial. He also decided he needed another drink.

Hence the Glaswegian stopped at the next roadside pub, which had fewer guests than a dry Scottish wedding. There he decided to have another drink. And another. Whereupon he noticed a stuffed osprey in a glass case displayed behind the bar. For reasons only the beer could explain – as he couldn't when specifically asked to do so in court later – he decided to grab the display case, lob it on the backseat and drive off at speed … straight into another tree. He was charged with theft and drink-driving. Fittingly, he is now doing bird.

★ ★ ★

The etymology of 'bird' (meaning jail time) is 'birdlime' – rhyming slang with a literal sixteenth-century origin. The sticky substance birdlime was used to cover low-lying twigs in order to catch songbirds. A 'birdlime' was archaic slang for a thief (i.e. sticky fingers) and the rhyming slang corruption implied the outcome of thieving: doing time.

FINGERPRINTING GOOD

A hungry forty-two year old (an age by which the culprit should surely have known better) decided to rob a branch of KFC in Avon. Scarpering from the scene, the villain succeeded in taking a bucket-load of cash and dropping his wallet at the counter. Needless to say, the wallet contained photo ID, a current address, his National Insurance number, workplace details and probably a map with a marked and highlighted route to his house.

Police were awaiting his arrival at his nearby home when he returned from his caper, matching him to three previous robberies that had occurred in the area that week. They cuffed him before he had time to consume his bargain bucket.

He will now be emptying out a different kind of bucket daily. In court, after receiving an eight-month sentence, he reputedly gave the sentencing judge the finger; which may have felt finger-stickin' good for the defendant, but added an extra three months to his sentence for contempt.

STEALING FORTY WINKS

An Irishman from Cork suffered self-induced boozy confusion whilst on holiday in Bulgaria. The thirty year old broke into the Bansko ski resort. There the shop assistant discovered him snoozing the next morning, and called the police to arrest him. He tried to make a run for it along the town centre pavement whilst wearing skis. Amazingly, the police were able to apprehend him.

Apparently, the plentiful presence of booze had delayed his robbery getaway by several hours. His departure from Bulgaria has now been delayed by several years.

EARLEY IN THE MORNING

A doubly dozy villain was easily apprehended after burgling a property near Reading, Berkshire. Having leant his head back to consume a small bottle of tranquillisers to calm his nerves pre-burglary (as plans go, this one is right down there with Jeffrey Archer's 'I know, I'll commit perjury – no one will ever find out about it'), the dim burglar then proceeded to rob a woman's house in Lower Earley – presumably after swallowing so many pills that he was rattling like Santana's rhythm section.

Having deposited some items into his traditional burglar's spoils bag, a thick fog of tiredness quickly descended. The next morning, the homeowner discovered the snoring crook and promptly hit the 9 button three times on her phone. The local village bobby from Lower Earley was soon on the scene, and if he was able to resist giving the assailant a slapped awakening, then he probably couldn't resist observing, 'It's still Earley where I am, but you're nicked.'

BEHIND POLICE LAUGHTER LINES

A burglar was caught in Accrington when a man told a joke downstairs, and heard someone laugh upstairs. This was a surprise, given he was at home with his wife and two visiting friends. A nearby police patrol car was diverted to the property, and the tickled thief was nicked.

DRAGON'S DEN OF INEPTITUDE

Allegedly contravening the 1996 Food Labelling Act, local business Black Mountains Smokery was forced by local trading standards enforcement officers to list on the packaging that their product Welsh Dragon Sausages 'doesn't contain any actual dragon'. Pork, apparently, now has a higher billing.

BUS AND THEM

In Tewkesbury, Gloucestershire, in 2009 an ambitious traffic warden slapped a parking ticket on a vehicle occupying a town centre bus stop outside Boots. The driver appealed against being ticketed – mainly because he had legally parked his vehicle in the bus stop, on account of the fact he was driving one of the town's official service buses.

Elsewhere, another careerist warden waited patiently like a spider in a web at a bus stop in Manchester's Lever Street. As soon as the No. 77 service bus briefly pulled into the officially designated bus stop, the traffic warden pounced with panther-like efficiency to slap a £40 parking ticket on the windscreen of the bemused bus driver's double-decker.

IT'S NO YOKE

A Cheshire man was arrested in 2007 'for being in possession of an egg with intent to throw'. Police reports stated he did not have an accomplice. So, no one was egging him on, then.

CAUGHT ON THE RUN

A Nottinghamshire athlete trousered £23,400 in illicit disability benefits, despite being a top marathon runner. A spokesman for the Department of Work and Pensions confirmed to the *Daily Mail* that the athlete had been claiming the highest stratum of disability allowance, in spite of being the top placed member of Sutton-in-Ashfield Harriers running club. Regularly running marathons in an impressive three and a half hours, he also diversified into becoming a successful road race and half marathon champion.

Claiming he was unable to walk without the aid of a wheelchair or two crutches, the self-confessed cripple competed in numerous competitions. Running in three London Marathons, he was eventually spotted on camera. He took only three and a half hours to cover the 26-mile stretch, but required ten months to cover the stretch handed to him by the judge. I'm surprised he didn't make a run for it.

JOYLESS JOYRIDERS

A group of teenage joyriders were charged to appear before Bournemouth Magistrates' Court. They had earlier appeared before Bournemouth's high-definition speed cameras, after the purloining petrol-heads had stolen and then burnt-out a Ford Escort.

Helping the prosecution's case appreciably, they provided a different sort of legal aid: the car thieves had deliberately triggered a speed camera to make it flash – at which point the teenage twerps faced the camera to pose intentionally for a gurning mugshot.

The resultant photo even recorded the car's speedometer displaying 40mph in a 30mph zone, allowing their self-supplied evidence to ensure a hat-trick of convictions for theft, arson and speeding.

BANGED TOO TIGHTS

Incompetent burglars decided to rob a Birmingham bookies with face masks that were restrictively tight. Chafing wasn't the worst of their problems, as one of the bungling buffoons struggled for breath, followed by guaranteed concussion when he blindly head-butted a protruding beam. Afterwards he attempted to pull off the restraining mask whilst departing the crime scene. Struggling continuously, he eventually succeeded in ripping off the mask. In a busy street. Crowded with witnesses. Packed with CCTV cameras.

At least he briefly succeeded in carrying out a robbery, before the inevitable capture. Unlike an American would-be-robber who went for the pantyhose identity-concealment approach – pausing outside the shop in full few of passing witnesses to remove a pair of tights from the packaging, and then stretch them over his face. The discarded packaging, rich with fingerprint samples, also gained him a littering conviction. Entering another shop he spotted a security guard, so then tried to act casually whilst browsing wearing a stocking over his head!

A policeman munching a doughnut like Chief Wiggum, whilst sitting in a very marked police car opposite the crime scene, radioed that there was a probable armed robbery in progress. He had barely finished his sugary snack by the time the stocking-faced reprobate emerged out of the shop and straight into the cross sights of positioned armed police. The nylon-headed nincompoop attempted to make a run for it, but the tights ensured he could barely see where he was going. Conveniently, he ended up behind the police van, which then transported him to prolonged custody.

WHAT'S YOUR POISON?

One thick criminal was formerly a long-suffering office worker, who begrudged a rival's promotion. Rather than working harder, applying himself to projects, or moving to other departments or employers, he instead decided to focus intensely on one workplace project: poisoning a co-worker.

Suspicions were aroused, culminating in a hidden camera being installed in the office kitchen area. This monitored the poisoning fiend applying a noxious concoction to his unfortunate co-worker's lunch whenever it was left in the fridge. Luckily, the increased doses were not consumed. This was because they tasted disgusting, and the presence of empty rodent poison packets were visibly left in the bin next to the fridge – hardly the work of a master criminal. Though it certainly helped the CPS.

He claimed in court that he was merely applying medicinal cocktails to the victim's lunches. His victimised co-worker recovered after falling ill from consuming the earlier lunches which had been contaminated with a lower dose. Meanwhile, the poisoner received an unpleasant dose of his own medicine – three years in prison.

The poisoner's wife has publicly declared that she will stand by her convicted husband – presumably whenever it's his turn to prepare dinner.

PUTTING THEIR NECKS OUT FOR THE LAW

When a teenage Sussex shoplifter fled the scene of a supermarket with some alacrity, he leaped over barriers, hurdled fences and was easily pulling away from a pursuing female police officer and two dutiful members of the public. The next obstacle to be encountered on his evidently pre-planned getaway route (intended to deter any would-be vigilante pursuers intent on winning a Crimestoppers award) was a shallow river.

The pilferer ran into the river towards the opposite bank, where he had earlier parked a getaway bike. Whilst the pursuing police and public breathlessly flagged behind and became progressively resigned to the villain evading his chasers and justice, a back-up crime-fighting team of swans suddenly became involved.

Just as the delinquent was about to mount his bike, he realised that he had disrupted an eyrie of nesting swans. Hissing angrily, the parent birds immediately attacked, shooing the swindler back towards the bank, where the waiting police-woman cuffed him.

Reportedly grateful to escape the destructive rage of the bellicose birds, he held out his hands for a cuffing. Doing bird, the villain could ruminate on meeting the long arm of the law (ably partnered by the long neck of the swan).

MAGNET PI

A shoplifter was busily lifting several designer garments when he was himself lifted up by a pair of burly coppers patrolling a Leeds shopping centre and dragged into the local police station for questioning. He was marched into the interview room, and the interrogating officers pressed 'play' on their analogue tape recorder (this was 1999) and commenced the interview. At this point, a loud 'thud' was audible on the tape, along with a yelp of pain from the five-finger discount specialist.

Suddenly the suspect was lying with his face pressed against the metallic table in the somewhat minimalist interview room. This was not a comeback for the 1970s style of police interrogation techniques favoured by DCI Gene Hunt, but instead caused by the accused's inadvertent collision with the table – from which he was desperately struggling to lift himself away. Whilst he attempted heaved leverage from his table-bound palms, his shirt pocket remained stuck to the metal table.

Here comes the science bit. Thieves sometimes use highly powerful magnets to deactivate the security tags on shop-displayed clothes. Leaning forward towards the metal table during the start of the interview, the criminal had failed to remember that he had placed these magnets in his shirt's top pocket.

'Do you still claim not to have any specialist de-tagging magnets, as commonly used by shoplifters, on your person?' enquired the policeman, with difficulty, through a rising smile.

'Nnnn … nno … nnnnooo … help me!' came the muffled and agitated reply.

'For the purposes of the recording, the suspect is now speaking whilst his face remains stuck to the table,' added the interviewer. Accompanied by the sound of much insufficiently suppressed giggling. And another thud. Which must have been difficult for the interviewing policemen to explain when the audio tape was played in court. 'No, not the face, please coppers! Ouch!'

Elsewhere, a similar de-tagging shoplifter in a Milton Keynes shopping centre once succeeded in expertly removing the magnetic security tags, but still failed to evade capture. Mainly because he had stuffed all the removed alarm-activating tags into his pocket!

MAKING AN ILLEGAL PASSING MANOEUVRE

Four seemingly mute villains were netted for committing petty crimes in a town centre shopping mall whilst enjoying a state of inebriation, and were brought individually to the police interview room.

Under caution, they were to be interviewed by a female detective constable. She quickly established that the men were not choosing to remain silent in accordance with their advised rights at the point of arrest, but because they were illegal immigrants incapable of speaking English. Hence a specialist translator was duly requested, but she seemed equally reticent in speaking.

When repeatedly asked to translate, and questioned as to why she and her countrymen were demonstrating a national trait of muteness, the translator eventually repeated what the suspect had said. A visibly reluctant interpreter informed the senior officer: 'I think you are very attractive lady. When I leave prison, would you like to go on date? You like to make love too, yes? You very sexy lady and me big sex fan. You give me phone number, yes?'

Her phone number? Surely that would be 999. When it comes to learning refined English social skills, this was more a case of deportation than deportment. The interpreter was asked to translate the following – which the culprit might have interpreted as a definite answer to his question: 'You are hereby charged with soliciting a police officer in a police station.'

TEA LEAF TAKES THE BISCUIT

There's an old cracker joke. Where do policemen live? Letsbe Avenue. (I didn't say it was a funny joke.) But it is representative of what policemen used to say, in former genteel Dixon of Dock Green times, when bobbies stood on street corners, hands behind their backs, intermittently stooping their knees up and down for no apparent reason, and saying 'Hello Hello Hello', 'Evenin' all', and 'Let's be having you' (hence the joke) whenever making an arrest.

Of course, in those far-off days now safely cocooned in our memories of the past, the worst the police could expect to encounter was someone who had mistakenly absconded with a prize marrow from the wrong allotment. In contemporary Britain, policemen don't say Hello x3 or 'Evening all' – nowadays, the most common phrases uttered by the police are: 'The Met is not institutionally racist' and 'I can't visit your crime scene today as I'm due to have lunch with the editor of the *News of the World*'.

Lincolnshire Police were called to an incident in the 1960s at a house near Grantham. The occupant was a known police regular, the pettiest of petty villains, who was generally viewed more as an eccentric harmless rogue than a threatening hardman. Hence the attending policemen were surprised to be greeted from an upstairs window with what looked like a gun.

'I ain't letting no copper take me!' he shouted down to the attending squad car, flashing what appeared to be a gun barrel. 'No way are the rozzers taking me alive. It weren't me what done it this time.'

'Is that a gun you've got there, Bert?' enquired an avuncular old-school officer in a tone more usually reserved for patiently confiscating fruit from remorseful apple scrumpers.

'No, it's a curtain rod – but if any of your senior officers turn up, tell 'em it's a rifle and I mean business.' Eventually he was persuaded to come down and attend the station in return for a nice cup of tea – and a biscuit.

'What sort of biscuit?' enquired Bert.

'We could extend to chocolate ones if you come straightaway.' Top police negotiation work. Old style gentlemanly villains and coppers – we miss 'em.

UP BEFORE THE INKY SMUDGE

After thieving a printer from a branch of PC World, an aggrieved thief felt that he had missed out on his entitlement to an instruction booklet, and an advertised set of free printer inks that came with the initial purchase. The word 'purchase' probably being significant in that last sentence.

But his main problem was getting his newly acquired printer to communicate with his existing PC. So, he rang up the technical support line, and provided the serial number of his stolen printer. He also requested his free inks and booklet.

Calmly, the call centre support worker took down all of the caller's details, especially his printer serial number and home address, and pledged he would call back to offer further assistance. In fact, it was the police that called next – in person at his given address.

Although they didn't deliver his free printer inks, they did find the stolen printer, criminally accompanied by a pile of fake drivers' licences that had been printed on an older, now broken, printer. Hence the required replacement.

Investigating officers also linked the phone number he had given the technical support company as one that had been used in a previously unsolved identity theft case. It didn't remain unsolved for much longer.

COPYCAT CRIME

There's no need to buy pairs of those tacky fake plastic breasts sold in joke shops that are so beloved by stag and hen night revellers in a desperately misguided attempt at wit. With the advent of 3D printers, boozed-up office girls can take advantage of this twenty-first century technological upgrade to photocopying, and just copy their own breasts and bottoms in plastic 3D for free.

But one immensely stupid 'criminal' – yes, even by the standards in this book – probably won't be using office machinery to photocopy body parts for a while. At least until she's checked out of hospital.

Determined to break through the workplace glass ceiling, a female office employee in a Berkshire trading estate decided to sit on the copier and photocopy her own posterior. She had attended a colleague's leaving party, and alcohol may well have been involved in the decision-making process. As it was in the decision to scan the resultant image to a rival worker she was currently in dispute with. So far, not a great plan.

Being a fully framed, large-boned lady, when she sat down on the small, somewhat vintage, photocopier, the glass surface broke and she fell inside the mechanism. That is how she came to spend an uncomfortable few hours in A&E later that evening, whilst the distinctly awkward embarrassed silence was broken every few seconds by medical staff with tweezers placing another retrieved glass fragment into a metallic medical dish with a satisfyingly loud 'ching' sound. Sitting down was apparently not an option for a few weeks, nor was returning to her job. Her company even attempted to prosecute her for criminal damage.

The lesson to be learnt here is that you're not supposed to try breaking through the workplace glass ceiling literally.

SWEET FANNY ADAMS FOR THE DEFENCE

Frederick Baker of Alton, Hampshire, wrote the following diary entry in July 1867: 'It was fine and hot. Killed a young girl today.' This entry enabled 18,000 residents of Winchester, Hampshire, to record in their diaries a few days later: 'It was fine and hot. Attended a public hanging today.' Baker's diary entry had referred to his horrendous crime of killing Fanny Adams, now immortalised in the common English phrase Sweet Fanny Adams.

MOTORIST GIVEN A WIDE PERTH

Driving back from the pub in Perth, a forty-six-year-old man displayed a tendency to zigzag across the road, bouncing from kerb to kerb. Flashing lights appeared and the police stopped and breathalysed him. He was over the limit and charged accordingly.

A few hours later, the same man was stopped again near Perth in the early hours of Sunday morning, driving a different car, but just as erratically. Again he was breathalysed and charged.

The next day, he and an accomplice broke into the car park where the police had impounded his vehicle and stole it. When inevitably arrested shortly afterwards, the ill-advised joyrider was given an automatic breathalyser test at the scene ... which proved positive again.

He had completed a hat-trick of certain drink-drive convictions in under twenty-four hours.

LANGUAGE BARRIER

Petrol station robberies are disturbingly common. Criminals will fill up their car and then floor the accelerator without paying. Some forecourts have retaliated by installing barriers in crime hotspots. Yet sometimes a physical barrier is not as effective a crime deterrent as the language barrier.

A robber in South East London entered a garage at around midnight and announced, 'This is a stick-up.'

'A what?' replied the harassed minimum-wage Eastern European cashier called Sveta (name changed), recently arrived from overseas with a work permit.

'A hold-up! Raise 'em!'

Pausing to mentally flick through The Bumper Book of English Idioms, Sveta could still not comprehend what the man was attempting to communicate. 'Why do you have sweater stuck to your face? Do you need help?' she enquired.

'What?! No, this is a stick-up. Give me the lolly, now!' barked the robber, realising the evening was already displaying the hallmarks of failure. The dialogue continued like this:

'We have ice creams, but no lolly.'

'Don't push me darling – or you'll be brown bread.'

'We don't sell bread – but shop along road, they do.'

'Are you taking the p★★★, love?'

'What is p★★★?'

'Give me the money.'

'Why do you have fingers inside bag?'

'Because I'm rob … it's not a finger, it's a gun.'

'No, Rob, it is fingers. Is your finger hurt as well as face?'

'Bloody immigrants!'

At this point another customer arrived and the xenophobic cockney tea leaf (or, as the cashier would probably say, 'how can man be tea leaf?') departed, cursing multi-cultural Britain. Whatever happened to your old-time upright cockney villain of the 1960s? Regularly visiting his mum between holding up the jellied eel stall and shooting a Kray associate, prior to robbing the bookies to nick a pony (admittedly that last crime would inevitably confuse Sveta too: 'What? Bookmakers race actual ponies in their shops?').

AGATHA CHRISTIE'S THE SCOUSE TRAP

A Scouse chancer ran straight into a perfectly set yet accidental trap, when he unwisely decided to rob a Liverpool off-licence.

Not only was the shopkeeper a former no-nonsense senior officer in the Zimbabwe police, he refused to hand over any money without a (rather too relished, in the mind of the assailant) fight. Two off-duty policemen were also customers in the shop at the time. Then a police cadet entered the Merseyside premises. Followed by a vigilante, with his companion – a martial arts specialist.

Next, a retired police officer entered, and then two currently serving uniformed officers and a special constable. All before an alarm had been raised, or 999 dialled. A passing patrol car stopped outside the offy, and picked up the hapless scally, who was cuffed with his hands reportedly still holding his head in despair. He endured the traditional palm-pressing-down-on-head manoeuvre as he was placed into a police car, whilst ignoring shouted advice from locals to 'buy a lottery ticket – it's definitely your lucky day!'

COURT JESTER

Elsewhere in Liverpool, a petty thief was back at the Magistrates' Court – a building where he had spent an unfeasibly large proportion of his youth. It was the early 1980s, and the charts were dominated by moody pop stars with too much hair gel – most of whom should never have been bought a synthesiser for Christmas.

The era's hit youth movie was *Quadrophenia*, celebrating tribal youth culture and narrowly defined fashion gang stratification. In the film, a character portrayed by Sting is stung in court by a sharp fine and coolly requests, 'If Your Honour would accept a cheque?'

Likewise, a Scouse thief – failing to separate fiction from real-life – decided to adopt a similar approach, and announced his intention to the empty press and public galleries in a Magistrates' Court by asking whether 'His Honour would accept Access?' (Access was the forerunner of Mastercard, for anyone young enough to not remember leaving home without their flexible friend.) I'd say the joke has not dated well, but that would imply that the joke succeeded at the time. All it succeeded in doing was adding an extra few quid to his fine for contempt.

A FINE EXAMPLE

A fine example (or example fine) of court contempt occurred in Oxford Crown Court in the mid-1990s. A juror had returned late from her lunch break a day earlier, and had been warned unambiguously by the judge that any repeated tardiness would result in a fine for contempt. Stubbornly refusing to learn her lesson, she returned to court five minutes late at 1.05 p.m. the next day. 'So good of one member of the jury to decide to join us,' enthused the judge with accompanying sarcasm so thick that he had to open his mouth dentist-visit-wide to orate the words.

'That's OK,' replied the woman, seemingly unaware of the existence of sarcasm as a concept.

'And could I ask madam why she was detained again from the exciting involvements of our court proceedings?' The sarcasm dial was now turned up past 10, beyond 11, to a newly conceived 12.

'I was sale shopping,' replied the juror.

'And I trust madam's exertions were rewarded?' enquired the judge.

'Yes, I saved £50,' answered the woman, clearly still immune.

'Not any more, you didn't!' responded the judge, banging his gavel for emphasis whilst declaring, 'Fine £50 for contempt of court!'

TIME FOR T

The police were baffled for several seconds when the victim showed them a photo of her vandalised car, with the neologism 'BICH' daubed crudely across the windscreen of her £18,000 Peugeot.

A twenty-seven year old from Preston had evidently missed his vocation as *Countdown*'s worst-ever contestant, and instead instigated a vindictive campaign against his ex-girlfriend, culminating in over £10,000 worth of damage to her property.

When the victim showed police text messages originating from the suspect, with the car's owner charmingly and chivalrously referred to as 'a bich' throughout, they knew they had got their man. Witnesses told the court: 'He kept missing out the 't' whenever he tried dissing her.' The silly cun. Perpetually missing the 't' out of insulting words? What a daf wat.

The case's prosecutor was genuinely called Tim Ashmole – though the accused, a pathological misspeller and middle letter neglecter, would doubtlessly omit the middle letter again – perhaps replacing it with another consonant whenever attempting to spell the prosecutor's unfortunate surname.

Not that you're allowed to do jokes about dyslexia these days – it's no longer considered to be CP. And the law is a bich.

POLICE SEE THROUGH CRIMINAL'S BAG OF TRICKS

A crook attempted to rob a London bookmaker's with a banana wrapped inside a carrier bag. Not only was the bag transparent, but he dropped his fruit-based 'weapon'.

His getaway was delayed by struggling to remove his balaclava, which was noticeably several sizes too small. Unsurprisingly, this was recorded in high definition on multiple CCTV cameras. Especially the bit where he removed the balaclava. Inside the shop. Surrounded by cameras and witnesses.

HOME SWEET GNOME

Although it's hard to keep pace with current EU workplace directives, prospective cat burglars ought to check if there is a weight limit to practising their profession.

A sizable Cornish resident and frequent pasty taster succeeded in making so much noise trooping along the roof of a cottage that he awoke the seventy-year-old owner inside. Angry and unnerved at being awoken in the middle of the night, she phoned the police, and then went outside.

Spotting the burglar on her roof, she felled the corpulent crook with an accurately tossed garden gnome (though to be fair, the target was a big one).

UNCHARITABLE BEGINNINGS AT HOME

An estimated one million Britons now forsake the daily commute in order to work from home, exchanging time otherwise spent in the daily dash to the workplace for extra working hours in their abode.

This was a switch James willingly made in 2009, when deciding to work from home in Cambridge. Whereas some professions can naturally accommodate working at home (writers, IT support workers, etc.), other jobs unquestionably can't (firemen, traffic wardens). But James worked out a way for his current job to be continued at home.

Unfortunately for his fellow housemates, James was a burglar. It only took the loss of three laptops from three flatmates in three days (unfittingly, he didn't get three years) with no obvious source of a break-in, for the police searchlight of suspicion to stay fixed upon James' squinting face.

Perhaps the 'laptops for sale' signs pinned to local lampposts and newsagents' windows, including two immediately outside his own apartment block containing his mobile number, had helped ensure a speedy conviction and were the reason for the jury being discharged by lunchtime.

PURR-GERY

Dogs are the traditional nemesis of burglars. Cats not so much – even amongst cat burglars.

One cranially challenged Brummie thief decided he would break into a house on the off-chance of stealing valuable jewellery – Wolverhampton council estate terraced streets presumably offer stately home Princess of Monaco-type hot rock pickings.

Sensibly ignoring properties displaying 'Beware of the Dog' signs, he targeted a quiet abode. Forcing the back door open, he was immediately attacked by two cats. The ferocious felines scratched the burglar, tearing his clothes to ribbons. Unsurprisingly, he then decided to run away, shredded trousers flapping as he legged it from the cat-astrophic crime scene, where a waiting patrol car picked him up (a vigilant neighbour had dialled 999 after witnessing the suspicious man entering next door's property).

All paws for thought indeed. And a need for a 'Beware of the Cat' sign. The crime-fighting moggies had helped apprehend a local menace, as it transpired police were able to charge him with several other break-ins. The crook was responsible for the local neighbourhood being cat-atonic with rage from his cat-alogue of crime. OK, I'll stop. Cat's it. (Sorry.)

MUCH TO DO ABOUT PUFFIN

Installing a webcam at a puffin nesting site successfully caught an egg-collecting thief. Well-known for previous convictions, he was already treading on eggshells, given he was serving a suspended sentence.

When police arrived at his house the morning after the nest heist, he unwisely decided to abscond. But he was soon out of breath and easily apprehended. He must have been puffin (come on, I'm allowed one).

The eggs were all safely retrieved, with the exception of one, which the thief broke when tripping. That must have left him with egg on his face (OK, not allowed two. Fair enough). No egg puns. No, don't egg me on, they'd be eggcruciating.

FIDDLER ON THE ROOF

A London burglar thought he had located an easy route into a shop to steal cigarettes, as he attempted to enter by the building's narrow skylight. Attempting to just drop in for some free fags, he realised his criminal career objectives had become too narrow. Narrow being very much the problem here.

Since the corpulent crook was at least twelve doughnuts and a supersized Happy Meal above the size of the skylight frame, he became stuck. Painfully stuck. The obese opportunist operator later heard the shop's proprietor testify in court: 'The skylight was deliberately too small to allow human access – it's a basic security message.'

LET YOUR FINGERS DO THE WANDERING

Wandering fingers undid an Essex villain who seemed unable to stop thieving … anything. The Rainham crook was witnessed and arrested by two officers in a patrol car after he had broken into a parked car and stolen a copy of the Yellow Pages.

That's right – he risked captivity for criminal damage, breaking and entering, and theft, for stealing something that is delivered to every household in the UK completely free of charge. They actually bring it to your house – for nothing. Hope they search the pathological purloiner when he leaves jail in case he's nicked any mailbags, porridge spoons, cell bars, bunk sheets, etc.

DRUGS FREE THE MIND (BUT NOT THE BODY)

Since jobs are destined to constantly evolve, there's no place for the Luddite in the modern workplace. Gone are the traditional tools of the stick-up industry, as proved when a musician named Michael decided to hold up a Mansfield pharmacy in an attempt to bag some free drugs.

He transcribed a ransom note on his phone (very twenty-first century), stating that he was armed and should be given six bottles of a specific drug. He also claimed, rather extravagantly, that his phone was a bomb – presumably the new Bomb App that international terrorists have been pestering Apple to produce.

Grabbing the bottles from a pharmacy assistant who'd been terrified into compliance, he then ran out of the chemist's shop. This is the point where he discovered he might have left his own planning meeting before the end.

There was no getaway vehicle or arrangements. Hence, he walked away and hailed a passing cab (very nineteenth century). The pharmacist noted the taxi company and rang the police. The cops ensured the cab company monitored the destination of the vehicle, and then promptly arrested the nefarious nicker as soon as he got out of the car. And I bet he didn't tip the taxi driver.

BAD PHARMA

In a spate of similar incidents, a fix-craving thief barged into a Tyneside pharmacy and thrust a stick-up note and pretend gun into the face of a traumatised pharmacist. She hurriedly collected the demanded drugs that were listed alphabetically on his hold-up note and handed them to the assailant.

Needless to say, the robber had requested highly specific, rare drugs, and when known-users were cross-referenced to the local database, police were able to see the handful of people in the area who had a known prescription for such drugs. Only one of them had form – more form than a top thoroughbred – and a record for armed robbery. This enabled the police to solve the crime so efficiently that they were at the culprit's house before the culprit, waiting for him to return home from the raid. He was duly arrested.

Cuffs were slapped on him, and he received the traditional push-down of the head when entering the police car. And here's the sting: he was entitled to receive all the drugs he stole as a free-of-charge prescription. What an idiot. He must be on drugs or something.

BACK TO SCHOOL

Two burglars broke into a Plymouth school, smugly believing that targeting an educational establishment in August would render the place deserted due to the summer vacation, and therefore devoid of troublesome witnesses.

This was the late 1990s, and they stumbled across a piece of era-led fancy technology: a digital camera. After posing for a considerable number of 'look at me, I'm robbing a computer' and 'this is me, stealing a child's vital educational tools' snaps, they decided to remove the incriminating photographic catalogue of their school crime spree. Unable to find the film inside the camera, they simply concluded that no film was loaded.

As soon as the school staff arrived, summoned by an intruder alarm, they discovered the DIGITAL camera and downloaded numerous images of the villains snapped in mid-thieving action. Unsurprisingly, the police recognised their over-exposed faces from their own abundant stock of file photos, and put the photogenic pair into detention for a very long time.

LETTERS OF THE LAW

There's a prison joke. A man returns to prison and is recognised by a warder. 'Welcome back,' says the screw, 'The last time you were in here we taught you to read and write. What are you in for this time?' 'Forgery, sir,' replies the inmate.

One inmate made use of the prison service's commitment to teaching adult literacy. The reason he was staying full board at Her Majesty's hotel for the next four years was mainly down to a combination of illiteracy and illegibility. He had asked an unreliable cellmate to write on a note the phrase: 'Put the money in this bag. I have a shotgun.' Unable to evaluate the accuracy of the message, the villain entered a London betting shop and produced a carrier bag for the booty which he slid, with the accompanying note, under the counter ledge.

'You've got some hot gum?' asked the bemused cashier.

'What? No! I've got a shotgun.'

'Well, it says here "hot gum", look.'

'No, I've got a shotgun.'

'In that case,' asked the cashier reasonably, 'where is it?'

At this point, he amended his mission from Operation Get Rich to Operation Scarper. Unsurprisingly for such an elaborately planned professional operation, the abandoned hold-up note contained multiple fingerprints that matched the police's files.

CRIME DOESN'T PAY AND DISPLAY

A Manchester thief decided that car park owners were the true thieves in society, so he instigated a Robin Hood approach to redistribute their wealth. By that, I mean he stole money from car park machines and redistributed it to pub landlords, tobacconist counters, bookies, and the occasional prostitute who didn't mind being paid in small change. Basically, a selfish Robin Hood/*Shameless* mash-up.

After incessantly clubbing a car park ticket machine like a seedy Manchester piñata, the cashbox eventually sprayed rewarding coins all around the tarmac.

The following week, he targeted another machine. Carefully lining up the angle of his first blow like a golfer about to hit a par

5 tee shot, he raised his sturdy baseball bat to the highest possible backswing arc, before smashing the club onto the metallic box with the immense force of every harnessed muscle in his body. Unfortunately, Newtonian physics ensured that the bat bounced off the strengthened solid metal, and a reactive force equal to the one applied cannoned the bat back and straight into his stupid criminal face.

Several teeth were broken. Much blood was spilled. Many months of liberty were lost. Other car park users dialled 999 and asked simultaneously for two of the emergency services.

Ironically, once he is released from prison, he will face a hefty and outrageous clamping release fee from the car park to retrieve his getaway vehicle – now, that is criminal.

FIFTY SHADES OF GROT

She was a twenty-something submissive student called Anastasia, who knew that she had been a very naughty girl and needed to be punished. As she slid seductively through the pages of E.L. James' inexplicably successful novel, she emitted a tiny, 'Ouch, this is painful stuff … Ow! Ouch!'

She shrilled harder, like she was enduring a bad simile but thought 'I can take it'. 'Ow-ow-ow,' she squealed, enduring a merciless third blow of trite over-plotting. But part of her craved yet more punishment. Her young, luscious yet vulnerable feminine frame shook in anticipation of receiving another sting of inelegantly expressed innuendo, overladen adverbs and jejune characterisation, causing a sigh of, 'I deserve it for being such a bad girl.'

Writhing, she experienced yet more lazily constructed character development landing on her, with no recovery time permitted before enduring a further stinging blow of contrite literary indulgence, as she recognised the unmistaken swoosh of hack writing. 'I think you're ready to move to the next level,' she seemed to hear the author remark, and duly reeled as another laborious metaphor got lost. Finally, when a misused correlative conjunction was unleashed, she realised she just couldn't take this much punishment. Anastasia called out, 'Please stop!' But she was in the hands of dominant author E.L. James and would be willingly returning, submissively suffering many more of her torturous books.

OK, so that's a parody of E.L. James – in no way motivated by the fact her sales figures are slightly greater than mine.

But *Fifty Shades of Grey* has sparked several legal events. Such as the genuine case of a man who successfully divorced his wife for her unreasonable rise in sexual expectation, after the novel had allegedly transformed her into a terrifying dominatrix.

The book has caused women to do things in the bedroom they would never have considered before (like cleaning the skirting board and dusting, rather than reading that ridiculous novel).

It also caused a middle-aged lady to experiment with doing naughty things for the first time. In this particular case, shoplifting. Entering a branch of a well-known British book chain in the East Midlands, she had intended to purchase the E.L. James bestseller (or so she briefed her defence counsel before the magistrates' hearing that cost her a fine far greater than the cover price of the book).

She testified in court that she had become embarrassed at being seen taking the title to the checkout, and was afraid of being judged by the assistants and assembled customers. So instead, she slipped a copy in her bag and legged it. Unaccustomed to getaways, and slowed by a recently replaced hip joint, she stopped to allow a security guard (who was gaining on her without seemingly having to move any faster than his normal walking speed) to apprehend her. Hence she was surprised when he ignored her, instead brushing past to pursue a slightly younger woman. A chase ensued, and the uniformed store security accosted the other woman. She had been attempting to steal a copy too. The guard then returned to apprehend the older erotic-fiction snaffler as well.

The vigilant store security had ensured that the only thing being pinched was the shoulders of inexpert debut shoplifters, preferring the shame of a court appearance to appearing in front of a cashier clutching *Fifty Shades of Grey*.

Both stolen editions were the more expensive hardback versions. Presumably they required a hardback rather than paperback so their partners could spank them with it.

Luckily, if it was punishment they were after, the law obliged and both received cautions.

ONLY CRIME WILL TELL

There are occasions when the authorities decide not to get involved, decreeing that the 'victim' deserved his encounter with criminality.

A man complained to both the local constabulary and Dorset Trading Standards in 1999. He had fallen victim to an advert enticing frustrated men to dial a phone chatline, where an adult female unambiguously promised 'phone to hear me moan'. Once connected to the premium rate 0891 number, he accessed a pre-recorded voicemail of a woman loudly berating and nagging her husband for not helping with the household chores.

The unfulfilled sex-line caller complained. Local police simply dismissed the complaint, concluding that 'he got what he deserved'.

Presumably he got to hear some more female moaning, only this time for free, when his other half discovered his itemised phone bill.

Police also warned him against troubling them with further unwarranted grievances. Though presumably, if he made additional superfluous protests, it would involve phoning up a woman in uniform to be informed that he'd been a naughty boy and would have handcuffs put on him – not bad phone dialogue for a non-premium rate call!

On a related note, has any man ever been arrested by a WPC without, at the moment the handcuffs are clicked on, remarking, 'Oh, that's kinky officer!' Just me then?

TWO

OVERSEAS STUPID CRIME FILES

GETTING SHOT OF THIEVES

When planning a robbery, all potential villains ought to conduct a risk assessment into their likelihood of incurring physical harm. This scale ranges from stealing candy from a baby (a traditional crime for the amoral thief – low risk) to robbing a heavily armed US gun store patrolled by firearm-packing staff and policemen in broad daylight (probable death). Yes, a reckless robber decided to hold up a firearms store in Washington.

Less committed criminals/idiots may have been slightly put-off by the marked police cars parked outside the store. Perhaps the presence of uniformed gun-carrying officers from the firearms squad at the counter may have prompted reconsideration. Then there were the heavily armed security guards patrolling the store, the trigger-happy, heat-packing customers, and the staff: some of whom were holding firearms and showing a customer how to release semi-automatic weaponry.

Demonstrating a recklessness to his own safety that Wile E. Coyote would have considered too high risk, the robber fired several shots into the ceiling and announced that this was a robbery. Several policemen, security guards, staff and customers immediately returned fire.

Needless to say, the robber is no longer with us. And his body has more holes in it than his plan and legal defence.

Other than slipping on his own banana skin whilst a passing trombonist plays long notes, it is difficult to envisage his crime going any worse. Unless his getaway vehicle was a clown car, shedding parts as it left the scene.

SCOOTER LOOTER

A scooter-riding thief had a plan: he would bag a bag from an old bag. Riding around the streets of Bari, the Italian traditionalist evidently wanted to continue the heritage crime his nation is known for, i.e. snatching bags from scooters.

When he saw a defenceless old woman ahead, he pressed down on the noisy accelerator. As the engine roared, he soon drew level with the elderly lady and swiped her bag.

Fortunately, the woman was able to obtain a clear view of the odious crook's registration plates, and immediately reported the lowlife to the authorities. Unusually when reporting a crime, she was also able to furnish the authorities with his home address. Given that he had just robbed his mother.

FACING JAIL

Turns out that the problem with wearing a robber's mask is that it conceals your identity. Yeah, I'd have thought that was obvious too.

One youthful thief spotted a friend passing the Chicago convenience store he had just robbed and called out to him, 'Hello!' But his friend discourteously blanked him. So he repeated his greeting a further three times in incrementally raised tones. Still no response. At this stage he realised that perhaps the ski mask he was wearing was obscuring his identity. So he removed it, resulting in his friend greeting him back.

The police also greeted him a few hours later, after they recognised one of their more regular customers from the street CCTV footage.

In Colorado Springs, another convenience store robber also somehow forgot that his disguise obscured his face. Nor did he find the convenience store that convenient. Demanding that the shopkeeper remove the till's contents into a bag, he also ordered him to hand over a bottle of whisky from the shelf behind the counter.

'No,' responded the till operative, 'as you need to be over twenty-one.'

No one likes an injustice – apparently not even an armed robber. 'But I am over twenty-one – it's obvious.'

'Not to me, Sir – I can't see your face.'

'Oh for God's sake, see … here's the proof,' confirmed the crook, showing the proprietor his driver's licence. Two hours later, the police arrested the man at his home.

CELL PHONE

Inmates at the city prison in Arapiraca, a sizable metropolis in the Mexican state of Alagoas, were enjoying a contraband supply line that had mystified police and guards for months. The jail was somewhat optimistically described as 'maximum security'.

Then one evening in 2013, the smuggler was discovered attempting to bring inside the prison saws, drills, batteries and other assorted hardware. Additional prohibited items confiscated from the busted contraband mule included a mobile phone complete with charger.

Unfortunately, the smuggler would not talk. Mainly because he was a white domestic cat. Even though he had been caught red-pawed smuggling the goods taped to his back.

'It's tough to find out who's responsible for the action as the cat does not speak,' a prison official informed the local newspaper *Estado de Sao Paulo*. You wonder how long it took them to figure that out, and whether they intend to try interviewing one more time; maybe bringing in a specialist police dog might encourage the mute moggy to start spilling the beans. Mexican beans, obviously.

Police announced that the entire prison population of 263 detainees were being investigated. One thing's for sure: the feds have felt the cat's (flea) collar.

ACUTE ACCENT ON CRIME

As if channelling behaviour synonymous with the duo from *Flight of the Conchords*, two Australasian thieves decided that the most sensible solution to their cash-flow problems was to rob a bank. Not just any bank, but their own home branch in Vail, Colorado, where they had become regular customers after moving to the US state to seek seasonal work a few months earlier. Possessing unique accents in small-town America had ensured they were well known around the town.

These incredibly distinctive New Zealand and Australian voices initially gave the game away as the dumb duo were clearly identifiable to the bank's tellers, even with their ridiculously shoddy disguises. Their decision to wear ski masks meant that they struggled to convince staff it was a robbery. One of the cashiers later told Australian TV: 'Seeing two guys wearing ski masks really didn't mean much in a ski town.' Then they demanded ALL the money in the bank! The startled teller later recollected: 'I remember thinking, "You're so stupid! You want to carry $5,000 in one dollar bills!".' She had a point – they couldn't carry the spoils from the bank.

Arguably intent on giving themselves away and aiding the prosecutor's workload, they subsequently took photos of each other displaying the loot in a McDonald's toilet, posing triumphantly with bundles of cash from the bungled $150,000 raid.

Their getaway plan was the snow-capped summit of idiocy atop Mount Stupid. They had planned to use the ski lift as a getaway vehicle, and then snowboard home!

Numerous other clues that were left before, during and after the bank raid were described by police as 'laughable' to the local newspaper, which dubbed the pair 'Dumb and Dumber'. Picked up by the Feds within eight minutes, the two Dumbs each received five years breaking rocks in a high-security US prison.

BLOW YOUR SOCKS OFF

When the notorious underpants bomber Umar Farouk Abdulmutallab was asked at airport security if he was carrying any hazardous substances, his reply must have been a lie. And it is appropriate that a liar should end up with his pants very much on fire. Still, you have to admire his balls – particularly when they were destined to become incandescent twin fire balls.

As acts of stupid criminality go, it certainly raises the bar several scorched notches higher for others to follow with Road-Runner-like cartoonish exploding slapstick ineptitude. He bought a one-way ticket. Paid £3,000 in cash. Had no luggage. And then looked forward to seeing seventy-two virgins in paradise – which must surely always constitute a hard sell to a suicide bomber's wife. This seventy-two-virgin reward would also have been incontestably compromised by the fact he would have just blown off his groin. Other than that – genius plan.

Although living with seventy-two girls may sound like a male fantasy, think of the bathroom queuing time. Plus some contemporary scholars argue that the conviction is based on a mistranslation, and martyrs will actually receive seventy-two grapes in paradise instead – which is barely enough to make half a glass of Chardonnay. And do female suicide bombers receive seventy-two male virgins, because that's hardly an incentive, is it? 'Hello. My name's Malcolm. I like trains and live with my mother.'

In 2012 a UK-born CIA operative succeeded in infiltrating Al Qaeda, and handed his underpants bomb to the authorities. Subsequently he was described in secret service press testimonials as 'undergoing a de-briefing'. They know how to detonate puns as well as bombs at the CIA.

AIMLESS YOUTH TAKES THE RAP

Deservedly taking his place in the pantheon of stupidest automobile-related crimes is a Minneapolis gangster-wannabe youth. Pumped by rap lyrics, he decided to 'put a cap in his ass' (no, not place a baseball hat on a donkey, but shoot a rival). So he drove around the neighbourhood, looking for his quarry. When he was located on a street corner, the rap fan instigated a drive-by shooting. Only he forgot to wind down the window first. So he succeeded in shooting out his own car windows with shattering stupidity.

As seeing through the shattered windscreen was impossible, the myopic youth crashed into a fire hydrant, immediately triggering an armed police response team. They did wind down their windows, before pointing their weapons at him. The windows where he is currently residing for the next few years do not open.

FOR YOU THE BAR IS OVER

A German drinker decided that 4.30 a.m. was, in his opinion, excessively early for a hotel bar to shut, and so he took matters (as well as the bar grille that had just descended to close the bar) into his own hands. He pulled off the metal rails and continued to help himself and his rowdy friends to free booze.

The barmaid contacted the polizei, who came and arrested the illicit nocturnal drinkers. It transpired that the boozy free-loaders were a gang celebrating a robbery, and were currently being sought by the police. They all got three years – that's drei in German, pronounced 'dry', as in their living conditions for the next three years. That accommodation is, however, replete with bars.

TABLET THEFT

Tablet thefts are becoming depressingly common. Even so, a Baptist churchgoer in Murfreesboro, near Knoxville, Tennessee was not expecting her tablet to be stolen.

Two weeks earlier she had piously erected a 3ft-high concrete slab outside her house, displaying the text of the Ten Commandments. Regrettably, thieves did not stop to consider all of the commandments – or at least they certainly did not read as far down as the eighth commandment.

Perhaps these bad boys are using the tablet as an impractically sized checklist to tick off all ten. Nobly, the victim of the crime informed the local press of her intention to forgive the perpetrators. Though it is unlikely anyone today would actively be coveting someone's ox – unless playing Scrabble.

THE TEXAS CHAIN STORE MASSACRE

Determined to prove there is such a thing as the perfect crime, a Texan spent months planning a heist so clever that the authorities would have to go head-hunting at Bletchley Park to stand any chance of solving it.

The moderately sized Texas town that he called home was still large enough to boast two separate branches of the same Mexican restaurant. And this gave the robber an idea. Given it's an idea contained in a book celebrating criminal ineptitude, you are correctly assuming it was not a particularly enlightened scheme.

In summary, this is the plan that would have been written on the blackboard in his hideaway: Obtain phone numbers of both branches of the Mexican chain restaurant. Anonymously telephone the cops and report that you are a witness to an armed robbery at one branch. Then (and you can almost see the smug, tongue-sticking-out moment of self-declared genius recognition when he first had this idea) rob the other branch across town, whilst the police are responding to a reported robbery at the fraternal branch.

Cometh the crime hour, cometh the policeman. As planned, he dialled the cops and reported a robbery, quoting the specific address of the first Mexican take-away branch from the eatery's own leaflet. He then waited five minutes to allow the peelers to respond to the initial incident and make their way across town. He even heard several cop car sirens, confirming that his plan was working since all available cars must presumably be on their way to an armed robbery response.

Pausing only to check that his gun was fully loaded, the IQ-challenged criminal then walked into the perceived other branch of the Mexican chain restaurant, shot a bullet into the ceiling and demanded the contents of the till. Within seconds, several armed police response marksmen stormed the building. The panicking purloiner realised his chances against them were impossible, so he willingly took up the loudhailer directive to put down the gun, before being unceremoniously bungled into a large choice of waiting police cars.

It took him several hours to work out why the plan had gone so badly awry: he had mistakenly dialled the OTHER branch of the chain, kindly announcing to the authorities that he would shortly be robbing a restaurant. He even helpfully provided the postcode for the police to put into their SatNav. Maybe he will be eligible to receive a Crimestoppers award?

A SHOWER OF BULLETS

When a burglar broke into a Texas home whilst the owners were at work, he ignored the housebreaker's charter of getting in and out as quickly as possible. Indeed, he took his time. This was going to be a leisurely burglary. As it was a Friday, and the burglar had turned up in T-shirt and jeans instead of his usual black burglar's hoodie, it was presumably also dress-down day in the workplace.

The robber put on the homeowner's slippers, liberally helped himself from the drinks cabinet, and, after filling a rucksack with jewellery and cash, decided to have a shower. Well, you would, wouldn't you? Perhaps he misunderstood the concept of making a clean getaway.

At the exact moment that the thief was frothing shampoo into his hair, and singing a Mariah Carey song (a detail for which the judge hopefully added a few extra months on his sentence), the owner of the property returned.

Whilst the burglar grabbed a lather, the returned homeowner grabbed a semi-automatic weapon.

Fearing that he would probably be shot – with this being gun-toting, pistol-packing, shrapnel-extracting Texas – the burglar dialled 911 himself to report a man trespassing inside the property. He decided this course of action was preferable to picking pellets out of his posterior.

Asked by the 911 operator to describe the man, he was – unsurprisingly – able to give quite an accurate description. Texas operates a law known colloquially as 'castle law', which governs homeowners' rights to basically massacre anyone in their property who they suspect may be trespassing. It's a 'shoot first, ask questions at the coroner's inquest later' type of vigilante's law and order policy.

The homeowner also dialled 911. The police came and arrested the showering cowering crook.

When the *Daily Mail* covered the story, its reader comments section drew the usual array of xenophobes, society-rejecting survivalists, and self-declared right-wing American nutjob 'freedom-lovers' who evangelised the right for gun ownership. One reasonable and well-adjusted British commentator remarked that had this scenario occurred in the UK, 'the householder would probably be prosecuted for not providing an anti-slip shower mat!'.

Meanwhile, 'Ann from Houston' sensitively adds her liberal opinion: 'Squatters aren't rare in Texas – they simply don't exist! Trespass is criminal here. BOOM, BOOM!!' The sinister addition of 'Boom Boom!!' is not a tribute to vulpine comedy genius Basil Brush, but more likely the illustrative sound of her firing a gun for emphasis as she types – her neighbours in the upstairs apartment probably being used to dodging bullets which appear vertically through their floorboards.

THE CLINTON ADMINISTRATION

Hillary Clinton has made several attempts to become the first
woman to be positioned behind the desk in the Oval Office (not
counting Monica Lewinsky). It would be a blow for her husband
too (… OK, I'll move on …) if she never became President.

A conspicuously stupid criminal thought that he could rob a
convenience store. And assumed that whilst he was out spending
the proceeds of the crime, Secretary of State Hillary Clinton
would be taking the rap. It was such a genius plan that failure
was beyond comprehension. Unfortunately, there were numerous
other concepts beyond this particular criminal's comprehension.
See if you can spot any.

Simply by putting on a cardboard photo mask of Hillary
Clinton's face, this well-built, heavy male believed his own face
was rendered indistinguishable from the actual Hillary. And
that the cops would be putting out an arrest warrant for her
as soon as 'she' entered the convenience store packing heat and
demanding the takings.

In reality, his inspired idea was so defective that it is perhaps
surprising to discover it is a recycled one. A few Republicans,
probably alarmed that giving a poor person some health
treatment meant America had become indistinguishable from
the Stalinist-era Soviet Union and was now actively toppling
towards a European ideology (or the self-styled EUSSR as they
would probably call it), had attended a protest wearing Hillary
Clinton face masks. They were campaigning that she had stolen
the American taxpayers' money and should therefore be held
responsible for 'crime'. This had provided the vacuous villain with
his second-hand idea.

When the day of the crime arrived, the robber entered a small
convenience store, pulled out a gun, and hollered for the takings
to be put into his distinctive bag that even had the name of a small
traceable gym emblazoned on it.

Driving his own conspicuous car back to his house, with
licence plates monitored by several CCTV cameras, he
proceeded to tip out the $18.24 that he had succeeded in stealing.

Apparently the cost of the Hillary Clinton mask, including shipping, had come to $19.99. Hence he had actually lost money in the robbery. Not to mention the next few years of his liberty, after being convicted of armed robbery. He discovered he had something else in common with Hillary Clinton: both were looking for a four-year term.

AS FREE AS A BIRD

Having secured a job at an exotic bird aviary, a thirty-five-year-old worker decided to take her work home with her. After being informed by fellow employees that one of the zoo's exhibited species could be openly traded on the Internet for in excess of £1,000 each, she decided to smuggle a bird out of the aviary.

To accomplish the transference of feathered specimen from workplace to home without ruffling feathers, she decided to ram the parrot down her bra, muffling the squawks of objection with a padded D-cup. Presumably she rejected stuffing the bird down her knickers as this risked halving its value – given a bird in the hand is worth two in the bush.

Once the contraband bird had been removed to her house, she logged on to the Internet to hook a buyer. Well, perhaps she first Googled a recommended treatment for soothing painful beak bites on sensitive areas, and *then* attempted to discover a buyer for her parrot.

Unbeknown to her – though probably very much beknown to anyone who would contemplate the scenario for just a few seconds – the aviary was monitoring the Internet for anyone suddenly offering a rare breed of Greenwing macaw for sale in the Florida area, after theirs had been mysteriously stolen that afternoon.

She quickly agreed to sell the pilfered parrot to a friend of the aviary owner, who was posing as a rare bird collector. He agreed to swap the parrot for a vintage 1964 Volkswagen requested by the thief – before notifying the authorities, who identified the pinched parrot from DNA traces.

She is now looking at a serious spell in a cage of her own. Though unlike the returned bird, she doesn't receive cuttlefish perks pushed through her cage bars every day.

A CRIME WITH HER NAME ON IT

There's a blonde joke. Two blonde girls decide to rob a bank. They demarcate the roles of getaway driver and robber by drawing lots. The blonde who drew the robber role enters the bank, whilst the driver waits nervously across the street. Moments later she witnesses her partner in crime dragging a heavy safe on a rope, scuffing it across the tarmac towards the getaway vehicle. A security guard, with trousers around his ankles, waddles like a penguin in slow pursuit. 'What happened?' she screams at her blonde accomplice. 'Well, I followed your plan just as you briefed.' 'No you didn't!' says the other blonde, 'you were supposed to tie up the SECURITY GUARD and then blow the SAFE.'

Two blonde female employees of a large German conglomerate managed something similar in real life. They were feeling underappreciated and underpaid. Hence they devised a lunchtime moonlighting opportunity, guaranteed to net them a substantial … stay in the cooler.

Their plan was to be deliberately visible in the staff canteen at the start of their lunch break, interacting with several potential witnesses who could later vouch that they were in the building at the time of the robbery, should an alibi be required. The purloining pair then bolted out of the building, held up a small post office a few doors down from their workplace, and scarpered back to work, where they stashed the loot in their desk drawers.

The Deutsche duo of dummkopfs had only just turned the key in their drawer to secure the stolen cash when their manager appeared, saying there were two uniformed officers and a detective extremely keen to see them.

Even, it transpired, with their meticulously planned operation, complete with decoy witnesses, the fiddling fräuleins had been apprehended. But how? How did the young fräuleins get fingered? (Oh, grow up.) Possibly because one of the women wore her logoed workplace name-badge throughout the robbery!

The German authorities didn't need to have ways of making her talk to secure a conviction. For her, the wheeze is over.

IRAN FROM THE COPS

Iran is not considered the best location to be an incompetent thief. Notorious for removing the hand of anyone caught thieving, presumably a twice-convicted Iranian thief then has to shoplift with his mouth.

One Iranian man adopted the ultimate thief's disguise: invisibility. He paid approximately £300 (5 million Iranian rials) to a self-styled local wizard, who promised the man his spell would render him invisible.

The next day he entered a shop in Isfahan, 200 miles south of Tehran, and commenced liberally helping himself to items and money from the till. Other customers aided staff in restraining him until the police arrived. Devastated to discover he was not invisible, the man admitted, 'I may have been conned.' May have?!

SPECIAL BRANCH BIRCH SUSPECT

Bizarrely, a crook decided to rob a New Hampshire bank disguised as a tree, with branches and foliage crudely stuck to his costume. Unsurprisingly, his disguise was unsuccessful at evading recognition in an urban environment. When he robbed a branch, police twigged immediately.

SEARCHING RUG-GED TERRAIN

Deciding that his girlfriend was paying too much for her cosmetics, Warsaw thief Miroslaw decided to obtain a discount on her expensive purchases: specifically a 100% discount.

Robbing a cosmetics shop ensured a police chase. Yet the thirty-two-year-old crafty crook managed to evade the cops and reach his bolt-hole hideout. Hoping to lie low at his aunt's flat until the heat was off (why do older women like their apartments to be so warm?), the product purloiner was startled to see four cops heading towards his aunt's home.

Needing to hide in a tiny flat, the skincare-swiper opted to roll himself up in a carpet. Police searched the premises and were about to leave, until an officer used the balcony to have a smoke after five hours of fruitless searching. There, he later testified, he noticed a large rug 'shivering'.

THE THONG GOODBYE

Several stick-up merchants tend to opt for wearing an identity-concealing stocking over their head (tights don't work, even if you have an accomplice). Rather pleasingly, a pair of hold-ups is required for a hold-up.

However, a pair of thieves in Colorado took something else from the lingerie drawer in a feeble attempt to disguise their identity. They each donned a pair of briefs over their faces to carry out an armed robbery at a petrol station. Dubbed the 'Thong Bandits', the bare-faced cheek of the robbers was easily recognisable on CCTV, and launched several YouTube parodies of their inept caper. The tiny Dairylea-triangle-sized thongs failed to mask their criminal identities. As a pair of robbers, they were pants.

REWARDING STUPIDITY

When a poster campaign promised a distinctly modest financial reward for information leading directly to the capture of a Taliban insurgent in Afghanistan, for a series of crimes against the coalition, it quickly brought forth its desired effect.

The wanted suspect was duly handed over to the American military personnel manning a checkpoint, who confirmed his identity with a biometric testing kit. Strolling up to an American military compound, the suspect then claimed his reward. For the wanted insurgent had handed himself in, in order to claim the offered $1,000 bounty on him!

A SNITCH IN TIME SAVES NINE

A company named Guns For Hire, which specialised in Western re-enactments, was astonished to receive a phone call from a forty-seven-year-old woman from Arizona asking them to shoot her husband.

'You mean you want us to stage a show involving your husband – is it for a special birthday or something?' they asked – rather optimistically.

'No,' came the sinisterly uttered reply, 'it'll be for his funeral. I want the lowlife dead.'

Establishing that this was a legitimate request, the theatrical company immediately informed the authorities. She is now doing a nine-year stretch. Although on release, she could pursue a case against Guns For Hire under the Trade Descriptions Act.

PLANTED EVIDENCE

When a tooled-up sixty-nine-year-old pensioner approached the airport security scanners in Portland, Oregon in 2012 he had a dilemma. Like a lot of Americans, he presumably believed that the only way everyone can remain safe is if everyone else carries a loaded gun – a belief strategy akin to everybody storing petrol and matches to protect themselves against fire.

Unusually, for a member of the stupid criminal genus, he decided to approach the authorities and report his dilemma. They informed him of his immediate obligation to surrender the gun. Fair enough, you're thinking.

Unfortunately, the gun-toting, trigger-trembling pensioner did not think. Instead, after publicly informing the authorities that he was packing a piece, he approached an ornamental plant. He then dug a hole in the soil and buried his gun. His plan – if we can generously stretch the elasticated word 'plan' to describe this idea – was to return to the airport after his holiday and retrieve the gun from the pot plant.

Sensing the Feds might be looking for him – as he had just informed the authorities in an airport crawling with security that he was in possession of a firearm – he decided to cancel his original plan and dig up the buried gun. But, like a forgetful dog, he frantically dug everywhere but failed to remember which plant pot he had initially selected.

'It was impossible to find,' he informed the *Oregon Tribune*. 'It was so well hidden.'

Fortunately the authorities, watching the escapade on CCTV, were more successful in locating the correct plant containing the gun, and they unearthed (quite literally) the 0.22-calibre handgun. The pensioner was handcuffed and charged with reckless endangerment.

His expensive handgun was confiscated – which must have been a fiscal setback, given handguns don't just grow on trees. Not even if they're meticulously planted.

Surely he used the excuse when the police came to arrest him: 'But officer, it's obviously a plant.' (Thank you. I'm here all week. Don't forget to tip your waitress.)

STIR CRAZY

What's the difference between a robbery and an armed robbery? Probably an average of five to eight years. Thus electing to carry a weapon on a raid constitutes a serious raising of the stakes. Then you have to select the right hardware for the job; does carrying a gun 'offer insurance'? If robbers need insurance that badly why don't they just phone Direct

Line? 'Could you give us a quote for an armed post office raid going wrong, and confirm that third party on the car covers its use as a getaway vehicle and any ensuing damage caused by police roadblocks?'

A Polish armed robber in 2012 decided to rob a bank with an item of cutlery. Oddly, this didn't cut it with bank staff. They merely laughed at the reprobate when he brandished a spoon in their faces, and refused to hand over any money. Yes, his choice of weapon did provide quite a stir.

On the plus side, it's currently handy for his porridge.

NEIN, NEIN, NEIN

A German bank raid ended when a robber threatened to detonate a grenade if his fiscal wishes were not instantaneously met. Fortunately for everyone present, the bomb turned out to be an egg painted to look like a grenade. He didn't even have the sense to use a hard-boiled one. Predictably it ended with the robber getting egg on his face.

WHAT A FUEL

A twenty year old from Kentucky was infuriated by rising fuel prices, so he devised a plan. Not a very good plan though. He decided to syphon petrol from a police car. So far, so stupid.

What elevates this crime from the pedestrian to potentially award-winning stupidity on a global stage is the choice he made next. He decided to record video footage of his crime, concluding by giving an obscene gesture to the camera directed at the police. So far, so exceptionally stupid.

He then uploaded it onto Facebook. The clip went viral. At least he's getting his heating and lighting fuel bills paid in the slammer.

AMERICAN GUN LOVERS

Ah … alcohol. Preserver of everything except secrets. Provider of sexual attraction for the otherwise unattractive.

Wayne was a man normally considered plainer than a bag of no-frills range ready-salted crisps. After drinking heavily in an

Irish-themed pub classily named the Paddy Wagon (a Paddy Wagon being the name given to the police vehicle deployed for picking up rowdy drunken Irishmen), he began to adopt a completely alien personality.

At leaving time, he planned to ask some females back to his nearby house in Port Charlotte, Florida with the dishonourable ambition of procuring some good old-fashioned emotionally detached sex. The beer was talking, and it said 'yes'.

Wearing beer goggles, he met a young lady and invited her into his car for a spot of hot monkey sex. Rather surprisingly, she agreed to this romantic entanglement. After trousers down, condom on and seats back, they commenced carnal exertions – at which point the woman beneath him put a .357 Taurus revolver to his head and demanded his wallet and car.

Panicking, the semi-naked victim dislodged the handbrake with his knee, causing the car to roll steeply downhill and crash violently into a palm tree. Upon impact the vehicle became airborne and destroyed two gardens. Police were soon on the scene, and the gun-toting amorous mugger sported two black eyes in her mugshot photo from the ensuing struggle.

'She's going down for this,' a sheriff informed the local media without any noticeable awareness of innuendo. Police returned the stolen money to the victim. Although it is too early to tell if the couple will have a second date.

SELF-CHECKOUT

Keen to promote their outreach activities to the local community, a police squad car was providing a demonstration of their latest high-tech surveillance equipment to passing children outside their Detroit precinct. This attracted an impressed twenty-one year old, who asked to participate in the demonstration.

The cops willingly obliged and asked him to key his driver's licence number into their computer. This revealed that he had been on the run for the past twenty-three months after committing an armed robbery in St Louis, Missouri. The police station was also allowing visitors to see inside their cells during the open day – an experience which they allowed the twenty-one year old to queue jump.

DO YOU KNOW THE WAY TO SAN JOSE JAIL?

One couple did. The married pair from San Jose, California decided that their matrimonial home needed some repairs. For starters the dishwasher was malfunctioning, and the kitchen door was broken. So they consulted the web and phoned a local handyman.

When he arrived, they kidnapped him for eight hours and forced the handyman to do DIY tasks around the house. Violence was threatened if he refused to comply. Eventually he escaped and the police arrested the impractical pair for false imprisonment, conspiracy to assault and making criminal threats.

Which is a role reversal to the usual scenario of plumbers being accused of extortion.

HIGH KARATE KID

A burglar, looking to fund an increasingly desperate drug habit, decided it would definitely be a good idea to break into a house in Manizales, Colombia. This decision was based on the observation that the resident, and his currently visiting friends, were all outside on the back lawn, thus ensuring the house was empty. In reaching this conclusion, he chose to ignore another observable fact: that they were engaged in martial arts stretching exercises on the small back lawn and were wearing karate outfits tied with black belts.

Needless to report, he was spotted immediately from the garden upon entering the house – the house (clearly a surprise for the burglar) being built with windows. Well, so few are!

The karate champion and his fellow black belts then commenced an encounter with the villain which was about as one-sided as a public hanging. They then restarted their stretching exercises, whilst the burglar started a stretch too: in the slammer.

NEW YORK, NEW DORK

Such was his need for a drugs fix that a youthful armed mugger decided he would hide behind a bench in New York's Central Park and await the sound of approaching footsteps. Then he would pop up from his hiding place, point a gun at the random unfortunate who next walked past his selected seat, obtain their wallet and buy drugs. Maybe there would be enough cash left over for a celebratory posh coffee too. Yeah, that was a great plan, definitely of the foolproof variety. He was smart – why hadn't anyone noticed how smart he was before?

Sure enough, he executed his plan/fast-track to the can. Footsteps were heard. It sounded like a couple; excellent, he thought, he was about to bag both a wallet and a purse. There would definitely be enough for a frothy coffee.

Like Zebedee after he'd taken several wrong turns in life, he sprang upwards from his concealment and pointed a gun at the couple. 'Give us your money, now!' he hollered.

'No!' replied one of the two patrolling uniformed policemen, who drew their weapons at Wild West re-enactment speed. That posh coffee will have to wait – at least for another six to eight years depending on good behaviour.

MUG SHOT

Bank robbers seem to believe they are professionally qualified for a career holding up financial institutions on the basis of seeing it done on television. Take two rubbish robbers from the American Mid-West who decided to hit their local small town bank as it was closing one Friday afternoon.

Storming into the bank and announcing, 'It's a stick-up!', a robber decided that he should show the tellers a gun to emphasise his point. Hence he reached into his pocket, located the weapon, found the trigger and immediately fired it. Whilst it was still in his pocket. Ouch.

His equally cerebrum-challenged accomplice misinterpreted the gunshot as security intervening, panicked and returned fire – hitting his colleague. 'Dial 911 for help!' squealed the now twice-shot bungling bandit. He was willingly squealing again a few minutes later, obligingly informing the cops of the identity of his sidekick, who had both shot and abandoned him at the crime scene.

A CUT ABOVE

So much choice, so little money – a common predicament faced by shoppers. But not by a twenty-four year old from Detroit, Michigan, who decided he was not going to choose which expensive hunting knife he could afford, but instead steal ten of them.

The problems with spontaneous crimes are many, but one that appears soon after the theft is where to hide the illicit loot. He opted to hide his shoplifted goods in his underpants. (Slight pause for male readers to grimace.) He was then spotted by staff, and a chase began.

This caused the robber to fall over with his perilous pants cargo, and a knife cut into his stomach. A few inches lower, and he'd be singing treble again for the rest of his life. Wisely deciding not to risk moving again, he was picked up by security and then bundled – very carefully – into a police van.

PLEA BARGAINING

About to enter its second week, the trial of an Oklahoma citizen for a spate of armed convenience store robberies was about to reach its conclusion. Just one convincing piece of witness testimony could swing the case either way, such was the frangible case for the prosecution. Until one of the store managers, who had been a victim of the accused, took to the stand.

He recounted the proceedings as he remembered them, which perplexed the accused in the dock to such an extent that he stood up and shouted, 'You're a liar! I should have blown your face off that day in the store, like I said I was gonna!' before sitting down, momentarily, then rising again to clarify, 'Er … if I had been in the store that day when the robbery took place, which, er, of course I, ahem, wasn't.' The jury required nine minutes.

PSYCHIC SIDEKICK

Here's the exact text from the *Miami Herald* reporting a crime that occurred in Port Richey, Florida:

Lewis Davis was ready to drive home from a party on November Drive at 2 a.m. Thursday when he saw a green Cherokee Chief pull up. 'Six men, their faces covered with red bandanas, got out of the Cherokee carrying a knife, baseball bat, club and rolling pin,' said Davis, 20. 'I knew when I saw the rolling pin that something bad was going to go down,' Davis said.

Shrewd observation skills there, perhaps bordering upon the psychic.

LIFE (AND DEATH) IN THE FAST LANE

Several cities have addressed the perpetual problem of traffic jams by encouraging a higher user-to-vehicle ratio. Thus carpool lanes are becoming a regular feature in many of the world's busiest metropolises.

Criminal stupidity has evolved to face the challenges set by the new traffic legislation. In Spain, a man was apprehended in the carpool lane for using a mannequin in the passenger seat. Maybe he got the idea from *Law for Dummies*.

However, Athens surely gains the prize for the best (by 'best' I do of course mean 'worst') excuse for being caught driving with an empty passenger seat in the carpool lane. A mortician was driving his refrigerated mortuary truck when traffic cops pulled him over for improper use of the lane. The driver explained his legal entitlement to use the lane, adamant he WAS carpooling since he had three passengers in the refrigeration unit in the back.

The court subsequently decided that in order to qualify as passengers, and thus be legally permitted to occupy the carpool lane, they must not be dead.

SMILE – YOU'RE GOING TO JAIL

CCTV has identified countless criminals, so the savvy modern crook will have long since devised a plan to avoid them. Or so you would have reasonably thought.

A bumbling gang in North Richmond, Texas decided that they would rob a store named Spy Supply – a surveillance superstore that deals exclusively in stocking CCTV monitoring cameras! I think that's worth typing again: stocking CCTV monitoring cameras.

The gang arrived by car, and took several attempts to park it close to the door; this fact is known from extensive footage shot from numerous angles on assorted cameras.

Because, as previously mentioned, this is a CCTV surveillance store.

Furthermore, the store arguably boasts the highest percentage per square metre of CCTV surveillance existing anywhere in America, including the White House and Pentagon. It is one of the primary sources of CCTV cameras – a bit like digging a hole into the middle of the planet's largest termite mound, jumping inside, and then being amazed to discover that there are some termites inside the termite tower. Oh, and now they're angry.

Police were supplied with multiple images of the villains taken in the sharpest definition on no less than 117 CCTV systems covering 360 degree angles. The thieves were recorded from an abundance of cameras loading $10,000 worth of CCTV equipment into a dustbin, and then spied from an additional 100 different angles loading it into their getaway car. A store spokesman told WNBC: 'It's absolutely astounding that these people have the audacity to steal from us and expect not to get caught. We are a security business. I'm confident they will get caught.'

The next time they appeared on camera was for the traditional police mugshot.

SHOULD HAVE KEPT MUM

An overbearing mother drove her son to crime – in at least one, if not both, senses of the phrase. For Dresden resident Daniela Langer was so concerned for her son's well-being after he was adamantly persevering with a dozy criminal plan to rob a DIY store, that she accompanied him to the scene of the crime. She even willingly chauffeured him to and from the crime spot.

In addition, she purchased items on a crime shopping list at her son's request (rope, duct tape, face mask, capacious black bag emblazoned with the word 'SWAG' – OK, possibly not the last item) and respected his not-at-all-suspicious directive to 'make sure you don't get fingerprints on any of the gear'.

Die Mutti informed the court that she could not believe what he was planning, but thought it best to accompany him throughout the crime to ensure he was safe. After all, armed robbery can be dangerous – armed robbery being one area where the Health & Safety Executives are frankly underperforming.

She admitted to being the driver and lookout during the robbery, where €29,000 worth of items were stolen from a jeweller's. If alarm bells were ringing in the mother's head over her son's safety, actual alarm bells were also triggered in the shop when store owner Joerg Weyrath, who was stabbed in the raid, managed to alert the nearby police station by setting off an alarm.

Der Polizei arrived instantly with expected German efficiency and bungled the overprotected mummy's boy and his pair of thieving teenage tearaway accomplices into the police van – German police being notably stricter than the mother with the ne'er-do-wells. His mother was refused a cell where she could oversee her criminal offspring, her new career as a getaway driver over before it started.

According to the *Daily Mail*, she informed the court: 'I could not talk him out of it, so I offered to drive him there and keep an eye on him. I was worried about him.' If in future years she's given jewellery for Mother's Day, she may want to insist on seeing an accompanying receipt.

CELL PHONE NUMBER

Most people know that you should not use the phone at work for making personal calls. An American villain forgot this rule when he made a call in his workplace: a warehouse he was robbing after breaking and entering.

With late-night radio for company, he knew the answer to a question posed on a local radio quiz for a chance to win a holiday, and couldn't resist phoning in and providing his name and address. The phone records later placed him conclusively at the scene during the time of the robbery. Although he didn't win the radio phone-in, he did win a paid stay at the state's expenses with full board, transfers included and an en suite cell available for three years!

JEWEL IN THE CLOWN

A thief stole several distinct items of jewellery from a store in the town of Pikeville. That is the town's real name. Yes, the place name is audibly demanding the insertion of a 'y' in the middle. So let's do that, and call it Pikeyville.

Pikeville (twinned with Pikeytown) is located in the US state of Kentucky. Kentucky is associated with horses, mountains, bluegrass and monumentally stupid criminals. Here's an example of the latter category.

A Pikeville local, whose face is professionally familiar to the town's CCTV operatives, enters a jewellery shop. He asks to see a tray of engagement rings. This ought to set alarm bells ringing – literally. Like the aforementioned CCTV operator, I have seen this man's face and body – and engagements may not be forthcoming. Imagine John McCririck after he's really let himself go (actually, don't do that). The felonious browser then grabs several highly distinctive rings and other items of jewellery and legs it to the door. So far, so bad.

Shortly afterwards, the same man enters the sister branch of the same jewellery store chain in the neighbouring Kentucky town. He then offers to sell back the stolen jewellery. Somewhat expectedly, they call the cops and he is arrested. A dazzling diamond of dim-wittedness.

WATCHING THE DETECTIVES

The Texan force regularly employs video surveillance to catch criminals and ... er ... the police. Officers in the Deer Park police precinct in Texas were annoyed that their food and drinks were regularly being removed by a hungry Chief Wiggum-type bandit. Hence they set up a CCTV monitoring system to catch the fridge raider. After only a few hours their expensive sting operation caught the porky pilferer hoovering up snacks and guzzling drink cans from the communal fridge.

The corpulent constable was caught doughnut-handed and charged. He was suspended from duty for a month, but spared prison food. The portly policeman's defence was poor; he protested that he was merely cleaning out the fridge – presumably by regular consumption of its contents, including numerous tins of soda belonging to fellow policemen.

The large lieutenant had gnawed his way through colleagues' packed lunches before the undercover operation to catch him red-sauce handed: an invitingly ketchuped bacon butty was snaffled from the shared fridge by the great-girthed grifter. A scrumptious waffle thickly spread with irresistible dripping honey was also left temptingly on the middle shelf – though this may have been perilously close to being a (literal) honey trap.

The refrigerator reprobate was eventually caught with his XXXXL police shirt covered with a dusting of sausage roll crumbs and remorseful tears, whilst the buttons strained to remain covering his enormous bulk. Cuffed, the fat felon realised how difficult it is to use a knife and fork whilst wearing handcuffs, and suffered the humiliation of being arrested in his own police station.

The station snacker discovered that his charge-sheet menu was a veritable smorgasbord of snaffled pastries, pies, cakes, trifles, yogurts, and ice creams – though significantly not salads.

And no, none of the obese officer's sandwiches contained truncheon meat.

STILL SEARCHING

In Peoria, Illinois, a series of signs were posted to lamp-posts and newsagents' windows reading: 'Lost in area – a search and rescue dog. If found, please contact …'

JUST IN THE NICK OF TIME

A youth, conditioned by a student lifestyle to rise late in the mornings, decided to rob a bank in the ironically named town of Liberty in Pennsylvania.

On the eve of the raid, the inexperienced criminal set his alarm clock earlier than usual. The next day, yawning at the unfeasibly early start, he made his way straight to the targeted bank. He had a gun. Check. A hold-up note. Check. A ski mask. Check. A bag for the hooky banknotes. Check. An imminent eight-year jail sentence. Check.

The drowsy thief arrived at the bank at just past noon. He had decided to rob it on a Saturday when the branch closed at 12 p.m. Staff inside noticed his aforementioned gun, note and ski mask. Whilst the tardy raider rattled the locked door of the closed bank, staff jotted down the registration number of his intended getaway vehicle and called the cops. He is no longer at Liberty or liberty.

DON'T DO THE CRIME IF YOU CAN'T TELL THE TIME

A fifty-seven-year-old would-be armed robber stormed into a 'bank' in Walchum, north-west Germany in 2011 with a toy gun and a ransom note. He had left the engine running in the getaway vehicle to facilitate a speedy fleeing of the crime scene – a detail indicative of meticulous planning.

Unfortunately for him, the building had not functioned as a bank for several years and was currently a physiotherapist's premises. Taken aback, he nevertheless asked the receptionist for money, and escaped in his stolen vehicle – though not for long, as he dropped his fingerprint-covered toy gun in the car and police arrested him within hours as the physiotherapist had noted his registration plate.

German newspaper *Das Bild* branded him 'Germany's stupidest bank robber'. Which is a bit unfair – he didn't even manage to enter a bank, yet alone rob one.

WENT LIKE CLOCKWORK

A Swiss thief should have been more receptive to the omens that were visible – including the uniformed police officer standing outside the jeweller's – on the day of his bungled robbery. For an operation whose implementation was supposed to run with fabled Swiss precision like clockwork, it is probably worth recognising in hindsight that clockwork is actually an antiquated, embarrassingly obsolete and unreliable technology, surpassed for centuries by scientific advancement.

Our omen-oblivious thief later told a court that he had mistimed the delivery van's arrival to the store because his train was late – remember his train was late in Switzerland, where the railways are supposed to run like clockwork … omen. Consequently, he decided to merely commit his robbery inside the store, rather than snatch the jewellery as it arrived outside the shop (the latter environment is far more conducive to casual robbery and subsequent getaways). Although the Swiss imbecile apparently hadn't planned a getaway, other than to presumably amble back to the station and then stand around looking at his watch and tutting in standard British commuter mode.

He told the court at his subsequent and inevitable appearance that he was surprised the jewellery was underneath glass, which disabled his sophisticated plan of 'grabbing it'. Instead, he asked staff for some expensive jewellery. They refused. If reviewing his crime for a How To Be A Successful Robber training seminar, he may consider bringing some sort of weapon to his future armed robbery attempts – it's just there's a slight clue in the name:

'armed robbery'. Yes, being armed would justifiably increase the
length of his custodial sentence, but it would have given him a
comeback when staff refused to hand over any jewellery. 'Have
you got a gun?' 'Hang on, I'll have a look. Er ... seems not.
Will that affect the robbery today?' At this point two uniformed
policemen entered the shop – fully fifty seconds after staff had
hit the panic alarm.

At the trial, the prosecution told the jury that the defendant's testimony was full of holes. Can't think of a Swiss humour
reference there.

FROM RUSSIA WITH LOUVRE

A Russian lady liked to spend her advanced years cutting out
pictures from magazines, and then pasting them onto some
inexpensively framed cardboard. It provided her home with
regular, quick and cheap makeovers. One month, her subscribed
magazine provided a free gift insert of Leonardo da Vinci's famed
masterpiece *Mona Lisa*.

Carefully cutting along the dotted line, she mounted the
poster on her wall. Soon afterwards, she left the apartment to
buy some cat food. Exploiting the time that the flat was unoccupied, a burglar broke in and stole just one item. That's right:
the 'priceless' Mona Lisa masterpiece usually seen hanging in the
Louvre in Paris. Oh to see him meeting the fine art collector who
had flown in especially for the meeting with the man who has
one of the world's great art treasures to fence!

VILLAIN LAS VEGAS

Alejandro Martinez decided he needed to turn his life around
and seek gainful employment. So he diligently completed a job
application form to work in a Las Vegas pizzeria. He also chose
to save a stamp and hand the application personally to restaurant
staff, thereby taking an opportunity to introduce himself. That
way he figured he could profess his sincerity towards working
there and provide himself with an advantage in the competitive
employment market.

However, you can always inadvertently say or do the wrong thing in the tension-charged environment of a nervous job interview, and he may possibly have slightly reduced his chances of securing the vacancy by choosing there and then to stick up the pizzeria and rob the joint. He demanded the contents of the till – which was only $110 as it was still early – and legged it out of the restaurant.

Police picked him up later that day, when they visited the home address listed on the application form he had handed in prior to the raid. Thick, crusty, deep prat with extra toppings of asininity and a side-order of crass stupidity.

His application was unsuccessful – for both the job and bail.

CRACK POT

Eloise Rose decided to avoid a confrontation with trading standards and marched directly into a North Carolina police station to register a complaint about poor-quality goods and services that she had been sold. She complained to the Putnam County deputy sheriff, citing her grievance was being made under the Sale of (Shoddy) Goods Act. It referred to recently purchased (… going to pause in order to build effect here … just a bit longer … it'll be worth it …) crack cocaine!

The fifty-year-old woman then removed a rock of crack from her mouth, angrily slammed it down on the counter, and fulminated that it contained wax as well as cocaine. Officers immediately gave her a drugs test, which – unlike the outcome of a common sense test – proved positive. Charged with possession, her bail was set at $1,500.

CALL THE PIGS

A burglar, breath flammable with cheap vodka, broke into the barn of a seventy-two-year-old pensioner in the Ulyanovsk region of Russia. His intention was to steal a giant hog – a terrifyingly large semi-wild 200kg boar. The plan called for a lot of pig and hence a lot of vodka.

Needless to say, events unfurled with a tragic predictability, and the boar trampled the thief to death. Russian police reports state that the boar dragged the thief into its slurry pit (only one of the wrestling pair could fairly be described as happy as a pig in sh★t).

Unusually for a suspected criminal killed by pigs, the unfortunate victim was white (phew, bit of satire there. Take that establishment).

HELEN'S FELONS

A Russian armed robber burst into a hairdresser's and demanded money with menace. Proprietor Helen, a reported twenty-eight-year-old lovely and skilled martial arts proponent, pretended to hand him the takings from the till. But her seeming compliance was a distraction, enabling her to assault the assailant. Instead of handing him any cash, she handed him a series of brutal high kicks rendering him barely sentient.

She then tied and gagged the thief with the cord from several hairdryers and handcuffed him to a radiator in the back office (apparently she supplied her own handcuffs). Returning to the front of the salon, she reassured customers that the situation was under control and the police were on their way. Only the police had not been summoned, and after her customers had departed and the shop had closed, Helen force-fed her captive robber numerous Viagra tablets. By the time the police got around to mounting their own investigation, Helen had already commenced mounting something else.

When the police eventually arrived (salon customers had notified them of the attempted robbery as witnesses, and were understandably inquisitive as to why no call had been placed from the salon), they discovered the sated stealer in a state described by the *Moscow Times* as 'squeezed like a lemon'.

Russian website Life.ru quoted a local police official: 'I don't know what's going to happen next – we could put them both behind bars: him for armed robbery and her for sexual assault.' For his sake, I hope they're held in separate cells. Still, they've both learnt their lesson the hard way (especially with that amount of Viagra involved).

GETTING THEIR FINGERS BURNED

The plan to get out of debt by robbing a Reno, Nevada casino left a gang of villains still very much in the red rather than the black.

Their masks fell off during the heist, the door ear-marked for escape was locked, their getaway car malfunctioned, and when they decided to torch the evidence they succeeded in burning themselves and … (a crime can never be said to have gone well when this scenario occurs) … they ended up dialling 999 themselves and asking for an ambulance.

ANTWERP'S TWERPS

Belgium has a Museum of Ironing with exhibits in twelve rooms. And they say Belgians are boring. Another common lazy prejudice directed at Belgians is their perceived failure to produce many celebrities (Tintin doesn't count as he's not real – like Anne Robinson).

Intent on rectifying this, two maladroit police officers arrived at the scene of a recent robbery, after raiders had absconded with the newsagent's takings. Oblivious to the presence of CCTV cameras – surely a reliable constant in the modern age of retail security – the burly officers proceeded to help themselves to adult magazines, fags and confectionery. One even jammed his hat full of illicit goodies.

The two wayward waffle-eaters were discovered as soon as the tapes of the earlier raid were played back at their police HQ. One can assume they knew their way to the station's cells.

PICNIC BASKET CASE

Showing that he was several sandwiches and a couple of scotch eggs short of a picnic, a forty-year-old Ohio man was arrested and charged with committing the same lewd public act on four occasions.

The man next door had filmed his naked neighbour outside the front of his house copulating with a picnic table. 'He just rolled the table outside his house, stripped naked and put in the hole where the umbrella is supposed to go his …' (I don't think we need to finish that sentence – although he's currently finishing his sentence: six months.)

He was charged with public indecency. Just think of the splinters. Ouch.

ATTEMPTED ROBBERY FOILED

When a passing housebreaker strolled past an abode in Budapest with some visible bling displayed in a wall-mounted cabinet, he decided to help himself. Smashing a side window, he entered the property, and was just scooping the final shiny object from the cabinet into his bulging plunder sack when he was interrupted by the homeowner.

Home alone, she appeared physically petite and slender. She was also holding an enormous sword. Instantly, she initiated a swash-buckling lunge at him, and, within seconds, had the interloper pinned to the floor with the tip of the blade pressing terrifyingly against his Adam's apple. 'OK, we'll call it a draw,' he probably said. The emergency services arrived, with the police transporting the burglar off to the clink after the ambulance crew had treated him for shock.

He had just targeted the home of a national fencing champion. She informed the media afterwards: 'I wasn't upset to see him as I needed the practice: I have a big championship coming up next week.' Which goes to prove that the pen is mightier than the sword at all times – unless you happen to get into a fight and your opponent has a sword.

BREAK-IN RECORDS

People wore some crazy outfits in the 1980s. Though not everyone got to experiment with the ever-changing fashions – some had to wear the same outfit every day. A prison outfit.

Two thieves had raided a fashion boutique in California in 1989, and were risking going back into the store to grab further spoils when they heard approaching sirens.

In response, they floored their getaway car's gas pedal, initiating a high-speed police pursuit. Realising that the cops were on their tail, and having driven for miles into unfamiliar territory, the daft duo decided to abandon the car, climb a fence and escape from the police on foot.

Although the fence was tall, and extremely well-fortified, their determined efforts ensured they made it over and jumped to the ground. 'Free!' they thought briefly, before looking up and seeing two prisons guards approaching them with a salivating mutt on a metal lead.

They had just broken INTO San Quentin State Prison. A police lieutenant informed the press: 'As far as I am aware, this has never happened before.'

DIRTY MAC

There was a time when Blackberries and Apples were simply the required ingredients for a nice crumble.

A modern conman from Houston decided to sell counterfeit MacBooks on the street. Although trading Apple's latest computer products isn't normally conducted on street corners in the more dubious areas of town, on the plus side you don't get hassled to buy extended warranty – and it's touch and go as to what constitutes the bigger crime.

Unfortunately for the Mississippi-born hooky hardware hawker, he was apprehended whilst attempting to sell three fake MacBooks to police officers. They also pointed out that MacBook is not spelt with an 'n'.

His fake 'MancBooks' were confiscated, along with his liberty for the next eighteen months.

MAN ENDS UP IN A WORSE STATE THAN WASHINGTON

Americans reserve an unsympathetic expression for their lower classes, referring to them as trailer trash. Hence the US police are well aware of the dwellings of some of their more regular customers, i.e. they know where several criminals park their homes.

One trailer-park resident near Seattle in Washington State decided he needed some petrol. Obviously this could have involved travelling to a nearby gas station and paying for it, but instead he opted to steal it from a neighbouring caravan. That was a much better plan, and obviously nothing could go wrong with that strategy.

Under cover of a moonless night sky, he tip-toed across a dozing trailer park and inserted his syphoning hose into a fellow resident's tank. Unfortunately for the lowlife criminal, he had mistakenly plugged the hose into the stationary vehicle's sewage tank outlet instead. He was immediately covered with human waste. Which demonstrates how a criminal lifestyle means you can quickly end up in the s★★★.

JUDGE REQUIRES AN ESCORT TO COURT

Being up before the Barnaby Rudge (I thought we'd employ some traditional rhyming slang, oft used in the shady villain-ous underworld) ought to be intimidating, with the bewigged Elmer Fudge (i.e. judge – do keep up) sitting up on high, in his special Inky Smudge chair, enjoying the real perk of the Vanilla Fudge's job: getting to bang his gavel.

However, a judge in the US was suspended after achieving stupid criminal status himself. This dishonourable 'Your Honour' was discovered banging more than just his gavel in the judge's chambers – which would have perhaps been a containable secret, had the woman involved not been both an escort and an illegal immigrant. Oh, and also wanted for questioning over an armed shop raid. M'lord was subsequently benched from the bench.

THREE

THE LAW IS AN ASS

The law is an ass. To quote a phrase coined, perhaps surprisingly, by Charles Dickens. In *Oliver Twist*, Dickens' character Mr Bumble is moved to fulminate: 'The law is an ass – an idiot. The worst I wish the law is that his eye may be opened by experience!'

Mr Bumble would likely repeat the remark if encountering any of the peculiar legislation in the following collection of perplexing laws, which prove that the law is an ass, and often a pain in the ass too.

✖ In Chicago, Illinois, it is illegal to eat in a restaurant whilst it is on fire.

✖ It is also illegal to drop dead in Parliament, according to the 1887 Coroners Act, though it is unclear what the punishment for offenders entails.

✖ In Alabama it is against the law to be knowingly employed at a grizzly bear wrestling match.

✖ Section 54 of the Metropolitan Police Act 1839 enshrines in law that carrying a plank of wood on a pavement in London is a criminal offence. The fine is a hefty 500 guineas. If enforced, this could have worked out very expensive for Eric Sykes. Rather than employing traffic wardens, the local authorities could surely swell public coffers by loitering around Ikea's car park.

✖ In Alabama it is illegal to wear a fake moustache in church.

✖ Thanks to Elizabeth I, a late sixteenth-century law ensures it is a criminal offence to be intoxicated whilst in charge of a cow. Much later, the bill was amended to include a steam engine. Though a cow driving a steam engine in an intoxicated state remains a legal grey area. The Scottish Alcohol Usage Licensing Act 1872 empowers magistrates with the authority to issue fines of up to 1,000 guineas to any drunken steam-engine drivers.

✖ In Mississippi it is expressly forbidden by law to shave in the middle of a busy road.

✖ A former by-law of Regent's Park sternly declared that it was illegal to stroke a pelican on weekends and bank holidays.

✖ If, in Scotland, someone knocks on your door and requests to use your toilet, they have a legal right to do so.

✖ In the city of York it is acceptable to murder a Scotsman within the ancient city walls, though only if carrying a loaded crossbow. And never on a Sunday. Obviously.

✖ In Ohio it is specifically forbidden by law to get a fish drunk.

✖ Doctors in Bahrain may only examine a woman's genitals in the reflection of a mirror.

✖ Whilst in Alabama, it is against the law to be blindfolded whilst in charge of a motorised vehicle.

✖ If visiting Florida, it is illegal for an unmarried woman to parachute on a Sunday.

✖ In Maryland it is illegal to take a lion to the cinema. Even if they really want to see *The Lion King*.

✖ It is illegal to have a donkey in your bathtub after 8 p.m. in Oklahoma.

✖ Vermont decrees that women must first obtain written permission from their husbands in order to wear false teeth.

✖ In France it is prohibited by law to name a pig 'Napoleon'.

✖ The Channel Islands' state of Jersey passed a law decreeing it illegal 'to assist witches in their ills and afflictions'. This statute was deployed to burn an unfortunate female on the fairly flimsy evidence that her pet black dog was seen walking on his hind legs by an intoxicated witness, which was therefore proof she had assisted witchcraft. In total, Jersey burnt sixty-six 'witches'.

✖ In California it is illegal to raffle a dog that has not been castrated.

✖ In the UK, pregnant women, and girls under six, are legally entitled to urinate wherever they wish. Despite the fact that this has been anecdotally spun to include a policeman's helmet, a bobby's hat is not specifically enshrined in law. They must be relieved – the policemen too.

✖ Following the Napoleonic Wars, a law was introduced in 1819 rendering it illegal to impersonate a Chelsea pensioner. The punishment, set a tad harsh to discourage fancy-dressers, was instant death.

✖ In Oklahoma, whaling has been declared illegal. It's probably worth pointing out to the state's legislators that Oklahoma is an entirely landlocked province whose closest point to the sea is over 500km away.

✖ Clothes and other items of personal apparel must not be washed in a birdbath in Oklahoma.

✖ According to Oklahoma statutes, all forms of transportation must be tethered with a rope when parked. An old law that goes back to Wild West frontier towns, that can no doubt be exploited by a keen modern-day traffic warden.

✖ The licence plates of all New Hampshire vehicles contain the state's official motto: 'Live Free or Die'. They are manufactured in the state's penitentiaries.

✖ Section 60, Sub-section 3, of the exhaustively complex Metropolitan Police Act 1829 renders it a criminal offence to beat a carpet in a London street. A punitive fine of 200 guineas is available for offenders, although an exemption is made for any Londoner indulging in this practice before 8 a.m. Clearly the pre-dawn hours were considered the ideal time for your neighbours to make lots of street noise. Unfortunately, legislators were noticeably more hesitant in outlawing domestic violence: an Act criminalising the beating of a spouse (1976) was not passed until roughly 150 years after making it illegal to beat a carpet!

✖ Allowing your pet to mate with a royally owned animal can ensure a spell in the clink. George I introduced an Act into the statute books promising 'severe penalties for any commoner who permits his animal to have carnal knowledge of a pet of the royal household'.

✖ In Tennessee it is illegal to consummate a marriage with a horse. Whether or not mating with Sarah Jessica Parker would constitute an offence is a legal grey area.

✖ It is illegal to build a pigsty in front of a house, although the law enables a construction 'if it is duly hidden'. So should anyone remark 'this place looks like a pigsty', as a point of law it is always best to deny it.

✖ Flying a kite in the street or hanging washing above a road or alleyway are both outlawed in the Town Police Clauses Act 1847 (Chapter 89, Section 28), and offenders are liable to receive a brutal £1,000 fine.

✖ New York City law decrees that women are legally entitled to appear topless in the street, but only 'if not for business reasons'!

✖ Following an unretracted royal proclamation issued by Edward II in the fourteenth century, any whale washed up on a British shore automatically becomes the property of the monarch. That's right, so you'd better take that beached whale you've got in the freezer straight to Buckingham Palace. The law was supposedly passed in order to provide a supply of whalebones for the Queen's corsets.

✖ Catch a sturgeon and sell it, and the police will catch you. A Plymouth fisherman in 2004 faxed the Queen's household to offer her a sturgeon – given they legally belong to the monarch if straying into UK waters. The offer was declined, but Devon police later investigated when the trawlerman attempted to sell the caviar-producing fish, as this is still an offence in the UK statute book.

✖ The 1799 Combination Act made it a criminal offence for two or more factory workers to join together and demand higher wages.

✖ Edward II implemented the Royal Prerogative Act in 1279, which became known after a 1313 modification as the Coming Armed to Parliament Act. This decrees that it is still illegal to enter the Houses of Parliament wearing a suit of armour.

✖ Annoyed by revellers attending fancy-dress parties? Me neither. But one party-spoiling, fun-depriving legislator evidently was in 1906 when he drafted the Seamen's and Soldiers' False Characters Act. A hefty fine is available for anyone dressed in military-impersonating garb, widening the remit to 'people giving the impression deemed in all likelihood to be mistook as a sailor'. So, Captain Birdseye can stump up the 500 guineas fine for starters.

✖ Visitors to Ottumwa, Iowa, please note: it is illegal to wink at unacquainted females.

✖ Surprisingly, mince pies are illegal. Their prohibited Class A status originated during the Interregnum, when Oliver Cromwell – not a man you'd want to spend Christmas with – pronounced them 'a papist symbol' and promptly oversaw the Purity Council introduce a permanent ban in 1657 for their Christmas consumption. Alas, Brussels sprouts remain perfectly legal.

✖ In Vermont disrobing is illegal, but public nudity is legal. The message state legislators are giving here is: disrobe before entering Vermont.

✖ Taxi drivers are forced in law to permanently carry a fresh bale of straw. If they don't, they could be looking at obtaining a different sort of bail. The law obviously originates from horse-drawn cabs. Also enshrined in English law: a taxi driver must make a mandatory enquiry as to whether his passenger is suffering from the plague. The Crown Prosecution Service is clearly a bit lax.

✖ In Youngstown, Ohio, it is illegal to run out of petrol.

✖ Bizarrely it is legal for a male to urinate in public – but his long arm must be touching the wheel of a car at the time, or the long arm of the law can touch him. And it must be the right hand too. This law allowed hansom cab and stagecoach drivers to relieve themselves without deserting their vehicles. Inconsiderately, this law does not extend to females – which probably explains why there is a greater statistical likelihood of encountering a queue in the Ladies than the Gents.

✖ Nevada state law specifically forbids people from riding a camel on the main highway.

✖ In California, primary schools must not host poker tournaments (which sounds like something Bart Simpson would be forced punitively to write on a blackboard).

✖ Detonating a nuclear device within the city limits in California will result in an automatic $500 fine.

✖ It is illegal in New Hampshire to inhale bus fumes in order to get high. However, if you are after a genuine legal high: buy a stepladder!

✖ When residing in North Dakota it is illegal to keep an elk in a sandpit at a domestic house.

✖ In Connecticut it is against the law to cross the road on a zebra crossing whilst doing a handstand. Presumably this law was hastily passed after a dexterous road-crossing acrobat fulminated: 'Well there's no law against it, officer!'

✖ The state of Utah has officially decreed that it is against the law for pharmacies to sell gunpowder as a headache cure.

✖ Widnes Council introduced a £5 automatic fine for anyone found asleep in a library reading room. Whenever they wish to increase their revenue, they could just leave some extra copies of Jeffrey Archer's books lying around the bibliotheque.

✖ Edward VI introduced one of the country's harshest yet maddest laws in 1549, ensuring that his breakfasting citizens were treading on eggshells each morning. To this day, any person discovered breaking a boiled egg at the sharp end could be sentenced to a minimum of twenty-four hours in the town's stocks.

✖ Prudish legislators in Wisconsin have rendered it illegal for any shop to display a naked mannequin.

✖ Throughout the UK it is illegal to be drunk on licensed premises.

✖ According to the Metropolitan Police Act of 1839, it remains illegal to fire a cannon close to a dwelling house (tip: so always sack a clergyman well away from such a property).

✖ The Library Offences Act 1898 enforces more than silence. The law ensures no betting or gambling can take place in a library reading room. Even if it's silent.

✖ Making, using or specifically enjoying a slide is forbidden by the Town Police Clauses Act 1847. Which means several tots in the park can be rounded up for questioning at the station.
   'Let's go through this one more time, sonny. You deny enjoying the slide, do you? You realise you could swing for this?'
   'Going on the swings isn't illegal, Sarge.'

✖ Donkeys are not permitted on the beach commercially between the hours of 10 p.m. and 6 a.m. Who are the enforcers of this law, enabling the British public to sleep sounder in their beds, snoozing safely in the secure knowledge that no donkeys are entering a beach at 10.01 p.m.?

Presumably WPCs, already used to having to deal with the donkey work, are the ones leading donkeys from the beach, rendering them susceptible to comments from beery lads: 'Nice ass, officer.'

✖ It is against the law in New Hampshire to check into a hotel under an assumed name. At least according to state legislators Mr and Mrs Smith.

✖ Until 1961 suicide was a capital offence in UK law. (Let's take an irony pause.) This meant that any failed suicide bids would be rewarded by the state doing the job properly for you – usually by the hangman. This must render suicide the only crime where failure to carry out the offence is instantly rectified by the courts. Akin to an armed robber bungling a bank job and being paraded before the courts, where a judge hands him a bag of hooky cash: 'There, that's the outcome you wanted, isn't it. You're welcome.'

FOUR

SILENCE IN COURT

The following comments are all reported, m'lord, to have occurred in the UK court system (with the occasional US example). Silence in court!

Counsel: What is your date of birth?
Accused: 18th February
Counsel: Which year?
Accused: Every year.

Barrister: 'And what did the apprehended say to you officer, after you'd tapped on the driver's window?'
Policeman: 'I swear to drunk I'm not God.'

A motorist was arrested on suspicion of dangerous and erratic driving, after causing an accident. He duly appeared in court and the cross-examination began:
Counsel: What gear were you in at the moment the impact occurred with the other vehicle?
Defendant: My Fred Perry top, black hoodie and Nike trainers.

'So, to clarify to the court, you claim to be unable to read or write.'
'That's right. I ain't never been able to read or write, man.'
'This note, retrieved from the scene of the robbery, which states "I have a gun. Put the money in this bag or get shot!".'

Can you confirm to the court that it is definitely not your handwriting?'

'No, definitely not my note.'

'But we cannot prove it is not in your handwriting, can we?'

'Yeah – I can show you my handwriting; it's nothing like that note.'

Confirming that even the professionals can have fun in court, this is reportedly a transcript from a rather under-prepared defence lawyer attempting to cross-examine a pathologist:

Counsel: How many autopsies have you performed on dead people?

Pathologist: All my autopsies have been performed on dead people.

The courtroom was tense. Would the prosecution have enough evidence to convince the jury? The defence called their star witness: 'Now take your time, madam. The two men who are alleged to have committed the robbery in the shop that day – are they in the courtroom today?' At that point, the two defendants stood up in the dock and made themselves known to the court. This prompted so much laughter that the judge called for an adjournment.

A villain resided in Liverpool. Scousers do ubiquitously seem to employ a shorthand of their own, in referring to Liverpool as 'the pool' (presumably 'cos someone's kicked the 'liver' from Liverpool). The middle-aged Liverpudlian was arrested near Albert Dock on suspicion of carrying stolen property in his car. In court he denied the charge.

'Do you have a receipt for the boxes of trainers in the car?'

'No.'

'Surely you have some invoices, purchase orders or a paper trail proof of legitimate ownership?'

'No.'

'Then you must have some traceable proof of legal possession?'

'No!' [getting annoyed]

'Why not?'

'Because it's best not to write anything down in my line of business.'

'And how do we know that you are no longer a criminal, Mr X?'

'I ain't been robbing for two years.'

'How exactly do you expect the court to believe your departure from such a villainous lifestyle has been sustained for fully two years now, Mr X?'

''Cos I've just spent the last two years inside.'

'You have already strongly implied to the court your displeasure at being accused of common burglary.'

'That's right – I ain't never been no burglar never.'

'Would you like to inform the court of your nickname?'

'I ain't ever been burgling in my life – the police made it all up.'

'If you'd kindly answer the question: by what nickname are you commonly known?'

'Burglar Pete.'

'Your husband was drunk and in an aroused state?'

'That's correct.'

'And did he proceed to make amorous advances towards you with the intention of securing er … animalistic empyrean pleasures?'

'You what?'

'Was his somewhat inebriated state complicit to securing a carnal objective?'

'Do you mean did he say "Do you want a f★★★?". Cos that's what he said.'

'Charmed, madam, I'm sure. And did your husband, this modern-day Keates, this contemporary Coleridge, this … how shall we say …

'F★★★ me?'

'Thank you madam – both the court and I are indebted for such elliptical economy with words expressed in madam's erudite elegance. Did he say – '

'Do you want to f★★★ me?'

'Obliged as I am by madam's kind offer, the court is interested to know what your husband said.'

'No – my husband said "Do you want a f★★★?".'

'And, pray, did he succeed in realising this oft-stated carnal objective?'

'I have no idea.'

'Why not?'

'I fell asleep.'

'You claim this man was your son and with you on the night of the robbery.'

'That's correct.'

'How old is your son?'

'Oh, he must be twenty-three … no, twenty-four.'

'And how long has he lived with you?'

'Er … It must be at least thirty years – probably longer.'

'Have you ever seen the accused before in your life?'

'Yes – he's my son.'

'What's his middle name?'

'I can't remember.'

'Where was he born?'

'I can't answer that as I didn't know him then.'

'But you still claim that you are the accused's mother?'

'Maybe.'

Q: 'How was your first marriage terminated?'

A: 'By death.'

Q: 'And by whose death was it terminated?'

Barrister: 'After your first wife's death, you eventually remarried and then went on a rather exotic and expensive honeymoon, did you not Mr X?'

Accused: 'That's correct, Sir. I went to Italy and then a romantic three-week cruise around the Mediterranean.'

Barrister: 'And did you take your new wife on this honeymoon trip?'

'And after you had read the arrested suspect his rights, what did he then say to you, WPC?'

'Could I repeat the beginning of the second sentence of the caution.'

'Would you care to remind the court as to what those words were?'

'Anything you say may be taken down and used in evidence.'

'And what did the accused reply to that?'

'Your knickers, officer.'

'And is this when the alleged knee to the accused's delicates occurred, WPC?'

'Yes – but undertaken by a member of the public at the scene.'

'A member of the public who doesn't appear to have been seen by any of the many witnesses present, WPC. Is that a fair summary of events?'

Barrister: 'So madam, you claim to identify my client as the man who supposedly exposed himself in the park, yet you cannot clearly confirm that he was the same man in the police's photo files?'

Witness: 'Well, it all happened in a flash.'

'Is it not true, Mr X, that your wife and yourself had been warned for indulging in so-called dogging activities at this lay-by before?'

'I cannot recall that. They must have warned another couple.'

'The police are convinced that this layby, where yourself and your lady wife were discovered in a state of semi-undress, was a well-known dogging spot. Can you explain why the police had sighted your car there on previous occasions?'

'It's a popular lay-by – especially now that the council has had all the bushes trimmed.'

Barrister: 'My client, Your Honour, has attended the drugs rehabilitation programme and declares that he has been clean for several weeks now. So I firmly believe his life of petty thieving and larceny is over, and that a custodial sentence will serve no real benefit to the community. [He then asks his client a question.] How long, exactly, have you been clean now, Mr X?'

Defendant: 'All the time now – I'd say eight weeks: I've been having regular showers ever since I've come off the skag.'

Barrister: 'When the vehicle hit the wall, what speed was it travelling at?'
Witness: 'Zero mph – it was stationary, 'cos of hitting the wall.'

Mitigating defence counsel: 'And that is why my client, Miss X, has convinced me – and I sincerely hope this court too – that her days of prostitution are over. Also, one of her former, now rehabilitated clients, is standing firmly behind her and intends to maintain this position going forward. He is convinced she'll come good, and has given her some money to fulfil this honourable intention.' And, as if to clinch the title of 'Worst Mitigation Ever', her defence counsel (no, he's not the prosecution) ended with the plea: 'Sending my client back to prison would be wasting what a fine young woman has to offer society. Instead of having her lying on her back all day being bored, she could be out in society, touching people … with her story.' If his career in law doesn't work out, there's always the possibility of work if they ever extend the Carry On franchise – his one-track Freudian mind being more Rumpy-Pumpy of the Bailey than Rumpole.